Kotlin for Enterprise Applications Using Java EE

Develop, test, and troubleshoot enterprise applications and microservices with Kotlin and Java EE

Raghavendra Rao K

BIRMINGHAM - MUMBAI

Kotlin for Enterprise Applications Using Java EE

Commissioning Editor: Richa Tripathi
Acquisition Editor: Sandeep Mishra
Content Development Editor: Tiksha Sarang
Technical Editor: Abhishek Sharma
Copy Editor: Safis Editing
Project Coordinator: Prajakta Naik
Proofreader: Safis Editing
Indexer: Priyanka Dhadke
Graphics: Jisha Chirayil
Production Coordinator: Shraddha Falebhai

First published: November 2018

Production reference: 1301118

Published by Packt Publishing Ltd.
Livery Place
35 Livery Street
Birmingham
B3 2PB, UK.

ISBN 978-1-78899-727-0

www.packtpub.com

ಹೊಸ ಚಿಗುರು ಹಳೆ ಬೇರು ಕೂಡಿರಲು ಮರಸೊಬಗು ।

ಹೊಸಯುಕ್ತಿ ಹಳೆತತ್ತ್ವದೊಡಗೂಡೆ ಧರ್ಮ ।।

ಋಷಿವಾಕ್ಯದೊಡನೆ ವಿಜ್ಞಾನ ಕಲೆ ಮೇಳವಿಸೆ ।

ಜಸವು ಜನಜೀವನಕೆ - ಮಂಕುತಿಮ್ಮ ।।

New leaves and old roots are what makes a tree magnificent.

New wisdom and ancient philosophy blend to become dharma.

If words of the sage reverberates in science and art,

It would be for the benefit of humanity. – Mankuthimma

To my mother, my father, and my beloved brother.

Foreword

Despite the rapid proliferation of mobile and web technologies, developing software systems and applications for these environments continues to be complex and challenging. One of the primary reasons for this is the need to have an application run on an innumerable number of diverse devices and an increasing number of platforms. The fact that a programming language like Java is used in billions of devices today is due to its ability to work on any device regardless of its hardware and software, with the only requirement being the presence of the JVM interpreter. Modern and prominent programming languages, such as Kotlin, are taking the development of systems to the next level.

Kotlin is a language that has been designed from the ground up to be a modern language, and in the words of the founders, it is *a pragmatic programming language for JVM and Android that combines OO and functional features focused on interoperability, safety, clarity and tooling support.* You can use it for developing server-side applications, desktop applications, and mobile applications on Android, where it is also creating a significant buzz in the developer community. An impressive feature is the near-seamless interoperability with Java, with capabilities such as the ability to create mixed Java-Kotlin projects, as well as the ability to use Java libraries in Kotlin and vice versa.

In the healthcare industry, the product life cycle is quite long, and this means that interoperability with existing code and infrastructure is critical for us to be able to re-use existing assets while developing newer features based on modern programming concepts. Kotlin does a fantastic job on this front. Also, the flexibility to use native functional programming features in Kotlin while still being in the Java ecosystem is a huge plus.

Raghavendra, the author of this excellent book, has broad experience with programming languages. The fact that he has chosen to write his first book on Kotlin bears witness to his passion and enthusiasm for this language. The book brings out the inherent beauty of the language, but also states its limitations. This will certainly help the reader to get a balanced view and use Kotlin in their projects in the most appropriate way. It is well written and accessible, making it suitable for readers of any background.

Kotlin is here to stay, and we will certainly be hearing more of it in the coming years. This book will prove invaluable to those who want to embark on this exciting journey.

Henk van Houten

CTO Royal Philips

Contributors

About the author

Raghavendra Rao K is a senior programmer who's skilled in Java, Kotlin, Groovy, Scala, Java EE, Spring Framework, Cloud Foundry, and Docker. He's a strong engineering professional with a bachelor of engineering degree focused on computer science and engineering. He's enthusiastic about code quality and loves refactoring.

About the reviewers

Dr. Uri Benchetrit has, over 35 years, assumed a wide range of research and development positions in academia and industry in diverse fields, including software development, software architecture, algorithms, robotics, cellular phones, optics, and medical devices. Uri has been working for Philips since January 2010. He has served as the chief software architect for the CT/AMI Business Group at Philips, and then as the head of software engineering research and technologies in the Software Center of Excellence (SW CoE) of the Philips Strategy and Innovation office.

Uri holds a BSc in computer engineering, an MSc in data communications, and a DSc in robotics, all from the Technion. His post-doctorate research was done at the University of Michigan.

J Vijayananda has been in the IT industry for over 22 years. He has been primarily in the medical and healthcare domain. Vijay has been primarily focusing on machine learning and deep learning in the medical domain. Vijay is currently the chief architect and fellow at Philips Healthcare and leads the data science and AI platform at Philips.

He completed his bachelor's degree in electronics and communications from Mysore University, and also has a master's in computer science from Georgia Tech University.

Acknowledgements

Writing this book was only possible with the support of many individuals who gave generously their time and expertise. I have been fortunate to work with wonderful human beings on this journey. My sincere thanks to everyone who helped me with this project with their effort, knowledge, and the time they contributed to the book.

First and foremost I thank the platform development team of Kotlin at JetBrains, who put their thought and effort into creating a pragmatic programming language.

I express my sincere gratitude to technical reviewers of my book, Dr. Uri Benchetrit and J Vijayananda, for their time and support.

I had the privilege of Henk Van Houten writing the Foreword for the book. Thank you Henk for reviewing the book content and writing the Foreword.

My sincere thanks to Simao Williams, Dr. Eldo Issac, and Kenneth Kousen for the sharing feedback on the content of the chapters.

I also want to thank the wonderful team at Packt Publishing. Thank you Tiksha Sarang for editing the content very well. I also would like to thank Sandeep Mishra, Prajakta Naik, Abhishek Sharma, Riddesh Dawne and Storm Mann for their support in getting this book published.

`mapt.io`

Mapt is an online digital library that gives you full access to over 5,000 books and videos, as well as industry leading tools to help you plan your personal development and advance your career. For more information, please visit our website.

Why subscribe?

- Spend less time learning and more time coding with practical eBooks and videos from over 4,000 industry professionals

- Improve your learning with skill plans designed especially for you

- Get a free eBook or video every month

- Mapt is fully searchable

- Copy and paste, print, and bookmark content

Packt.com

Did you know that Packt offers eBook versions of every book published, with PDF and ePub files available? You can upgrade to the eBook version at `www.packt.com` and, as a print book customer, you are entitled to a discount on the eBook copy. Get in touch with us at `customercare@packtpub.com` for more details.

At `www.packt.com`, you can also read a collection of free technical articles, sign up for a range of free newsletters, and receive exclusive discounts and offers on Packt books and eBooks.

Table of Contents

Preface

It is always exciting to embark on a new journey, and learning a language is no different. This process is a fun-filled journey that brings with it the true satisfaction of learning.

In the process of developing the software or an application, choosing a programming language has always been a topic for debate. Several JVM-based programming languages have been available for application development, such as Java, Groovy, and Scala. When there are so many languages around, why do we need another one? Well, the answer is that any language is conceptualized for a specific task and audience. Typically, the language gets richer over a period of time as a result of the developer community. But one language typically will not have all the features required. Kotlin combines several nice features that are there in different languages. Its elegant syntax and the non-verbosity of the code makes application development faster and efficient to manage.

Kotlin combines the features of the object-oriented and functional style of programming to choose from, based on the context suitable for enterprise application development. Kotlin is developed with the intention of making the programming experience easier and solving the problems that programmers face while developing and maintaining an application or a microservice. This adds to the value proposition in an application's life cycle by saving time and keeping it productive while developing the solution. Kotlin is a very pragmatic language that caters well to the needs of enterprise applications.

Kotlin aids application development by having a lot less code compared to any other JVM-based languages, which essentially means that developing the application would become faster and maintenance easier. Language is non-verbose and hence, it is less error-prone. Elegance in syntax improves the readability of the code. Kotlin is a statically-typed language, so type safety is guaranteed.

For all these reasons, Kotlin is a great fit for enterprise application development.

Thank you for selecting this book. I hope you will enjoy reading it and apply the learnings to developing enterprise systems.

Who this book is for

This book is designed for programmers, application developers, architects, and technical managers. It assumes a degree of familiarity with the fundamentals of the programming and basics of Java and JDK in general, but does not assume any knowledge of the Kotlin language.

For application developers and architects, this book covers the various aspects of developing enterprise applications. It covers the fundamentals of the Kotlin language required to get started with this book and goes on to discuss various aspects for developing enterprise applications. The book can be used as a reference guide for developing enterprise applications using Kotlin and Java EE, with elegant and expressive syntax that the Kotlin language offers.

What this book covers

The book starts with the fundamentals of Kotlin language and a brief about Java EE platform, then focuses on using Java EE with Kotlin. It also covers RESTful services, securing services and implementing Microservices. Lastly it covers Application monitoring, Profiling and Design Patterns.

Chapter 1, *Kotlin – a First look*, we'll be introducing you to the world of Kotlin. We learn the basics of Kotlin and take a quick dive into various features that the Kotlin language offers.

Chapter 2, *Kotlin – The Game Changer*, explains how Kotlin would be a game changer in terms of developing real-world, enterprise applications. We discuss where Kotlin scores over Java and why it is becoming increasingly popular. After addressing key practices, and the advantages it has, we'll be building a basic Kotlin project using IntelliJ IDEA and Eclipse. We then cover the Coroutines (a very lightweight thread) used for programming asynchronously. We will also learn about intermixing Java and Kotlin.

Chapter 3, *An Overview of Java EE and Kotlin*, gives a bird's eye view of the Java EE platform. We'll be introducing Kotlin in our Java EE applications. We discuss the challenges that Java EE needs to tackle to make Kotlin work in unison. The Kotlin plugins that will aid in the cause will be integrated into our Java EE applications as we begin our journey to build apps using Kotlin and embrace the new programming language. We also cover creating a web application using Servlets, and EJB with Kotlin.

As Kotlin is based on JVM, it is fully compatible with existing Java-based frameworks such as JSF.

Chapter 4, *Kotlin with JSF and CDI*, discusses how to make Kotlin work with JSF and dependency injection using CDI. We then discuss how we can use CDI to create domain events. We also cover interceptors and a use case where they can be applied. This chapter will be another significant step in our journey of developing Java EE applications using Kotlin.

Chapter 5, *Kotlin with JPA and EJB*, explains how to bootstrap JPA with Kotlin. We then move onto modeling JPA entities. We also discuss transaction management and handling exceptions in an application. Along the way, we'll integrate each of the preceding frameworks to build a real-world application.

Java EE 8 introduced JMS 2.0, which greatly simplified the development of applications involving messaging functionality.

Chapter 6, *Enterprise Messaging with Kotlin*, covers the development of messaging models using Kotlin and the Java Messaging Service (JMS). We will discuss messaging queues and topics. We will implement Point-to-point and Publish-Subscribe messaging models. We will also cover the acknowledging of messages and transactions.

Chapter 7, *Developing RESTful Services with JAX-RS*, discusses the concepts of REST specifications and examples of JAX-RS API. Furthermore, we'll be looking at Jersey—a popular implementation of JAX-RS API, while implementing them in web services using Kotlin.

Java EE 8 introduces a new security API that standardizes application security across all Java EE 8-compliant application servers. The new Java EE 8 API includes support for authentication mechanisms, allowing us to authenticate users in a standard way. Several authentication mechanisms are supported, such as basic HTTP authentication, client certificates, HTML forms, and more. We will discuss what the Security API is all about, along with developing a web application that implements the same using Kotlin in chapter 8.

Chapter 8, *Securing Java EE Applications with Kotlin.* It also covers implementation of the JSON Web Token (JWT) to secure the RESTful APIs.

The main purpose of a microservice architecture is to break down an application into smaller standalone components that are easier to handle, deploy, scale, and maintain in the long term.

Chapter 9, *Implementing Microservices with Kotlin*, examines ways to refactor monolith applications into microservices. We will implement microservices using Kotlin.

Chapter 10, *Performance Monitoring and Logging,* discusses how to find memory leaks. We'll be exploring the performance and monitoring tools used for enterprise applications. We'll look into garbage collection (GC), tuning the GC, and profiling.

Design patterns may be viewed as a structured approach to computer programming. A software design pattern is a general reusable solution to a commonly occurring problem within a given context in software design.

Chapter 11, *Design Patterns with Kotlin,* dives into the various design patterns. We will learn the different types of patterns, specifically among the creational, structural, and behavioral patterns, and implement them using Kotlin.

To get the most out of this book

To run examples from this book, you will need a computer running Windows, Linux, or macOS. You will also need IntelliJ IDEA (preferably IntelliJ Ultimate edition) or Eclipse. You will need a basic knowledge of GitHub and Git to clone project samples discussed in the book.

To run examples and programs covered in the book requires Kotlin 1.3 and Java 1.6 or higher. Most of the examples will also work with the earlier version of the Kotlin. The instructions to download necessary software and tools are provided in technical requirements of the each chapter.

Download the example code files

You can download the example code files for this book from your account at www.packt.com. If you purchased this book elsewhere, you can visit www.packt.com/support and register to have the files emailed directly to you.

You can download the code files by following these steps:

1. Log in or register at www.packt.com.
2. Select the **SUPPORT** tab.
3. Click on **Code Downloads & Errata**.
4. Enter the name of the book in the **Search** box and follow the onscreen instructions.

Once the file is downloaded, please make sure that you unzip or extract the folder using the latest version of:

- WinRAR/7-Zip for Windows
- Zipeg/iZip/UnRarX for Mac
- 7-Zip/PeaZip for Linux

The code bundle for the book is also hosted on GitHub at `https://github.com/PacktPublishing/Kotlin-for-Enterprise-Applications-using-Java-EE`. In case there's an update to the code, it will be updated on the existing GitHub repository.

We also have other code bundles from our rich catalog of books and videos available at `https://github.com/PacktPublishing/`. Check them out!

Conventions used in the book

There are a number of text conventions used throughout this book.

`CodeInText`: Indicates code words in text, database table names, folder names, filenames, file extensions, pathnames, dummy URLs, user input, and Twitter handles. Here is an example: "We will create a message `Producer` class."

A block of code is set as follows:

```
class Producer {
  @Inject
  private lateinit var initialContext: InitialContext
}
```

When we wish to draw your attention to a particular part of a code block, the relevant lines or items are set in bold:

```
class Producer {
  @Inject
  private lateinit var initialContext: InitialContext
}
```

Any command-line input or output is written as follows:

```
> kotlinc -script 14c_SecondaryConstructor.kts
```

Bold: Indicates a new term, an important word, or words that you see on screen. For example: "The **Java Messaging System (JMS)** is the standard API for messaging systems."

 Warnings or important notes appear like this.

 Tips and tricks appear like this.

Get in touch

Feedback from our readers is always welcome.

General feedback: If you have questions about any aspect of this book, mention the book title in the subject of your message and email us at customercare@packtpub.com.

Errata: Although we have taken every care to ensure the accuracy of our content, mistakes do happen. If you have found a mistake in this book, we would be grateful if you would report this to us. Please visit www.packtpub.com/submit-errata, selecting your book, clicking on the Errata Submission Form link, and entering the details.

Piracy: If you come across any illegal copies of our works in any form on the internet, we would be grateful if you would provide us with the location address or website name. Please contact us at copyright@packtpub.com with a link to the material.

If you are interested in becoming an author: If there is a topic that you have expertise in, and you are interested in either writing or contributing to a book, please visit authors.packtpub.com.

Reviews

Please leave a review. Once you have read and used this book, why not leave a review on the site that you purchased it from? Potential readers can then see and use your unbiased opinion to make purchase decisions, we at Packt can understand what you think about our products, and our authors can see your feedback on their book. Thank you!

For more information about Packt, please visit packt.com.

1
Kotlin – A First look

Kotlin is a new language based on the **Java Virtual Machine (JVM)** that is fascinating the developer community with its concise, clear syntax, its lack of boilerplate code, and its full interoperability with the Java language.

The following topics will be covered in this chapter:

- The features offered by Kotlin
- Installing and running Kotlin
- The various constructs of the language

Technical requirements

Knowing the basics of the Java language will help you to understand Kotlin and compare the two JVM-based languages. We will work with the command line to illustrate the language features that are highlighted in this chapter.

Introduction to Kotlin

Kotlin is a statically-typed programming language that runs on the JVM and works across different platforms. The fact that it is statically typed means the types are resolved during compilation. JVM is a specification that provides a runtime environment for running applications that are developed in Java and other JVM-based languages. The most well known reference implementation of JVM is OpenJDK, which was originally developed by Sun Microsystems and is now supervised by Oracle. Kotlin is another JVM-based language that is simple to write and concise in nature.

Kotlin combines object-oriented and functional programming features. Kotlin is designed to be interoperable with Java and relies on the Java code from the existing **Java Class Library (JCL)**.

Kotlin provides a more expressive syntax than Java. It is concise and has strong type inference, which reduces code verbosity. It also has a wide variety of useful features, such as operator overloading, string templates, extended functions, and coroutines.

The history of Kotlin

Kotlin was developed by JetBrains in 2010. They initially released it under the name Project Kotlin in July 2011. They needed a language that was concise, elegant, expressive, and also interoperable with Java, as most of their products were developed in Java, including the Intellij Idea. They were looking for an alternate language to reduce the amount of boilerplate code required and to introduce new constructs, such as higher-order functions, to make language more expressive and concise. One of the goals of the Kotlin language was to be able to compile code as quickly as Java.

JetBrains open-sourced the project under the Apache 2 license in February 2012. Kotlin v1.0 was released on February 15, 2016. This was the first official stable release from JetBrains. Kotlin v1.2 was released on November 28, 2017. This release added a feature to allow code to be shared between JVM and JavaScript platforms.

Features of Kotlin

The key features of Kotlin are as follows:

- **Interoperability with Java**: The most important feature of Kotlin is its deep interoperability with Java. Kotlin compiles to JVM bytecode and runs on the JVM, using Java libraries and tools.
- **Concise**: Unlike Java, which is verbose, Kotlin reduces the amount of boilerplate code. This results in a leaner code syntax and improved readability.
- **Safe**: Kotlin improves code safety through the proper initialization of properties, null safety, and strong type inference.
- **No runtime overhead**: Kotlin imposes no runtime overhead. The standard Kotlin library is small. The Kotlin runtime exists only to support the language features. It has mostly focused on extensions to the Java standard library. Many of its internal functions are inline.
- **Collections**: In Kotlin, we have higher-order functions, lambda expressions, operator overloading, lazy evaluation, and lots of other useful functions for working with collections.
- **Extension functions**: Kotlin allows us to extend the functionality of existing classes without inheriting from them. Extensions do not modify classes; they extend them and are resolved statically.
- **Open source**: Kotlin is an open-source programming language. The Kotlin project is open-sourced under the Apache 2.0 license. It is on GitHub and is open for community contribution.

Getting started with Kotlin

Before installing Kotlin, we need to have JDK installed, as Kotlin relies on JDK.

In this course, we will be using OpenJDK. OpenJDK can be downloaded from `http://jdk.java.net/`. Alternatively, we can use Oracle JDK, which can be downloaded from `http://www.oracle.com/technetwork/java/javase/downloads/index.html`.

After installing the JDK, set the **PATH** variable to include the JDK installed and we can check its version using the `java --version` command.

Once we have JDK installed, we need to set up Kotlin. We will look at how to install it in the following section.

Installing Kotlin

Kotlin can be downloaded using the following link: `https://github.com/JetBrains/kotlin/releases`.

Installing Kotlin on Linux

To install Kotlin on Unix based systems such as Linux, Solaris, OS X etc., run the following commands in a terminal.

```
$ curl -s https://get.sdkman.io | bash
```

Then open a new terminal and execute below commands to install Kotlin:

```
$ sdk install kotlin
```

We can run the following command to see the version of Kotlin:

```
$ kotlin -version
```

To install Kotlin on Ubuntu, execute the following command from a terminal:

```
$ sudo snap install --classic kotlin
```

Installing Kotlin on Windows

To install Kotlin on Windows, perform the following steps:

1. Extract and set the **PATH** variable to include the Kotlin runtime.
2. Check its version using the `kotlin -version` command.

 The source code for the Kotlin project can be found at the following link: `https://github.com/JetBrains/kotlin`.

Installing Kotlin on Mac

To install Kotlin on a Mac system run the following command in a terminal:

```
$ sudo port install kotlin
```

Compiling and running

Now that we have JDK and the Kotlin compiler set up, let's try writing our first program in Kotlin and learn a few different ways to compile and run it.

Let's consider the `HelloWorld.kt` program, which just prints the *hello* message and the first argument passed to it:

```
fun main(args:Array<String>){
    println("Hello${args[0]}")
}
```

There are different ways to compile and run Kotlin code:

- **Command line**: By including the runtime, we don't have to provide the classpath; it gets bundled into it. To bundle the JAR, execute the following command in the command prompt/console:

  ```
  kotlinc HelloWorld.kt -include-runtime -d HelloWorld.jar
  ```

  We pass the class name and include the runtime and the name of the JAR as command-line arguments.

  In order to run the program, execute the following command:

  ```
  kotlin -classpath helloworld.jar HelloWorldKt World
  ```

  ```
  > kotlin -classpath helloworld.jar HelloWorldKt World
  Hello World
  ```

  Alternatively, we can use the following command:

  ```
  java -classpath helloworld.jar HelloWorldKt World
  ```

  The output is as follows:

  ```
  > java -classpath helloworld.jar HelloWorldKt World
  Hello World
  ```

  We can also compile Kotlin code without the runtime. When we want to run it using Java or Kotlin, we have to specify where the class file,`HelloWorldKt`, is located:

  ```
  kotlinc HelloWorld.kt -d classes
  kotlin -classpath classes HelloWorldKt World
  ```

The output is as follows:

```
> kotlinc HelloWorld.kt -d classes

> kotlin -classpath classes HelloWorldKt World
Hello World
```

- **Read-eval-print-loop**: Kotlin has an **read-eval-print-loop** (**REPL**) that we can use. Simply type `kotlinc` in the terminal and it will become an REPL. We can now run the Kotlin code interactively and experiment with it, as demonstrated in the following:

```
Type :help for help, :quit for quit
>>> println("hello")
println("hello")hello
>>>
```

We can type `:quit` to exit the REPL.

- **Scripts**: We can create a script file to compile and run a Kotlin program. Create a file called `HelloWorld.kts`. The `s` in the file extension stands for *script*. Then add the following `print` statement to it:

```
println("Hello World from Script")
```

`HelloWorld.kts` just has one print line statement. In the console, execute the following command:

```
kotlinc -script HelloWorld.kts
```

This gives the output shown in the following screenshot:

```
> kotlinc -script HelloWorld.kts
Hello World from Script
```

This way, we can directly run the Kotlin file as a script.

In this section, we have learned the following:

- How to install Kotlin
- How to compile and create byte code and run it

- How to code and play with REPLs directly
- How to write Kotlin code as a script and run it

A quick tour of Kotlin

In this section, let's take a quick look at the world of Kotlin and understand the basics of the language.

Declaring variables

To declare a variable in Kotlin, we use either the `val` or `var` keywords.

Let's take a look at the following example:

```
val number = 10
println(number)
```

The preceding code prints the value that is assigned to a variable number, as can be seen in the following screenshot:

```
> kotlinc -script 3_valnVar.kts
10
```

However, if we try to change the value assigned to the number, we will get a compilation error. Take a look at the following code:

```
val number = 10
println(number)
number = 11
println(number)
```

The output is as follows:

```
> kotlinc -script 3_valnVar.kts
3_valnVar.kts:3:1: error: val cannot be reassigned
number = 11
^
```

This is because `val` is immutable in Kotlin. This means that once a value is assigned, it cannot be modified. The keyword `var`, however, can be used to create a mutable variable.

Now consider the code for `3_valnVar.kts`:

```
val number = 10
println(number)

var anotherNumber = 15
println(anotherNumber)

anotherNumber = 20
println(anotherNumber)
```

The output for the preceding code is as follows:

```
> kotlinc -script 3_valnVar.kts
10
15
20
```

Let's examine what happens if we assign a string value to the preceding code:

```
val number = 10
println(number)

var anotherNumber = 15
println(anotherNumber)

anotherNumber = "20"
println(anotherNumber)
```

Compile this and see what happens:

```
> kotlinc -script 3_valnVar.kts
3_valnVar.kts:7:17: error: type mismatch: inferred type is String but Int was expected
anotherNumber = "20"
                ^
```

In this case, the compiler throws an error saying that the type is mismatched. This is because the `anotherNumber` variable was inferred to be of type `int` and, as a result, we cannot assign a different type.

The type is inferred from the context and type safety is also guaranteed.

Both `var` and `val` are used to declare variables in Kotlin. `val` creates immutable variables, and `var` creates mutable variables. Variables declared using the `val` keyword cannot be changed once a value is assigned to them. This is similar to a final variable in Java. `val` is used to create constants. Variables declared using the `var` keyword can be changed later in the program. This corresponds to a regular Java variable.

Data types in Kotlin

The basic data types in Kotlin are numbers, characters, Boolean, arrays, and strings. These are described as follows:

- **Number**: Kotlin provides the following built-in types that represent numbers, similar to Java:

Type	Byte
Double	8
Float	4
Long	8
Int	4
Short	2
Byte	1

Unlike in Java, characters are not numbers in Kotlin.

- **Byte**: Byte is a one-byte or 8-bit type for which values range from -128 to 127
- **Short**: Short is a two-byte or 16-bit type for which values range from -32768 to 32767
- **Int**: Int is a four-byte or 32-bit type for which values range from -2^{31} to $2^{31}-1$
- **Long**: Long is an eight-byte or 64-bit type that can have values from -2^{63} to $2^{63}-1$

- **Double**: Double is a double-precision, 8-byte, or 64-bit floating point
- **Float**: Float is a single-precision, 4-byte or 32-bit floating point
- **Char**: Char is used to represent a character in Kotlin, two-byte or 16-bit long, and is used to represent unicode characters

`Char` is a type used to represent characters. This is represented as follows:

```
val ch = 'a'
```

- **Boolean**: Kotlin has a Boolean type to represent Booleans. It takes either `true` or `false`:

```
val isValid = true
val flag = false
```

 If you are using IntelliJ IDEA, you can place your cursor inside the variable and press *Ctrl + Shift + P* to see its type.

Warnings

If we have created a variable and not used it, or if we forget to initialize a variable, we will get warnings, which can be useful to prevent errors. Kotlin provides many such warnings during compile time to avoid possible runtime errors. This increases program reliability.

Type inference

Kotlin is a statically-typed language. It executes the type inference for us, so we don't have to specify types. Consider the code for `3a_TypeInference.kts`:

```
val message = "Hi there"
println(message)
```

When we run this code, we get the following output:

```
> kotlinc -script 3a_TypeInference.kts
Hi there
```

We can also explicitly specify the type. Consider the following code:

```
val message : String = "Hi there"
println(message)
```

This is an example of creating a variable of the `String` type and printing it in the console. This looks like Scala syntax and it is quite different from what we do in Java.

In Java, we would write this as follows:

```
String message = "Hi there";
```

Languages such as Kotlin emphasize that the name of a variable is more important than the nature of the variable. Kotlin puts the name of a variable or constant first and the type after in the `var` declaration syntax. The type is, in fact, optional; we don't have to specify it. We might think that this is the same as the dynamic type, where the type is resolved during runtime. Kotlin, however, actually infers the type at compile time.

Kotlin uses the String class from the JDK library. We can query the class that it uses as follows:

```
val message = "Hi there"
println(message.javaClass)
```

The output is as follows:

```
> kotlinc -script 3a_TypeInference.kts
class java.lang.String
```

As a general rule, it's a good idea to specify type information when we write public-facing interfaces and, when using local variables, we can let the language infer the type.

String templates

Kotlin has support for templates for the String type. This is useful because it helps us to avoid concatenation in code.

Let's look at an example for `4_StringTemplate.kts`:

```
val name = "Atrium"
println("Hello ${name}")
```

The output is as follows:

```
> kotlinc -script 4a_StringTemplate.kts
Hello Atrium
```

 The curly brackets are optional here. `println("Hello ${name}")` can be written as `println("Hello $name")`, but it is good practice to use them to indicate the boundaries of the expression.

Let's look at `4a_StringTemplate.kts`:

```
val name = "Atrium"
println("Hello $name")
```

The output is as follows:

```
> kotlinc -script 4a_StringTemplate.kts
Hello Atrium
```

Now consider the following code in Java:

```
myName= "tanbul"
System.out.println("my name is" + myName);
```

Here, we meant to print `tanbul`, but due to a formatting error, this code prints `my name istanbul`. We want to correct the code as follows:

```
myName= "tanbul"
System.out.println("my name is " + myName);
```

Kotlin's string template really helps to avoid any possible formatting errors from string concatenation. In Kotlin, we write the preceding code with clear syntax as follows:

```
myName= "tanbul"
println("my name is ${myName}")
```

This prints the following:

```
my name is tanbul
```

Multi-line String Literals

We can also define multiline string literals without having to use + + for concatenation. Let's create a multiline string in the example `4b_MultilineString.kts`:

```
val name = "Atrium"
val message = """This is an example of
 multiline String $name
"""
println(message)
```

The output is as follows:

```
> kotlinc -script 4b_MultilineString.kts
This is an example of
multiline String Atrium
```

Observe the indentation in the preceding example. If we don't want to use indentation, we can put | and use the `trimMargin()` function to trim the margin as follows:

```
val name = "Atrium"
val message = """This is an example of
 |multiline String $name
"""
println(message.trimMargin())
```

The output is as follows:

```
> kotlinc -script 4b_MultilineString.kts
This is an example of
multiline String Atrium
```

One more thing that we can do is customize the character that we are going to use for margin separation and pass it to the `trimMargin()` function as follows:

```
val name = "Atrium"
val message = """This is an example of
 ^multiline String $name
"""
println(message.trimMargin("^"))
```

This gives the following output:

```
> kotlinc -script 4b_MultilineString.kts
This is an example of
multiline String Atrium
```

Expressions over statements

A statement is an element of a program that represents an action. An expression is a part of the statement that gets evaluated to a value. Statements introduce mutability. The more statements a program contains, the more mutability it will have. Mutability in code increases the chance that it is erroneous. Expressions, on the other hand, do not produce mutability. In purely functional constructs, there are no statements, there are only expressions. More expressions in a program mean less mutability and code that is more concise.

Consider the code for 5_Expressions.kts:

```kotlin
val number = 5
val evenOrOdd = if(number % 2 == 0) "is even number" else "is odd number"
println("$number $evenOrOdd")
```

The output is as follows:

```
> kotlinc -script 5_Expressions.kts
5 is odd number
```

In this case, the code has expressions and we are not mutating any state. We are simply assigning the result of an expression to a variable and printing it.

Similarly, try...catch is also an expression. try...catch is used for handling the exceptions. The last statement in the try block becomes the expression for the try block.

Functions

The fun keyword is used to define functions in Kotlin. In this section, we'll discuss writing a function, type inference, and specifying the return type.

In the following example, we create a function that takes two arguments of the String type and prints them to the console.

Consider the following code for `6_Function.kts`:

```
fun welcome(name:String, msg:String) {
    println("$msg $name")
}
welcome("Bob", "hello")
```

Note that we used string template to print the values without concatenating string literals.

The output of the preceding code as follows:

```
> kotlinc -script 6_Function.kts
hello Bob
```

This is a simple example of creating a function and invoking it. Now, let's create a function that returns a value.

Consider the code for `6a_Function.kts`:

```
fun welcome(name: String, msg:String) =
"$msg $name"
println(welcome("Bob", "hello"))
```

The output is as follows:

```
> kotlinc -script 6a_Function.kts
hello Bob
```

The = symbol says that Kotlin should infer the type from the context and identify the return type of the function. This is more suitable for single-line functions. For complex functions, we can specify the return type, in this case a `String`, and the `return` statement in the function, as shown here.

Consider the code for `6b_Function.kts`:

```
fun welcome(name: String, msg:String) : String {
    return "$msg $name"
}
println(welcome("Bob", "hello"))
```

The output is as follows:

```
> kotlinc -script 6b_Function.kts
hello Bob
```

We specified the String return type after the arguments prefixed by the colon (:) and the return statement in the function body.

Let's take a look at a function that doesn't return anything. We are interested in writing the void function.

Consider the code for 6c_Function.kts:

```
fun addNumbers(x: Int, y:Int) : Unit {
    println("Sum of numbers is ${x+y}")
}
addNumbers(2, 3)
```

The output is as follows:

```
> kotlinc -script 6c_Function.kts
Sum of numbers is 5
```

Unit is the representation of void in Kotlin. We can also write a void function without the Unit, as shown here.

Consider the code for 6d_Function:

```
fun addNumbers(x: Int, y:Int) {
    println("Sum of numbers is ${x+y}")
}
addNumbers(2, 3)
```

The output is as follows:

```
> kotlinc -script 6d_Function.kts
Sum of numbers is 5
```

Default arguments

Default values to the arguments is a nice way for an API to evolve. If we already have a function with two arguments and we need a third argument, we can make the transition easy by making use of default values to arguments. The existing code still works and, at the same time, we can invoke a function with new arguments. Default values to arguments make the API simple and expressive.

Let's write an example to provide a default value to an argument to the function.

Consider the code for `6e_DefaultArguments.kts`:

```
fun welcome(name: String, msg:String = "Hey") {
    println("$msg $name")
}
welcome("Bob", "hello")
welcome("Berry")
```

In this case, we are not providing the second argument, `msg`, to the `welcome()` function. It therefore uses a default message instead. The output is as follows:

```
> kotlinc -script 6e_DefaultArguments.kts
hello Bob
Hey Berry
```

As shown in the preceding example, a default value to an argument can be specified with an = symbol in the argument declaration. In this case, if we don't pass the second argument while invoking the function, a default value will be provided.

Named arguments

We can use a named argument to invoke a function and pass the arguments by naming them. Since the arguments are named, the order doesn't need to be maintained.

Let's take a look at the following example. Consider the code for `6f_NamedArguments.kts`:

```
fun welcome(name: String, msg:String = "Hey") {
    println("$msg $name")
}
welcome(msg = "How are you", name = "Mark")
```

The output is as follows:

```
> kotlinc -script 6f_NamedArguments.kts
How are you Mark
```

We can also mix named arguments with arguments without a name. Consider the code for `6g_NamedArguments.kts`:

```
fun welcome(name: String, msg:String = "Hey") {
    println("$msg $name")
}
welcome("Joseph", msg = "Hi")
```

The output is as follows:

```
> kotlinc -script 6g_NamedArguments.kts
Hi Joseph
```

In this case, we invoked the function with one positional argument with the value `Joseph` and one argument named `msg`. When we are dealing with multiple arguments in a method, we can choose to send some arguments positionally by maintaining the order and to send others as named arguments. The language gives us the flexibility to invoke functions with type safety.

varargs and spread

Kotlin supports a variable number of arguments. `vararg` is the keyword that is used for a variable number of arguments. Using `vararg`, we can pass multiple arguments to a function.

Let's see an example of `7a_VarArgs.kts`:

```
fun findMaxNumber(vararg numbers : Int) =
        numbers.reduce { max , e -> if(max > e) max else e }

println(findMaxNumber(1,2,3,4))
```

The output is as follows:

```
> kotlinc -script 7a_VarArgs.kts
4
```

The `findMaxNumber()` function takes a variable number of arguments and finds the maximum. We invoked `reduce` on the numbers and wrote a lambda expression. In Kotlin, a lambda is specified using curly braces.

If we have an array of numbers, we can invoke the `findMaxNumber()` function using the `spread` operator without changing the function argument type.

Consider the following code for `7b_Spread.kts`:

```
fun findMaxNumber(vararg numbers : Int) =
        numbers.reduce { max , e -> if(max > e) max else e }

val numberArray = intArrayOf(25,50,75,100)
println(findMaxNumber(*numberArray))
```

The output is as follows:

```
> kotlinc -script 7b_Spread.kts
100
```

Note that * acts as a spread operator here. We can combine this with discrete values, as shown in the following `7c_Spread` file.

Consider the code for `7c_Spread.kts`:

```
fun findMaxNumber(vararg numbers : Int) =
        numbers.reduce { max , e -> if(max > e) max else e }

val numberArray = intArrayOf(25,50,75,100)
println(findMaxNumber(4,5,*numberArray,200, 10))
```

The output is as follows:

```
> kotlinc -script 7c_Spread.kts
200
```

The for loop

Let's write a `for` loop to print numbers. Consider the code for `8a_ForLoop.kts`:

```
for(num in 1 .. 5){
    println(num)
}
```

The output is as follows:

```
> kotlinc -script 8a_ForLoop.kts
1
2
3
4
5
```

`..` is used to specify the range, meaning the program prints numbers from 1 to 5 inclusively.

To exclude a range, the `until` keyword is used. Consider the code for `8b_ForLoop_Until.kts`:

```
for(num in 1 until 5){
    println(num)
}
```

The output is as follows:

```
> kotlinc -script 8b_ForLoop_Until.kts
1
2
3
4
```

If we want our numbers to be inclusive, we use (..). If we want to exclude the range, we use `until`.

If we want to traverse the range in a given step size, we can use `step`. Consider the code for `8c_ForLoop_Step.kts`:

```
for(num in 1 .. 10 step 2){
    println(num)
}
```

The output is as follows:

```
> kotlinc -script 8c_ForLoop_Step.kts
1
3
5
7
9
```

If we want to iterate in reverse order, we can use downTo.

Consider the code for 8d_ForLoop_downTo.kts:

```
for(num in 25 downTo 20){
    println(num)
}
```

This gives us the following output:

```
> kotlinc -script 8d_ForLoop_downTo.kts
25
24
23
22
21
20
```

If we want to iterate in reverse order in a given step size, we can use downTo and step.

Consider the code for 8e_ForLoop_downTo_Step.kts:

```
for(num in 25 downTo 15 step 2){
    println(num)
}
```

The output is as follows:

```
> kotlinc -script 8e_ForLoop_downTo_Step.kts
25
23
21
19
17
15
```

.. works on a range in ascending order.

Now, consider the code for 8e1_ForLoop_downTo.kts:

```
for(num in 25 .. 20){
    println(num)
}
```

The output is as follows:

```
> kotlinc -script 8e1_ForLoop_downTo.kts

>
```

This code compiles without any errors, but when you run it, there will be no output.

For downTo and step, the value has to be a positive number. If we give a negative number, such as -2, it will produce a compilation error.

Consider the code for 8e2_ForLoop_downTo_Step.kts:

```
for(num in 25 downTo 15 step -2){
    println(num)
}
```

The output is as follows:

```
> kotlinc -script 8e2_ForLoop_downTo_Step.kts
java.lang.IllegalArgumentException: Step must be positive, was: -2.
        at kotlin.ranges.RangesKt__RangesKt.checkStepIsPositive(Ranges.kt:102)
        at kotlin.ranges.RangesKt___RangesKt.step(_Ranges.kt:455)
        at _8e2_ForLoop_downTo_Step.<init>(8e2_ForLoop_downTo_Step.kts:1)
```

Iterating over a list

Collections are used for storing and processing a set of objects. Kotlin provides an elegant syntax for iteration over a collection.

Consider the code for `9_IteratingOverList.kts`:

```
val names = listOf("Mark", "Tina", "Williams")
for(name in names) {
    println(name)
}
```

The output is as follows:

```
> kotlinc -script 9_IteratingOverList.kts
Mark
Tina
Williams
```

If we are interested in getting the index value, we can do that by running the `indices` command on the collection.

Consider the code for `9a_IteratingOverListIndex.kts`:

```
val names = listOf("Mark", "Tina", "Williams")
for(index in names.indices) {
    println(index)
}
```

The output is as follows:

```
> kotlinc -script 9a_IteratingOverListIndex.kts
0
1
2
```

As the index is a String, we can write an expression to print it. Consider the code for `9b_IteratingOverListIndex.kts`:

```
val names = listOf("Mark", "Tina", "Joseph")
for(index in names.indices) {
  println("$index")
}
```

The output is as follows:

```
> kotlinc -script 9b_IteratingOverListIndex.kts
0
1
2
```

We can also add names to the expression to get items out of the collection, as in the following example, in which we are printing `index` and `name`. Consider the code for `9c_IteratingOverList.kts`:

```
val names = listOf("Mark", "Tina", "Joseph")
for(index in names.indices) {
 println("$index: ${names.get(index)}")
}
```

The output is as follows:

```
> kotlinc -script 9c_IteratingOverList.kts
0: Mark
1: Tina
2: Joseph
```

When clause

`when` is a pattern matching clause in Kotlin. This helps us to write elegant code when dealing with pattern matching, meaning we can avoid using a lot of `if else` statements.

Let's write a function that takes an input, the type of which is not known. `Any` is used to indicate this and a `when` block is used to handle different patterns.

Consider the code for `10_when.kts`:

```
fun processInput(input: Any) {
    when(input) {
        10 -> println("It is 10")
        98,99 -> println("It is 98 or 99")
        in 101 .. 120 -> println("More than 100")
        is String -> println("This is ${input} of length ${input.length}")
        else -> println("Not known")
    }
}
processInput(10)
processInput(98)
processInput(99)
processInput(102)
processInput("hey there")
processInput(Thread())
```

The output is as follows:

```
> kotlinc -script 10_when.kts
It is 10
It is 98 or 99
It is 98 or 99
More than 100
This is hey there of length 9
Not known
```

Alongside the pattern matching, we can also perform type checking using the when block:

```
is String -> println("This is ${input} of length ${input.length}")
```

Note that the argument input is of the Any type. After type checking, the input is automatically cast to String, and we can use the length property, which is defined in the String class. The Kotlin language does the auto-typecasting for us, so we don't have to do any explicit type casting.

The nullable type

In Kotlin, we can declare a variable to hold a null value using the nullable type.

Let's write a program to check whether the given input is Web. If it is, it should return Web Development. If not, it should return an empty string.

Consider the code for 11_NullType.kts:

```
fun checkInput (data: String) : String {
    if(data == "Web")
        return "Web development"
    return ""
}
println(checkInput ("Web"))
println(checkInput ("Android"))
```

The output is as follows:

```
> kotlinc -script 11_NullType.kts
Web development
```

So far, so good. Let's say that we want to return `null` if there is no match for the given input:

```
fun checkInput (data: String) : String {
    if(data == "Web")
        return "Web development"
    return null
}
println(checkInput ("Web"))
println(checkInput ("Android"))
```

Let's compile and run this code:

```
> kotlinc -script 11_NullType.kts
11_NullType.kts:4:12: error: null can not be a value of a non-null type String
    return null
         ^
```

Here, we get a compilation error because the return type is non-null by default in the function declaration. If we want to return null, we have to specify the type as nullable using `?`:

```
fun checkInput (data: String) : String? {
    if(data == "Web")
        return "Web development"
    return null
}
println(checkInput ("Web"))
println(checkInput ("Android"))
```

The output is as follows:

```
> kotlinc -script 11_NullType.kts
Web development
null
```

This code has compiled and run successfully. When we invoke the `checkInput` function with `Web`, it prints `Web development`. When we pass `Android`, it prints `null` to the console.

Similarly, when we receive data in response, we can also receive a nullable type from the function and perform a null check. Kotlin provides a very elegant syntax to do null checks.

Consider the code for `11a_NullCheck.kts`:

```kotlin
fun checkInput (data: String) : String? {
    if(data == "Web")
        return "Web development"
    return null
}
var response = checkInput ("Web")
println(response)
response ?.let {
    println("got non null value")
} ?: run {
    println("got null")
}
```

The `checkInput()` function returns a string if there is a match for `Web`, otherwise it returns `null`. Once the function returns a value, we can check whether it is null or non-null and act appropriately. `?.let` and `?:run` are used for this kind of scenario.

The output is as follows:

```
> kotlinc -script 11a_NullCheck.kts
Web development
got non null value
```

Consider the code for `11a_NullCheck.kts`:

```kotlin
fun checkInput (data: String) : String? {
    if(data == "Web")
        return "Web development"
    return null
}
var response = checkInput ("iOS")
println(response)
response ?.let {
    println("got non null value")
} ?: run {
    println("got null")
}
```

We now pass `iOS` instead of `Web`.

In this case, the output is as follows:

```
> kotlinc -script 11a_NullCheck.kts
null
got null
```

Lambda expressions in Kotlin

Functional programming can be advantageous when we are performing lots of different operations on data that has a known, fixed amount of variation. It provides a very elegant way to write code with immutability. It also allows you to write pure functions.

A lambda expression is an anonymous function that represents the implementation of **single abstract method** (**SAM**) of an interface. Lambda expressions deal with expressions and promote immutability, which turn functions into higher-order functions.

Let's write a lambda expression. Consider the following code for
`12_LambdaExpressions_HelloWorld.kts`:

```
val greetingLambda = { println("Hello from Lambda") }
greetingLambda()
```

The output is as follows:

```
> kotlinc -script 12_LambdaExpressions_HelloWorld.kts
Hello from Lambda
```

We can invoke lambda functions directly, as in the example shown in the preceding code, or we can use `invoke()` as follows—`greetingLambda.invoke()`:

```
val greetingLambda = { println("Hello from Lambda") }
greetingLambda.invoke()
```

In the next example, we will write a lambda expression that takes an argument. Consider the following code for `12a_LambdaExpressions.kts`:

```
val greetingLambda = { user: String -> println("Hello ${user}") }
greetingLambda.invoke("Tom")
```

The output is as follows:

```
> kotlinc -script 12a_LambdaExpressions.kts
Hello Tom
```

We will now write an inline lambda function to print only even numbers. Consider the following code for `12b_LambdaExpressions.kts`:

```
listOf(0,1,2,3,4,5,6,7,8,9)
.filter{ e -> e % 2 == 0}
.forEach{ e -> println(e)}
```

Here, we created a list of numbers from 0-9, and then we used `filter` to retrieve only the even numbers. Finally, we used `forEach` to iterate over the numbers and print the values to the console.

The output of the preceding code is as follows:

```
> kotlinc -script 12b_LambdaExpressions.kts
0
2
4
6
8
```

Extension functions

In Kotlin, we can easily add functionality to existing classes through its extension functions. The language provides the ability to add additional functions to classes without modifying the source code. In this section, we will look at how to extend the functionality of classes so that they provide the exact functionality that we are interested in. Kotlin supports extension functions and extension properties.

To create an extension function, we start with the `fun` keyword, and then we prefix the name of the extension function with the name of the class to be extended (known as the receiver type), followed by the dot operator (represented by the `.` character).

An example of this is `receiverType.customFunctionName()`.

Consider the following code for `13_ExtensionFunctons.kts`:

```kotlin
fun String.myExtendedFunction() = toUpperCase()

println("Kotlin".myExtendedFunction())
```

Here, `myExtendedFunction()` is an extension to the existing String class. We added `myExtendedFunction()` as an extension function and invoked it on a String literal.

The output for the preceding example is as follows:

```
> kotlinc -script 13_ExtensionFunctons.kts
KOTLIN
```

This can be pictorially represented as follows:

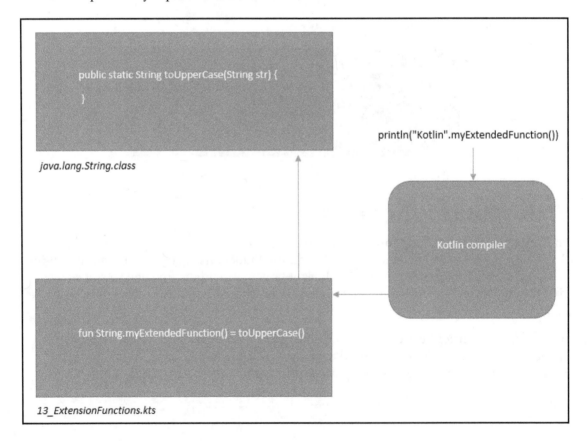

- Extension functions do not get added to the original classes. Instead, new functions are made callable by adding a dot on the `receiverType` variables.
- Extension functions are resolved during compilation time. They are statically typed. This means that the extension function being invoked is determined by the `receiverType` of the expression on which the function is invoked, not by the nature of the result of evaluating the expression at runtime.
- The extension functions cannot be overloaded.

Classes in Kotlin

Classes in Kotlin are created using the `class` keyword, which is depicted as follows:

```
class User {

}
```

The structure of the class is as follows:

```
Class className {
        //properties and constructor
        //member functions
}
```

Let's write a class for `User`.

Consider the following code for `14_Class.kts`:

```
class User {
    var name = "George"
}

val user = User()
println(user.name)
```

The output is as follows:

```
> kotlinc -script 14_Class.kts
George
```

This class has a property called `name`. Classes are instantiated with just the class name, followed by parentheses. Note that there is no `new` keyword in Kotlin to create an object, unlike in Java.

Classes in Kotlin are final by default. We cannot extend from a class directly. To inherit from the classes, we have to open the classes explicitly. Classes need to have an `open` keyword in their declaration, as shown in the following code:

```
open class Person {

}
```

Alternatively, we can use *all-open compiler* plugins to make all the classes extendable or accessible to frameworks such as JPA and Spring. We will discuss compiler plugins further in the next chapter.

Constructors

Constructors are used to initialize class properties. As in Java, a constructor is a special member function that is invoked when an object is instantiated. However, they work slightly different in Kotlin.

In Kotlin, there are two constructors:

- **Primary constructor**: This is a concise way to initialize the properties of a class
- **Secondary constructor**: This is where additional initialization logic goes

The **primary constructor** is part of the class header. Here's an example:

```
class User() {

}
```

The block of code surrounded by parentheses is the primary constructor. Consider the following code for `14a_PrimaryConstructor.kts`:

```
class User(var firstName: String, var lastName: String) {

}

val user = User("Norman", "Lewis")
println("First Name= ${user.firstName}")
println("Last Name= ${user.lastName}")
```

The output is as follows:

```
> kotlinc -script 14a_PrimaryConstructor.kts
First Name= Norman
Last Name= Lewis
```

The constructor goes here as part of the class header. The constructor declares two
properties—firstName and lastName. Let's look at another example
for 14b_PrimaryConstructor.kts:

```
class User(var firstName: String, val id: String) {

}
val user = User("Norman", "myId")
println("First Name = ${user.firstName}")
println("User Id = ${user.id}")
```

The output of the preceding code is as follows:

```
> kotlinc -script 14b_PrimaryConstructor.kts
First Name = Norman
User Id = myId
```

For the primary constructor, properties have to be declared using var or
val. Otherwise, the code fails to compile.

The secondary constructor is created using the constructor keyword. The class can
declare a secondary constructor to initialize its properties. This is shown in the following
code:

```
class AuditData {
    constructor(message: String) {
        //init logic
    }
    constructor(message: String, locale: String) {
        // init logic
    }
}
```

In the preceding code snippet, we wrote two constructors. One had a message as an argument and one had two arguments—message and locale. Consider the following code for `14c_SecondaryConstructor.kts`:

```
var audit = AuditData("record added")
println("Message ${audit.message}")

audit = AuditData("record updated", "en-US")
println("Message: ${audit.message}")
println("Locale: ${audit.locale}")
```

When we call `AuditData` with only a message, the constructor with one argument will be invoked. Similarly, when we pass two arguments, a message and a locale, the constructor with two arguments will be invoked.

The output is as follows:

```
> kotlinc -script 14c_SecondaryConstructor.kts
Message: record added
-----------------------
Message: record updated
Locale: en-US
```

Static functions

Static functions are functions that can be invoked without creating multiple instances of a class. Static functions avoid code duplication and can be reused.

Let's take a look at how to write a static function in Kotlin.

Consider the following code for `15a_StaticMethods.kts`:

```
object MyUtil {
  fun foo(){
        println("Static function foo() is invoked")
    }
}

MyUtil.foo()
```

Note that we declared an object `MyUtil` and defined a function `foo()`. This is known as object declaration.

We invoked the function `foo()` directly using the object `MyUtil`.

The output of the preceding code is as follows:

```
> kotlinc -script 15a_StaticMethods.kts
Static function foo() is invoked
```

There are different ways to write static functions in Kotlin. We can define a `companion object` inside a class and define a static function in it. Consider the following code for `15b_StaticMethods.kts`:

```kotlin
class Person {
    companion object {
        fun foo(){
            println("Static function foo() is invoked")
        }
    }
}
Person.foo()
```

The output is as follows:

```
> kotlinc -script 15b_StaticMethods.kts
Static function foo() is invoked
```

We can also give a name to the companion object. Consider the following code for `15c_StaticMethods.kts`:

```kotlin
class Person {
    companion object Util {
        fun foo(){
            println("Static function foo() is invoked")
        }
    }
}
Person.Util.foo()
```

The output is as follows:

```
> kotlinc -script 15c_StaticMethods.kts
Static function foo() is invoked
```

We can invoke the static method shown in the preceding example with `companion` as `Person.Companion.foo()`. The static method `foo` can be invoked using either the class name or a named companion object prefixed with the class name, such as `Person.Util.foo()`.

In this section, we have covered the constructs that Kotlin provides. We will be using these constructs in the next few chapters.

Kotlin programming style and Syntax

Let's now discuss some of Kotlin's syntactic rules and coding guidelines:

- **Class name**: As in Java, class names begin with an uppercase letter. We can create it with a lowercase letter, but it is recommended that we use an uppercase letter, as per the Java coding convention. This is to keep the convention the same when dealing with both Java and Kotlin files.
- **Packages**: Specify the package at the top of the class. Packages are written in lowercase letters separated by a dot(.):

```
package org.rao.kotlin.intro
```

Note that the semicolon is optional in package declarations in Kotlin.

- **Imports**: The imports should be after the declaration in the class file. If there is no package statement, the import statement should be the first statement. An example of an import statement is as follows:

```
import java.util.List
```

- **Variables**: In Kotlin, `var` and `val` are used to declare variables. Use camelCase when declaring variables and provide meaningful names for them. Some examples are shown in the following table:

Examples	Explanation
`val number = 10`	Here, the type `Int` is inferred. We can use this syntax in local contexts in code.
`val number: Int = 10`	Here, the type `Int` is declared explicitly and a value is assigned.
`val number: Int`	Here, a variable is declared but not initialized. Declaring the type is required in this case.
`var userName = "Bob"`	Here, we used `var` to create a mutable variable, which is initialized. Because of this, the type is optional and is inferred from the context. In this case, the type inferred is `String`.

- **Comments**: Kotlin has support for single-line and multiline comments:

```
// This is single line comment
/* This is a multi-line
comment. */
```

Unlike Java, Kotlin also supports nested comments:

```
/*
Top level comment section
/*
        Nested comments section
*/
        */
```

- **Operators**: Use the `in` operator to check whether a number is in a specified range or in loops for iteration:

```
if(number in 1..5)

for(number in 1..5)
```

Similarly, use the `is` operator to check the type. When we use the `is` operator, explicit type casting is not required:

```
fun processInput(input: Any) {
    if(object is String) {
        var data: String = object
    }
}
```

Note the automatic type conversion that is applied when using the `is` operator in this context. Outside this context, the type will be `Any`. This is a super type in Kotlin, like `Object` in Java.

Kotlin provides an easy and flexible syntax compared to Java. This helps us write concise and more expressive code that is easy to maintain.

Summary

In this chapter, we have discussed the following:

- A brief introduction to the Kotlin language
- A quick tour of the language, with various examples enabling us to familiarize ourselves with the Kotlin world
- A brief look at Kotlin syntax

Kotlin – The Game Changer

2

Enterprises typically develop their applications or microservices based on Java. Java is the first choice of language for development because it is robust, safe, and backward compatible. Java's platform independence makes it suitable for developing web services and enterprise applications. Having said that, however, have we ever considered whether there might be a better way to write code, one that makes it easy not only to develop an application, but also to maintain it over a period of time?

With its elegant syntax and numerous features, Kotlin makes it much easier to work with. Writing code with Kotlin is much simpler. We can develop complex applications quickly and maintain them easily:

The following topics will be covered in this chapter:

- What makes Kotlin stand out among other JVM-based languages
- A comparison with Java
- How to configure Kotlin in IDEs
- What Coroutines are and how to use them in an application
- Using Java and Kotlin to set up a project

Technical requirements

We will use IDEs, such as IntelliJ IDEA and Eclipse, to set up the project. A knowledge of working with these IDEs is helpful.

Why Kotlin is the game changer

Kotlin offers many features of modern languages. It has null safety, a functional style of coding, non-verbose code, and is clean and easy when it comes to using Java's stream operations, including `filter`, `map`, `reduce`, and more. All of these can help to improve your development life cycle and productivity.

Kotlin was developed with the intention of adding features that are not found in existing JVM languages. It is a modern JVM language that has full interoperability with Java, ensuring that existing applications or services don't face any problems with coexisting with Kotlin. If we are familiar with functional paradigms, it will be easier to make use of the power of the language.

Interoperability with Java

Kotlin is completely interoperable with Java. It hasn't changed any of the existing Java functionality. This means that if we are in the middle of an application or microservice written in Java, we can switch to Kotlin and use its new features.

If we have an existing Java project and want to leverage the advantage that Kotlin offers, we can add new code in Kotlin to an existing Java project. In an application, part of the code can be written in Java, part in Kotlin, and they will work seamlessly together.

Functional paradigms

Kotlin supports a functional style of programming that allows you to write more elegant, concise, and expressive code.

In Kotlin, we don't have to write lengthy code to provide simple functionality. Pure functions and higher-order functions avoid mutating the states, thereby reducing the complexity of the code and improving its readability.

Lambda expressions are anonymous functions that represent the implementation of a **Single Abstract Method(SAM)** interface. We can pass lambda expressions to functions. In doing this, we are not passing objects, but instead we are passing behaviors to the functions that are evaluated without mutating the state of an object. This turns a function into a higher-order function.

Consider the following lambda expression:

```
val greetingLambda = { println("Greet from inline lambda") }
```

This can be invoked using the following:

```
greetingLambda() or
```

```
greetingLambda.invoke()
```

The output of the preceding lambda expression is as follows:

Let's write an inline lambda expression to print even numbers:

```
listOf(0,1,2,3,4,5,6,7,8,9)
.filter{ e -> e % 2 == 0}
.forEach{ e -> println(e)}
```

The output will be as follows:

```
Run:      LambdaEvenNumbers  ×
    [INFO]
    [INFO] --- exec-maven-plugin:1.6.0:java (default-cli) @ myJavaApp ---
    0
    2
    4
    6
    8
    [INFO] ------------------------------------------------------------------
    [INFO] BUILD SUCCESS
    [INFO] ------------------------------------------------------------------
    [INFO] Total time: 20.819 s
    [INFO] Finished at: 2018-09-02T23:36:24+05:30
    [INFO] Final Memory: 37M/308M
    [INFO] ------------------------------------------------------------------
```

Immutability

Immutability is the opposite of mutation. **Mutation** is where we modify the state of an object. Mutation is error-prone and makes debugging difficult. Kotlin emphasizes immutability with `val`, which makes a variable immutable. Its collection types are also immutable by default. Once the `val` or collection is initialized, it is guaranteed to hold the same value. Immutability makes code easier to write and use and the internal state of the application will be more consistent.

Let's consider the following code sample:

```kotlin
object ImmutabilityTest {
    @JvmStatic
    fun main(args: Array<String>) {
        val msg = "Hello"
        msg = "hi"
        println(msg)
    }
}
```

In the preceding code, we created a immutable variable, `msg`, assigned a value. We then try to change its value.

If we compile this code, it gives us a compilation error that the value of msg cannot be changed:

```
[INFO] Changes detected - recompiling the module!
[INFO] Compiling 2 source files to ..\Intermixing Java and
Kotlin\myJavaApp\target\classes
[INFO]
[INFO] --- kotlin-maven-plugin:1.2.41:compile (compile) @ myJavaApp ---
[ERROR] ..\Intermixing Java and
Kotlin\myJavaApp\src\main\java\ImmutabilityTest.kt: (5, 9) Val cannot be
reassigned
```

Consider the following example as well:

```
object ImmutabilityTest {
    @JvmStatic
    fun main(args: Array<String>) {
        val msg: String
        msg = "Good Morning"
        msg = "Good Evening"

        println(msg)
    }
}
```

In the preceding code, we created a immutable variable, msg, which is of the String type. Note that we declared the type explicitly here and varied the initialization of msg. When we are varying the initialization, we have to declare the type explicitly. We then try to change its value.

If we compile this code, it also gives us a compilation error that the value of msg cannot be changed:

```
[INFO] Changes detected - recompiling the module!
[INFO] Compiling 2 source files to ..\Intermixing Java and
Kotlin\myJavaApp\target\classes
[INFO]
[INFO] --- kotlin-maven-plugin:1.2.41:compile (compile) @ myJavaApp ---
[ERROR] ..\Intermixing Java and
Kotlin\myJavaApp\src\main\java\ImmutabilityTest.kt: (6, 9) Val cannot be
reassigned
```

Null safety

Generally, when we write code, we declare the fields in a class. We are not sure whether or not the field is initialized during execution. To find out, we use null checks and annotations such as `@Nullable` or `@NotNull`. Kotlin provides elegant syntax for declaring fields with nullable and non-nullable types, which prevents the problem of accidental **NullPointerExceptions (NPEs)**. Kotlin catches possible null pointers when the code is being compiled, meaning that no null pointer issues will occur after the application has been deployed. This means that there are almost no cases of `NullPointerException`.

Consider the following code:

```
object NullabilityTest {
    @JvmStatic
    fun main(args: Array<String>) {
        var msg: String = null
        println(msg)
    }
}
```

Let's compile the preceding code:

```
[INFO] ------------------------------------------------------------------------
----
[ERROR] Failed to execute goal org.jetbrains.kotlin:kotlin-maven-
plugin:1.2.41:compile (compile) on project myJavaApp: Compilation failure
[ERROR] ..\Intermixing Java and
Kotlin\myJavaApp\src\main\java\NullabilityTest.kt:[10,28] Null cannot be a
value of a non-null type String
```

This code gives a compilation error. If we want to assign a null value to a variable, it has to be declared as follows:

```
var msg: String ?= null
```

The `msg` variable can be declared with a null value. Let's consider another example:

```
object NullabilityTest {
    @JvmStatic
    fun main(args: Array<String>) {
        var userList:ArrayList<String> ?= null
        println(userList.get(0))
    }
}
```

Variables can be declared to hold a null value. If we invoke any function on these variables, such as `userList.get(0)`, it doesn't throw `NullPointerException` at runtime. Instead, it just fails to compile:

```
Error:(6, 25) Kotlin: Only safe (?.) or non-null asserted (!!.) calls are
allowed on a nullable receiver of type
kotlin.collections.ArrayList<String>? /* = java.util.ArrayList<String>? */
```

Kotlin catches possible null pointers during compile time. It warns us that we should initialize the `var` before accessing it. The language provides clear constructs to define which variables can hold a null value, and which can hold a non-null value. When a variable is null, the language provides a safer way to deal with it, avoiding null pointer issues at runtime. This means that there are almost no cases of `NullPointerException`.

Since the variables have been declared to hold a null value, we need to perform a null check before accessing any function on this variable. Kotlin provides an elegant syntax for null check (`?.`), as follows:

```
userList?.get(0)
```

Kotlin provides an elegant syntax to perform an operation on the variable that can hold null values safely. Consider the following code:

```
fun main(args: Array<String>) {
    var userList:ArrayList<String> ?= null
    var user = userList?.get(0)

    user ?.let {
        println("got the user details")
    } ?: run {
        println("there is no user")
    }
}
```

Here, we create a list of users, `userList`, and try to get the first object and do something with it. In this case, the `user` instance is null, so when we use `?.` on it, it doesn't throw `NullPointerException`. If the `user` instance is not null, it prints a `got the user details` message to the console. If it is null, it prints a `there is no user` message.

In short, Kotlin is a feature-packed language, with its simple and concise language constructs. If we already have an application written in Java, we can include Kotlin to get the benefits that it offers. Once the code is compiled, everything is bytecode and no distinction is made between Java or Kotlin. This is possible because Kotlin is interoperable with Java and provides an elegant way of writing code that reduces the development life cycle and is less error prone.

Kotlin versus Java

When we think of developing an application, Java is one of the programming languages that comes to mind for various reasons, including its robust and secure nature, and the independence of its platform. Most enterprise applications are built using Java, and this particular programming language has been around for more than 20 years.

Kotlin is designed to be interoperable with Java, meaning Kotlin can seamlessly co-exist with Java. We can add Kotlin to our existing applications and we can use Java-based frameworks for application development. With this *bi-directional use* of Kotlin, we can invoke Java constructs from Kotlin, or Kotlin constructs from Java.

Although Java and Kotlin are both JVM-based languages used for application development, there are several differences between them. Kotlin has addressed some of the limitations previously associated with Java.

Null safety issue

Accessing a member variable of a null reference will result in a null reference exception. In Java, this is `NullPointerException`. Java allows us to assign a null value to any variable that we declare, but when we try to use an object reference that has a null value, it throws `NullPointerException`. This is a common problem to do with programming languages. The language allows us to assign a null reference to a member variable, while also allowing us to access that variable without checking whether it is initialized. It would be preferable if the compiler reports such issues. This is exactly what Kotlin compiler does for us.

In Kotlin, all the types are non-nullable by default. If we try to assign or return a null in the code, it fails to compile. The compiler differentiates between nullable references and non-null references, and the language provides an elegant syntax for null checks. This makes it almost impossible to encounter NPEs in Kotlin. In fact, if we do encounter an NPE, it is likely to be because we explicitly asked Kotlin to throw one, or because the NPE originates from external Java code.

Arrays in Kotlin are invariant

Arrays in Kotlin are not built on native types, but are instead based on a Java array. Although these are similar, they do behave slightly differently. In Java, we can assign an array of a type to an array of its parent type. Arrays in Kotlin are invariant, which means that an array of a specific type cannot be assigned to an array of its parent type. It is not possible to assign `Array<Integer>` to `Array<Any>`. This provides implicit type safety and prevents possible runtime errors in the application. Kotlin also provides specialized classes to create arrays of primitive data types, including `ByteArray`, `ShortArray`, and `IntArray`.

Extension functions

Kotlin gives us the ability to extend a class with new functionalities without modifying it. These *extension functions* are not available in Java.

No checked exceptions

In Java, exception handling is tedious and controlled by strict rules. Whenever we are dealing with checked exceptions, we can either handle exceptions in `try...catch` blocks, or they can be declared to be thrown. In this case, the code is repeated. Kotlin doesn't have any checked exceptions. The `Exception` class is extended from the `java.lang.Exception` class of the JDK library via `typealias`. We don't have to declare or handle the exceptions, thereby reducing a lot of boilerplate code.

Kotlin also provides other benefits, as explained in the following subsections.

Functional paradigms

Kotlin is both an object-oriented and functional programming language. It combines the functional and object-oriented paradigms. Kotlin offers support for lambda functions and higher-order functions, making it a great choice for functional programming.

Concise code

Kotlin code is elegant and clear and has a lot less boilerplate code than Java. When we compare a Java class and a Kotlin class that perform the same task, the one written in Kotlin will typically be much more concise, clear, and compact than the one written in Java. Kotlin greatly reduces the boilerplate code, meaning we don't need to write getters, setters, or `toString()`, `hashCode()`, or `equals()` functions. Kotlin generates all these constructs by itself, making the language more clean and concise.

We can choose which language to use for application development. If we already have an application written in Java, we can include Kotlin to get the benefits that it offers so that the code becomes clear, concise, and easy to maintain.

Configuring Kotlin in the project

Now that we have learned about the benefits that the Kotlin language offers, let's see how to configure Kotlin in a project. In this section, we will look at how to create a simple Kotlin project and a Maven project using IntelliJ IDEA.

Creating a simple Kotlin project

It's easy to create a Kotlin-JVM project using IntelliJ IDEA by observing the following steps:

1. Click on **File** | **New** | **Project**.
2. In the **New Project** window, select **Kotlin/JVM,** and choose **Next**. This is shown in the following screenshot:

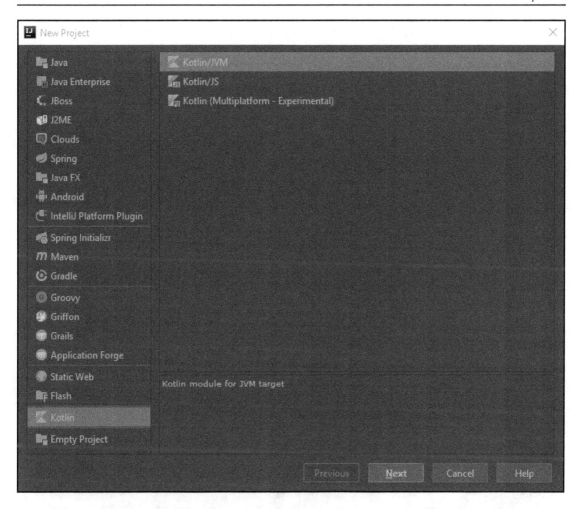

3. In the next wizard, specify the **Project name** and the **Project location**. Choose **JDK** and **Kotlin runtime** and click on **Finish**.

4. In the modules settings, click on **Facets** and add Kotlin to the module.

5. We have now created a simple Kotlin project. We can write the code here in Kotlin:

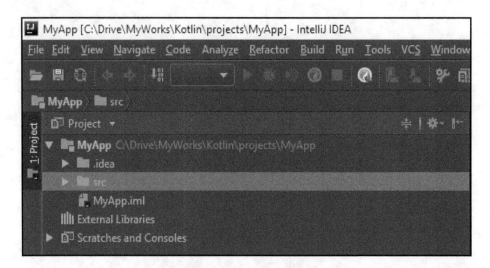

6. Under the source (`src`) directory, we can create the Kotlin files:

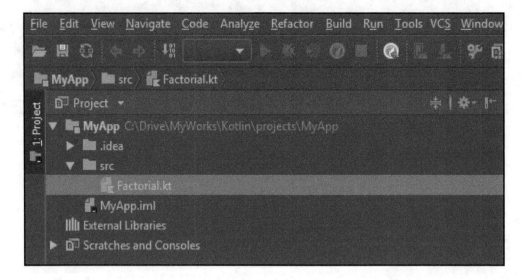

Now let's write a simple program to find the factorial of a number. Consider the following `Factorial.kt` file:

```kotlin
fun main(args: Array<String>) {
    val number = 5
    var factorial: Int = 1
    for (i in 1..number) {
        factorial *= i
    }
    println("Factorial of $number = $factorial")
}
```

The output is as follows:

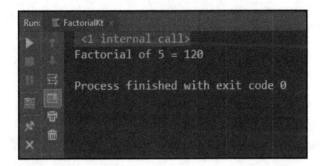

Maven project

Now, let's create a Kotlin project using the Maven build tool. Make sure we configure Maven in the system.

Create a Maven project by observing the following steps:

1. Click on **File** | **New** | **Project**.
2. In the **New Project** window, select **Maven** and enable **Create from archetype**.

3. Select `org.jetbrains.kotlin:kotlin-archetype-jvm` as the archetype and click on **Next**:

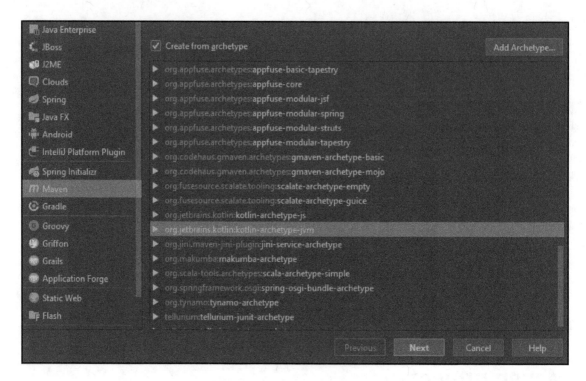

4. Specify the **GroupId**, **ArtifactId,** and **Version** for the Maven project and then click on **Next**.

5. Verify the project's name and location and click on **Finish**

We have now successfully created a Maven project:

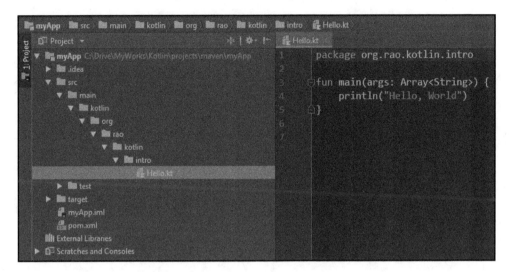

Configuring Kotlin in Eclipse

We can also use Eclipse to work with Kotlin. Eclipse supports Kotlin via a plugin. If we don't have Eclipse, it can be downloaded from `https://www.eclipse.org/downloads/`. Observe the following steps to configure Kotlin in Eclipse:

1. To install the Kotlin plugin, click on **Help,** and then **Eclipse Marketplace.**

2. Search for `Kotlin` in the **Search** field and install the plugin.

3. Restart Eclipse after installing the plugin in order for the changes to take effect.

4. After restarting, select **Kotlin** in **Open Perspective**:

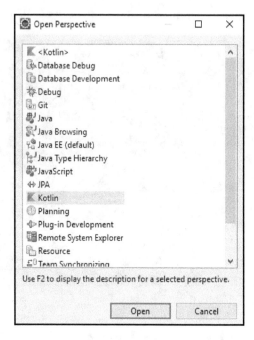

We have now successfully configured Kotlin in the Eclipse IDE.

Let's now take a look at how to create a simple Kotlin project in Eclipse:

1. Select **File**, then **New,** and then **Kotlin Project.**
2. Enter the **project name**, choose its **location,** and click on **Finish.**

3. This creates the following project structure:

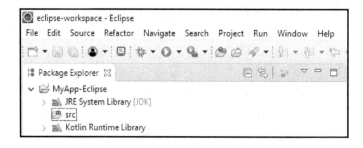

The steps to create a Kotlin file are as follows:

1. Right-click on the project, and then select **New | Kotlin File:**

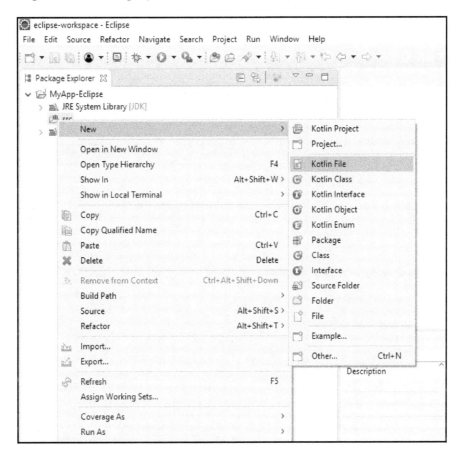

2. Enter the name of the file and click on **Finish**.
3. Let's now write a Kotlin program to check whether a given number is prime or not. Consider the following code for `PrimeNumber.kt`:

```
fun isPrime(number:Int):Boolean{
    for (i in 2..number / 2) {
        if (number % i == 0) {
            return true
        }
    }
    return false;
}
```

```kotlin
fun main(args:Array<String>){
  val number = 11
  if(!isPrime(number)){
    println("$number is a prime number")
  }else {
        println("$number is not a prime number")
  }
}
```

4. To run the program, right-click on the source file, choose **Run As**, and then click on **Kotlin Application**:

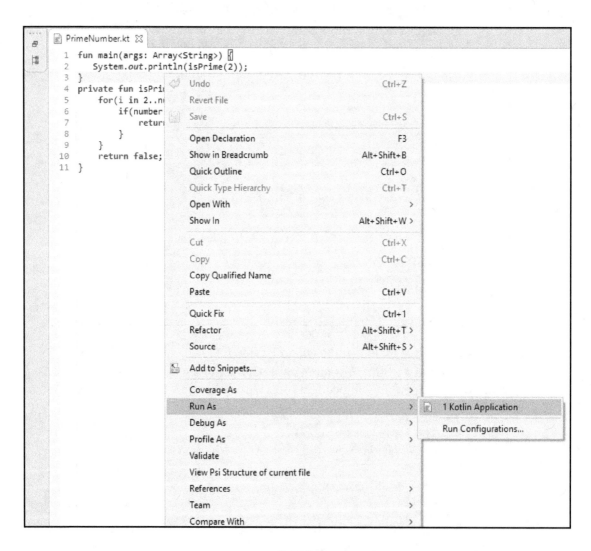

The output is as follows:

```
Console ⌗
<terminated> Config - PrimeNumber.kt [Java Application] C:\Users
11 is a prime number
```

Working with coroutines

A program in execution that initiates long-running operations, such as file IO, network IO, or CPU- or GPU-intensive work, requires the invoker to block until the operations complete. Programming languages handle this via concurrency.

The JVM has support for concurrency. Java has had strong support for multithreading and concurrency since its first release. Any process that is running inside the JVM can create a number of threads to execute multiple tasks in an asynchronous fashion. However, developing concurrent code in an optimal and error-free manner and debugging it is really challenging. Java provides various constructs to write concurrent code and, along with other JVM languages and third-party libraries, has tried to come up with innovative and elegant ways to achieve concurrency.

Java 5 made a lot of progress with regard to writing concurrent applications. It has higher-level constructs, such as the executor framework, which makes it easier to write concurrent code and allows us to decouple thread management code from the business logic. Java 8 has introduced parallel streams to turn the code to concurrent much more easily. RxJava brings reactive extensions to Java, allowing us to write very concise code for asynchronous functionality. Kotlin supports almost all of those approaches and offers a few of its own as well.

Coroutines in Kotlin

Kotlin offers a better way to perform asynchronous tasks, called **coroutines**. Coroutines are a new and fluent way of writing asynchronous and non-blocking code in Kotlin. They are much lighter than threads and are easy to manage. Both coroutines and threads are multitasking, but they differ in that threads are managed by the kernel and coroutines are managed by the code itself, thereby giving programmatic control.

Coroutines were introduced in Kotlin 1.1 as an experimental feature. There are two types of coroutines:

- Stackful
- Stackless

A stackful coroutine is a normal function that can be suspended during execution. It will be suspended with its entire stack, including its local variables, and the parameters passed from the invoking function. The stackful coroutine waits for the scheduler to resume its execution, similar to what a thread does. The scheduler can resume either the same coroutine or another suspended coroutine. A stackless coroutine, on the other hand, doesn't have its own stack, so it doesn't have to map on the native thread and doesn't require context switching on the processor.

Coroutines in Kotlin are based on the idea of suspending functions that can stop execution when they are invoked and resume execution once the task is complete. This utilizes the CPU better than blocking the execution in its entirety.

Functions can be suspended using the `suspend` keyword, and may only be invoked inside other suspended functions or inside a coroutine. Coroutines can run concurrently, similar to threads in Java, and wait for one another, communicating during execution. They are light compared to threads, meaning we can create thousands of them without worrying about the slow performance of an application.

As mentioned earlier, coroutines have been introduced as an experimental feature in Kotlin and are provided as a library. We need to include this dependency in the Maven or Gradle, or with the classpath in your project:

```
<dependency>
    <groupId>org.jetbrains.kotlinx</groupId>
    <artifactId>kotlinx-coroutines-core</artifactId>
    <version>0.22.5</version>
</dependency>
```

Let's create a Maven project to demonstrate coroutines:

1. Create a Maven project using the **kotlin-archetype-jvm** archetype.
2. Specify the `groupid` and `artifactid`.
3. This will create a project with the following structure:

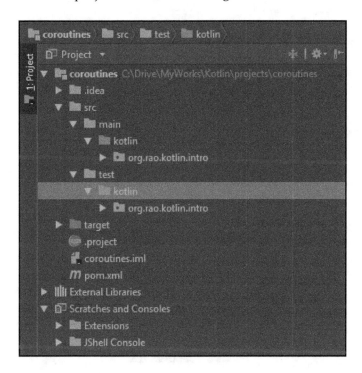

As coroutines have experimental status in Kotlin 1.1, the compiler reports a warning every time coroutines are used by default.

To avoid the compiler yelling at us whenever coroutines are used, we have to add `kotlin-maven-plugin` to the coroutines flag enabled in `pom.xml`:

```
<plugin>
    <groupId>org.jetbrains.kotlin</groupId>
    <artifactId>kotlin-maven-plugin</artifactId>
    <configuration>
        <args>
            <arg>-Xcoroutines=enable</arg>
        </args>
    </configuration>
</plugin>
```

Note that the `kotlinx-coroutines-core` JAR is published at `http://jcenter.bintray.com`. We have to add it to the `repository` section in our `pom.xml` file:

```
<repositories>
    <repository>
        <id>jcenter</id>
        <url>https://jcenter.bintray.com/</url>
    </repository>
</repositories>
```

The Kotlin library provides different ways to create the coroutines. The most simple way of creating this is the `launch {}` function.

Now, let's write our first coroutine:

```
fun main(args: Array<String>) {
    println("Inside main")

    launch {
        println("Coroutine in execution")
    }

    Thread.sleep(2000)
    println("main completed")
}
```

The program prints the output as follows:

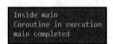

This program starts a coroutine and prints the message. The main thread must wait until the coroutine finishes the execution, otherwise the program will end prematurely.

The `launch` function starts a new coroutine. By default, it runs in a shared pool of the thread that is in execution. Threads exist in a program and each thread can run multiple coroutines. This means that the coroutines are much lighter.

There is a construct in Kotlin that can be used to suspend the coroutine—the `delay()` function. This function takes time as input which can be of `long`/`int` type:

```
fun main(args: Array<String>){
    println("Inside main")

    launch{
        println("delay in 2 seconds")
        delay(2000L)
        println("Coroutine in execution")
    }

    Thread.sleep(2000)
    println("main completed")
}
```

The output is as follows:

```
Inside main
delay in 2 seconds
main completed
```

The `delay()` function can only be called inside a coroutine. If we try to use it outside the coroutine, the code fails to compile. The `delay()` function is declared with the `suspend` keyword in its declaration. Any function declared with `suspend` can only be invoked from the coroutines or other `suspend` functions.

When a coroutine is in a waiting or suspended state, the thread is returned back to the pool. When the waiting/block state is over, the coroutine resumes its execution on a thread that is available in the pool.

Let's create functions that can be called from a coroutine:

```
private suspend fun game1(): String {
    delay(1000)
    return "game1"
}
private suspend fun game2(): String {
    delay(2000)
    return "game2"
}

fun main(args: Array<String>) {
    println("Inside main")
```

```
    launch(CommonPool) {
        val one = game1()
        val two = game2()
        println("Game ----- " + one)
        println("Game ----- " + two)
    }
    Thread.sleep(4000)
}
```

The output is as follows:

```
Inside main
Game ----- game1
Game ----- game2
```

So far, we have discussed how to create and run coroutines. Note that all the coroutines that we have created so far execute in a serial fashion. In the preceding example, we created two coroutines—game1() and game2(). These were executed serially in the main thread. Let's now create coroutines that run concurrently in the main thread.

We can use async() to create and execute two coroutines concurrently, as follows:

```
private suspend fun game1(): String {
    delay(1000)
    return "game1"
}
private suspend fun game2(): String {
    delay(2000)
    return "game2"
}

fun main(args: Array<String>) {
    println("Inside main")

    launch(CommonPool) {
        val one = async(CommonPool){
            game1()
        }
        val two = async(CommonPool){
            game2()
        }
        println("Game ----- " + one.await()+": "+two.await())
    }
    Thread.sleep(4000)
}
```

This gives us the following output:

```
Inside main
Game ----- game1: game2
```

The asynchronous function returns an instance of the `Deferred<T>`, type, which has an `await()` function that returns the result of the coroutine.

Now let's look at one more example, where we can really use the power of parallel execution:

```
fun main(args: Array<String>) {
    println("Inside main")

    launch(CommonPool) {
        val deferred = (1..1_000_000)
                .map { n -> async { n }
                }
        var sum = deferred.sumBy { it.await() }
        println("sum ----- " + sum)
    }
    Thread.sleep(4000)
}
```

The output is as follows:

```
Inside main
sum ----- 1784293664
```

When we are performing long-running operations, we need to run these as background tasks.

In this section, we have learned different ways to create and manage coroutines in Kotlin in order to execute a number of operations in the background, both serially and concurrently.

Using Kotlin with Java

We will now discuss how to work with Kotlin and Java in the project that we created.

In this section, we will learn how to use Kotlin in an existing Java project, and Java in an existing Kotlin project.

One of Kotlin's important features is its interoperability with Java. If we have an existing Java project, we can add new code in Kotlin or we can convert the existing Java code to Kotlin.

Kotlin in an existing Java project

Let's look at an example of how to add Kotlin code to an existing Java project created using Maven. We have created a simple Maven project that has some code written in Java. This is shown here:

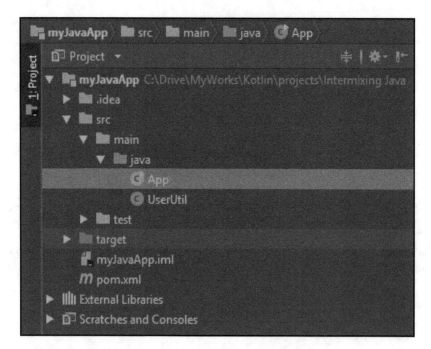

We can add Kotlin code to it as follows.

1. Right-click on `src/main/java` and then click on **New** | **Kotlin File/Class**. We call it `NewApp.kt`:

2. After creating a Kotlin file, IDEA prompts us to configure the Kotlin runtime:

3. Click on **Configure** and choose **Maven**.
4. Choose the desired Kotlin version and hit the **OK** button. We have now configured Kotlin runtime in a Java project.
5. The `App.java` and `NewApp.kt` files are *hello world* classes. This means that they just print a `hello world` message to the console, shown as follows:

    `App.java`:

    ```java
    public class App {
      public static void main (String[] args) {
        System.out.println ("Hello World from Java!");
      }
    }
    ```

```
NewApp.kt:

object NewApp {
    @JvmStatic
    fun main(args: Array<String>) {
        println("Hello World from Kotlin!")
    }
}
```

We can also write the `main` function without the class structure, as follows:

```
fun main(vararg args: String) {
    println("Hello World from Kotlin!")
}
```

Also, note that we can use `vararg` for arguments to `main` function. `vararg` is followed by the argument name and the type.

Let's run both the Java and Kotlin codes now. The output from the Java code will appear as follows:

```
Run:    App.main ×
    [INFO] --- exec-maven-plugin:1.6.0:java (default-cli) @ myJavaApp ---
    Hello World from Java!
    [INFO] ------------------------------------------------------------
    [INFO] BUILD SUCCESS
    [INFO] ------------------------------------------------------------
    [INFO] Total time: 17.939 s
    [INFO] Finished at: 2018-08-26T23:28:49+05:30
    [INFO] Final Memory: 43M/262M
    [INFO] ------------------------------------------------------------
```

The output from the Kotlin code will appear as follows:

```
Run:    NewApp ×
    [INFO] --- exec-maven-plugin:1.6.0:java (default-cli) @ myJavaApp ---
    Hello World from Kotlin!
    [INFO] ------------------------------------------------------------
    [INFO] BUILD SUCCESS
    [INFO] ------------------------------------------------------------
    [INFO] Total time: 40.859 s
    [INFO] Finished at: 2018-09-02T22:37:10+05:30
    [INFO] Final Memory: 32M/256M
    [INFO] ------------------------------------------------------------
```

As we can see, both Kotlin and Java can exist in the same project, and we configured the Kotlin runtime in a Java project. We can also load and use any Java class or a library written in Java from a Kotlin class.

Java in a Kotlin project

Let's look at an example where we add Java code to an existing Kotlin project using Maven. We previously described the steps to create a Kotlin project in the *Configuring Kotlin in your project* section. We have created a Maven project in Kotlin using the **kotlin-archetype-jvm** archetype:

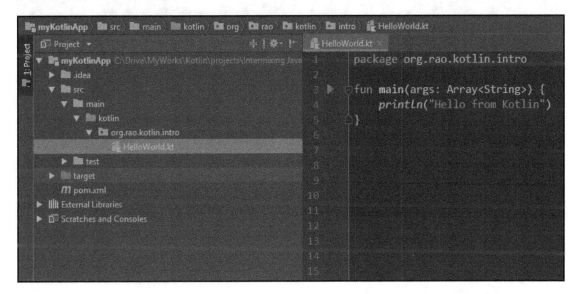

We will add a Java file to it and build the project as follows:

In this section, we have learned how to intermix Kotlin and Java using Maven.

Summary

In this chapter, we have discussed the following:

- What Kotlin offers and why it is a game changer in enterprise applications
- How Kotlin language compares with Java
- How to configure Kotlin in a project
- What Coroutines are
- Intermixing Kotlin and Java

An Overview of Java EE and Kotlin

3

Java Enterprise Edition (Java EE), formerly known as **Java 2 Platform Enterprise Edition (J2EE)**, is a platform used to build distributed web and **enterprise applications (EA)**. The current version is Java EE 8.

Technical requirements

A grasp of Servlets, EJB, and the MVC pattern will help you to understand Java EE with Kotlin. A knowledge of the IDEs used to create web applications will also be an advantage.

Overview of Java EE

The Java EE platform was developed through the **Java Community Process** (**JCP**), which is responsible for all Java technologies. JCP has created **Java Specification Requests** (**JSRs**) to describe the various proposed Java EE technologies. Typically, these specifications are implemented by the product vendors (the web-server, application-server, or database-system vendor). These vendors compete to implement the Java EE specifications. The Java Community works under the supervision of the JCP program, and JCP helps to ensure the Java technology's standards, stability, and cross-platform compatibility.

Java EE was maintained by Oracle under JCP after it took over Java from Sun Microsystems in 2009. On September 12th, 2017, Oracle Corporation announced that it would submit Java EE to the Eclipse Foundation. This Eclipse top-level project was named **Eclipse Enterprise for Java** (**EE4J**). On February 26th, 2018, Eclipse Foundation renamed it Jakarta EE.

Java EE (Jakarta EE) is a set of specifications that go beyond the Java **Standard Edition** (**SE**), giving us access to distributed computing and web services for enterprise applications. It is designed to create large, distributed, multitiered, secure, transactional, scalable, reliable, and highly-available enterprise applications that are intended to solve critical business problems. The intention of Java EE is to abstract the complex logic for distributed transactional details, leaving the programmer to work on the actual business logic.

Some of the core technologies of the Java Enterprise Edition include the following:

- Java Servlets
- JSP
- JDBC
- JavaMail
- RMI
- EJB

Java EE is made up of different frameworks that are used to develop enterprise applications. It provides a simplified programming model to build applications. It has a rapid application development time and is based on a secure and reliable model. It allows us to focus on the business implementation rather than on setting up the system. Let's take a look at some of the benefits of using Java Enterprise Edition as a platform for developing applications:

- **Dependency injection**: Through dependency injection, all the required resources can be injected into the components, thereby separating the resource-creation logic from the application code. This helps to create loosely-coupled applications that are easy to maintain. Java EE has **Contexts and Dependency Injections (CDI)** through which the required bean dependencies are injected into the components.

- **Configurations**: Java EE provides a way to define configurations using annotations. It also allows us to use XML-based configurations. The Server reads all the configurations and binds them to the components during the deployment of the application.

- **The Java persistence API**: Java EE provides an easy way to manage data layers and has a well-defined ORM framework known as **Java Persistence API (JPA)**. JPA allows us to define entities, mapping them to the database for persistence.

- **Support for web services**: Through its rich frameworks, the Java EE platform provides a way to develop web services. Using Java EE, we can create SOAP-based web services and from Java EE 6 onward, we can create Restful Web Services as well.

When we combine Java EE with the Kotlin language, we can write concise and clean code, and we can create enterprise applications quickly and easily.

New features and enhancements in Java EE 8

Java EE 8 has improved its APIs and programming models to suit the needs of modern enterprise applications. It provides an infrastructure for microservices and cloud-based environments.

Java EE 8 has a new security API and a new standardized API for binding JSON to model objects. The Servlet 4.0 API now comes with HTTP/2 support. A new Reactive rest client API and asynchronous API have been introduced in this release of the platform as well.

Java EE 8's new **dependency injection** (**DI**) feature, along with its improved security and reliability, makes it easier to develop applications.

Java EE 8 is also now aligned with Java 8, which means that Java 8 features, such as streams, lambda, and the new data-time API, can be used in Java EE 8's APIs as well, and it has enhanced support for these features.

Introduction to the Java EE architecture

Modern enterprise applications are often developed using a layered architecture. The most commonly-followed architecture is a three-tiered architecture. In this model, the responsibilities of an application are divided into three layers—view, business logic, and persistence. The view or presentation layer deals with presenting a user interface and is responsible for interacting with the end user and the application. The business layer consists of the core business and the domain logic of the enterprise application. This includes the code that defines the processes to run and deals with how data is created and operated on for the business problem in question. The persistence layer defines how data is stored using a database. This three-tiered architecture is as follows:

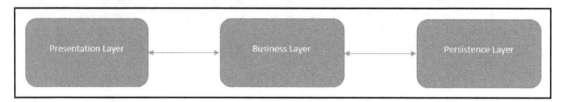

Java EE provides services to enterprise applications that are developed using a layered architecture. Servlets, **Java Server Pages** (**JSP**), or **Java Server Faces** (**JSF**) can be used for the presentation layer of the application. Typically, these components are deployed on a web container and the end user interacts with the web container using the web browser. Enterprise Java Beans are used for the business logic of the application and run in an EJB container. The JPA, meanwhile, is used for the persistence layer of the application, which maps between entities and relational database tables. This is depicted in the following diagram:

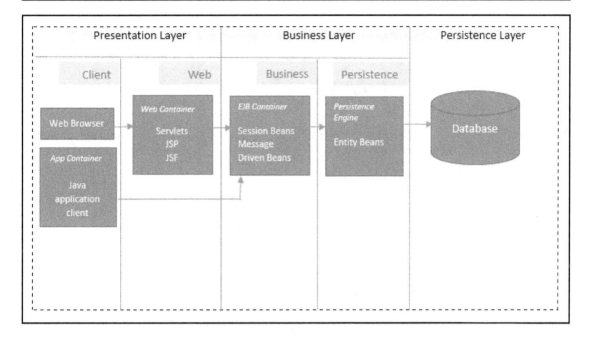

 A Java EE container offers many other services. These include the **Java Messaging Service (JMS)**, **Remote Method Invocation (RMI)**, resource adapters, and web services.

Integrating Kotlin plugins

In this section, we will take a look at a couple of plugins that make JavaBeans behave as standard Java classes.

Kotlin is interoperable with Java. Although a Java class can easily be converted to Kotlin, Kotlin classes are not readily compatible with Java EE. Plugins are available to make them compatible, meaning that we don't have handle this manually in the code.

Inversion of Control (IoC)-based frameworks load the beans, initialize them with all the required properties, and inject them into the required places. In Java EE, we use the `@Inject` annotation to inject the dependencies. In order to mock these beans, dependency injection needs to be reconfigured. The Kotlin compiler has support for different plugins, which simulate the structure and construct the objects that are suitable for the frameworks to use in an application.

The all-open compiler plugin

When we define a class or declare a data member, it is final by default in Kotlin. We declare classes as final to make them non-extendable. Similarly, we make functions final so that they can't be overridden. Fields are declared as final to prevent the value from changing once it is initialized.

The **Aspect-Oriented Programming** (**AOP**) library and the Reflection API require classes to be non-final. These frameworks create proxy objects, so the classes and member variables have to be open and accessible.

The *all-open compiler* plugin makes sure Kotlin complies with the requirements of these libraries and frameworks when dealing with proxy objects. It makes classes and member variables that have specific annotations accessible to create proxy objects without explicitly specifying the open keyword in the code.

Let's take a look at an example of how we can use an *all-open compiler* plugin. When we are dealing with the CDI framework, we need classes that are annotated with specific annotations, such as @Inject or @Dependent, to make them open and accessible. Let's look at the *all-open plugin* support for both Maven and Gradle.

Using the all-open plugin in Maven

The *all-open plugin* for Maven can be used as follows:

```
<plugin>
    <artifactId>kotlin-maven-plugin</artifactId>
    <groupId>org.jetbrains.kotlin</groupId>
    <version>${kotlin.version}</version>
    <configuration>
        <compilerPlugins>
            <plugin>all-open</plugin>
        </compilerPlugins>
        <pluginOptions>
            <option>all-open:all-
open:annotation=javax.inject.Inject</option>
            <option>all-open:annotation=all-
open:annotation=javax.ejb.Stateless</option>
        </pluginOptions>
    </configuration>
    <dependencies>
        <dependency>
            <groupId>org.jetbrains.kotlin</groupId>
            <artifactId>kotlin-maven-allopen</artifactId>
            <version>${kotlin.version}</version>
```

```
        </dependency>
      </dependencies>
   </plugin>
```

Using the all-open plugin in Gradle

The *all-open plugin* for Gradle can be used as follows:

```
buildscript {
    dependencies {
        classpath "org.jetbrains.kotlin:kotlin-allopen:$kotlin_version"
    }
}
apply plugin: "kotlin-allopen"
```

We have to add the plugin artifact in the `buildscript` dependencies section of the Gradle file. We can also enable the *all-open plugin* using the plugins section, as follows:

```
plugins {
    id "org.jetbrains.kotlin.plugin.allopen" version "1.2.41"
}
```

Following this, we can specify a list of annotations that will make our classes open and accessible:

```
allOpen {
    annotation("javax.ejb.Stateless")
}
```

We can specify multiple annotations using the `annotations` section in the `allOpen` plugin:

```
allOpen {
    annotations("javax.ejb.Stateless",
    "javax.inject.Inject")
}
```

We can then define custom annotations. The *all-open compiler plugin* is used to open the classes that are annotated with the custom annotations:

```
allOpen {
    annotation("org.rao.kotlin.javaee.Annotation")
}


@org.rao.kolin.javaee.Annotation
annotation class MyAnnotation
```

```
@MyAnnotation
class  Person{ }
```

Now, the `Person` class will be open.

The `MyAnnotation` class is annotated with a meta-annotation—`@org.rao.kolin.javaee.Annotation`. It is now an all-open plugin annotation that can be used in other classes to make them open and accessible.

No-arg compiler plugin

Constructors are used to initialize the states of an object. Sometimes, however, we need to have default constructors that take no arguments. The *no-arg compiler plugin* is used to generate no-arg constructors (the default constructors) for classes that are annotated with a particular annotation. When we have a *no-arg compiler plugin* enabled, a no-arg constructor is added during compile-time. The generated default constructor can only be invoked by the reflection APIs and are not accessible directly from the Kotlin code. The *no-arg compiler plugin enables* the CDI or the JPA to instantiate the classes, though it doesn't have any default constructors defined in the code.

 In Java, a default constructor will always be added to the compiled code by the compiler and no additional plugin is required to do this. In Kotlin, however, when we have the *no-arg compiler plugin* enabled, a default constructor will be added to the compiled code.

Using the no-org plugin in Maven

Using the *no-org compiler plugin* is the same as the *all-open* plugin. The `kotlin-maven-noarg` dependency has to be added to the `pom.xml` file and we specify the plugin in the plugin section:

```
<plugin>
    <groupId>org.jetbrains.kotlin</groupId>
    <artifactId>kotlin-maven-plugin</artifactId>
    <version>${kotlin.version}</version>
    <executions>
        <execution>
            <id>compile</id>
            <phase>compile</phase>
            <goals>
                <goal>compile</goal>
            </goals>
        </execution>
        <execution>
```

```
            <id>test-compile</id>
            <phase>test-compile</phase>
            <goals>
                <goal>test-compile</goal>
            </goals>
        </execution>
    </executions>
</plugin>

<plugin>
    <artifactId>kotlin-maven-plugin</artifactId>
    <groupId>org.jetbrains.kotlin</groupId>
    <version>${kotlin.version}</version>

    <configuration>
        <compilerPlugins>
            <plugin>no-arg</plugin>
        </compilerPlugins>

        <pluginOptions>
            <option>no-
arg:annotation=org.rao.kotlin.javaee.MyClass</option>
            <!-- <option>no-arg:invokeInitializers=true</option> -->
        </pluginOptions>
    </configuration>

    <dependencies>
        <dependency>
            <groupId>org.jetbrains.kotlin</groupId>
            <artifactId>kotlin-maven-noarg</artifactId>
            <version>${kotlin.version}</version>
        </dependency>
    </dependencies>
</plugin>
```

Using the no-org plugin in Gradle

Add the plugin in the `buildscript` dependencies section in the Gradle file:

```
buildscript {
    dependencies {
    classpath "org.jetbrains.kotlin:kotlin-noarg:$kotlin_version"
       }
  }

  apply plugin: "kotlin-noarg"
```

Alternatively, we can enable the *no-arg plugin* using Gradle as follows:

```
plugins {
    id "org.jetbrains.kotlin.plugin.noarg" version "1.2.41"
}
```

We can then specify the list of annotations in the plugin section. The *no-arg plugin* generates the default constructor for the classes that are annotated with the annotations that we specified in the `noArg` annotation section of the plugin:

```
noArg {
    annotation("org.rao.kotlin.javaee.MyClass")
}
```

If we want to execute the initialization of member variables from the default constructor, we can use the `invokeInitializers` plugin option:

```
noArg {
invokeInitializers = true
}
```

The kotlin-spring compiler plugin

The *kotlin-spring compiler plugin* is a wrapper on top of the *all-open compiler plugin*. This plugin is used for Spring-based applications.

Using the kotlin-spring plugin in Maven

In Maven, we can enable the *kotlin-spring compiler plugin* as follows:

```
<compilerPlugins>
    <plugin>spring</plugin>
</compilerPlugins>
```

Using the kotlin-spring plugin in Gradle

In Gradle, the *kotlin-spring compiler plugin* can be enabled by using `buildscript` with the `allopen` artifact, as shown here:

```
buildscript {
    dependencies {
    classpath "org.jetbrains.kotlin:kotlin-allopen:$kotlin_version"
    }
}
apply plugin: "kotlin-spring"
```

Alternatively, the plugin can be enabled using plugins as follows:

```
plugins {
    id "org.jetbrains.kotlin.plugin.spring" version "1.2.41"
}
```

This plugin specifies the following annotations:

- @Component
- @Transactional
- @Async
- @Cacheable
- @SpringBootTest

The classes that are annotated with these annotations are made open and accessible to the Spring framework so that we can create proxy objects.

Using the kotlin-spring plugin in CLI

The *all-open compiler plugin* is a JAR file that comes with the Kotlin compiler. In order to use the *all-open plugin,* we need to provide the path to the jar file using the -Xplugin option:

```
-Xplugin=$KOTLIN_HOME/lib/allopen-compiler-plugin.jar
```

We can specify the *all-open* annotations either with the annotation plugin option, or by enabling the preset. *Spring* is the only preset that is currently available for the *all-open plugin.*

The plugin option format is as follows:

```
-P plugin:<plugin id>:<key>=<value>
```

```
-P
plugin:org.jetbrains.kotlin.allopen:annotation=org.rao.kotlin.javaee.MyClas
s
-P plugin:org.jetbrains.kotlin.allopen:preset=spring
```

JPA plugin

The *kotlin-jpa plugin* is a wrapper on top of the *no-arg compiler plugin.* This plugin specifies the @Entity, @Embeddable, and @MappedSuperclass annotations. We need to add this plugin in the plugin section of the Maven or Gradle file.

Using the kotlin-jpa plugin in Maven

In Maven, we can enable the *kotlin-jpa plugin* as follows:

```
<compilerPlugins>
    <plugin>jpa</plugin>
</compilerPlugins>
```

Using the kotlin-jpa plugin in Gradle

In Gradle, we can enable the *kotlin-jpa plugin* using `buildscript` with the kotlin-noarg artifact, as follows:

```
buildscript {
    dependencies {
    classpath "org.jetbrains.kotlin:kotlin-noarg:$kotlin_version"
    }
  }
apply plugin: "kotlin-jpa"
```

Alternatively, we can use the Gradle plugins section to enable the *kotlin-jpa compiler plugin,* as follows:

```
plugins {
    id "org.jetbrains.kotlin.plugin.jpa" version "1.2.41"
  }
```

Using the kotlin-jpa plugin in CLI

We can use the -Xplugin option to enable the *kotlin-jpa plugin* in order to use the JPA plugin in the command line. This is shown in the following snippet:

```
-Xplugin=$KOTLIN_HOME/lib/noarg-compiler-plugin.jar
 -P
plugin:org.jetbrains.kotlin.noarg:annotation=org.rao.kotlin.javaee.MyClass
 -P plugin:org.jetbrains.kotlin.noarg:preset=jpa
```

The SAM-with-receiver compiler plugin

Java 8 introduced lambda expressions, which are geared toward the functional programming paradigm. With lambda expressions, we can write higher-order functions, which means we can pass a function to another function. Lambda expressions can be applied to interfaces with a single abstract method, which are known as SAM interfaces.

Before Java 8, when we wanted to use the SAM interface or the functional interface, we had to write an anonymous inner class, which requires a lot of verbose code. For example, let's write a SAM interface:

```
@FunctionalInterface
interface Greet {
    fun hello(str: String): String

}
```

To use the interface type as a method argument, we need to use the anonymous inner class, as shown here:

```
var Greeter = str :Greet
{
    override
    fun hello(name: String): String {
        return "hello $name"
    }
}
```

In functional programming, however, this can be written as follows with the Kotlin SAM conversion:

```
var Greeter = Greet { name - > "hello $name" }
```

Using the SAM-with-receiver plugin in Maven

In Maven, we can enable sam-with-receiver as follows:

```
<plugin>
    <artifactId>kotlin-maven-plugin</artifactId>
    <groupId>org.jetbrains.kotlin</groupId>
    <version>${kotlin.version}</version>
    <configuration>
        <compilerPlugins>
            <plugin>sam-with-receiver</plugin>
        </compilerPlugins>
        <pluginOptions>
            <option>sam-with-
receiver:annotation=com.my.SamWithReceiver</option>
        </pluginOptions>
    </configuration>
    <dependencies>
        <dependency>
            <groupId>org.jetbrains.kotlin</groupId>
            <artifactId>kotlin-maven-sam-with-receiver</artifactId>
```

```
            <version>${kotlin.version}</version>
        </dependency>
    </dependencies>
</plugin>
```

Using the SAM-with-receiver plugin in Gradle

In Gradle, we can enable the *kotlin-sam-with-receiver plugin* using `buildscript` with the `kotlin-noorg` artifact, as follows:

```
buildscript {
    dependencies {
        classpath "org.jetbrains.kotlin:kotlin-sam-with-
receiver:$kotlin_version"
    }
}

apply plugin: "kotlin-sam-with-receiver"
```

We can then specify the annotations that apply to the classes that are annotated with this list of meta-annotations to enable the plugin:

```
samWithReceiver {
    annotation("org.rao.kotlin.javaee.MySamInterface")
}
```

> The kotlin-sam-with-receiver compiler plugin doesn't have any built-in annotations. We need to specify a list of custom annotations to effectively apply the plugin.

Using the SAM-with-receiver plugin in CLI

We can use the *Xplugin* option to enable the *kotlin-sam-with-receiver plugin*. We need to point to the sam-with-receiver-compiler-plugin jar that is available in the Kotlin compiler distribution. We can then specify a list of custom annotations as follows:

```
-Xplugin=$KOTLIN_HOME/lib/sam-with-receiver-compiler-plugin.jar
-P
plugin:org.jetbrains.kotlin.samWithReceiver:annotation=org.rao.kotlin.MySam
Interface
```

The Jackson plugin

The Jackson plugin is not available with the Kotlin compiler distribution, but it is available as part of the Jackson module. It provides an automatic binding between the parsed JSON data and the constructor arguments of a class. All Kotlin types are supported. We need to specify `JsonProperty` on the constructor arguments in order to bind the JSON data.

This plugin is useful for mapping JSON data to the members of a class:

```
data class Person(
    @param:JsonProperty("firstName") override val firstName: String,
    @param:JsonProperty("lastName") override val lastName: String
) : Person
```

Bytecode prior to Java 8 did not contain names for the arguments of the constructor. Frameworks cannot bind the data to the constructor arguments automatically.

The Kotlin compiler and the Java 8 compiler add more metadata to the bytecode during compilation. This metadata can be used by frameworks to carry out the required binding of the data after parsing the JSON. In order to automatically map this data to the constructor, we can rewrite the preceding code as follows:

```
data class Person(
    override val firstName: String,
    override val lastName: String
) : Person
```

In order to bind the parsed JSON data to the constructor arguments and to enable the Jackson plugin, we need to add the `jackson-module-kotlin` and `kotlin-reflect` dependencies. We also need to enable the Kotlin module in the `Application.kt` file.

Using the Jackson plugin in Maven

In Maven, we add the following dependencies:

```
<dependencies>
 <dependency>
   <groupId>com.fasterxml.jackson.module</groupId>
   <artifactId>jackson-module-kotlin</artifactId>
   <version>${jackson_version}</version>
 </dependency>
 <dependency>
   <groupId>org.jetbrains.kotlin</groupId>
   <artifactId>kotlin-reflect</artifactId>
   <version>${kotlin_version}</version>
```

```
    </dependency>
  </dependencies>
```

Using the Jackson plugin in Gradle

In Gradle, we add the following dependencies:

```
dependencies {
    compile("com.fasterxml.jackson.module:jackson-module-
kotlin:$jackson_version")
    compile("org.jetbrains.kotlin:kotlin-reflect:$kotlin_version"
 }
```

Enable the Kotlin module in the `Application.kt` file:

```
@ApplicationPath("home")
class Application :MyApp(){
    private val classes = setOf(PersonService: :class.java)
    private val singletons = setOf(ContextResolver())
        override fun getClasses() = classes
        override fun getSingletons() = singletons
}

class ContextResolver :ContextResolver<ObjectMapper> {
    val objectMapper = ObjectMapper()
        init{
          objectMapper.registerModule(KotlinModule())
        }
        override fun getContext(p0:Class<*>?) = objectMapper
 }
```

The frameworks and their configurations offer loose coupling, dependency injections, and so on. We can use Kotlin compiler plugins to take advantage of the benefits that these frameworks provide. This reduces the number of classes that have to be modified.

Kotlin and Servlets

Java EE is an extension of the Java SE and is used for creating web applications, RESTful web services, and microservices.

In this section, we will discuss how to create a web application with HTTP servlets. A servlet is a server-side Java program. Java EE HTTP servlets can be used in Kotlin much like any other Java library or framework. We will create a controller to respond to this request using `HttpServlet`.

Kotlin for server-side development

Kotlin is a feature-packed language that is great for developing server-side applications, as it allows us to write code in a very concise and expressive manner while maintaining full compatibility with existing Java-based technology stacks. Using Kotlin to develop components on the server side has the following benefits:

- **Less time to develop**: With its elegant syntax and new features, such as its support for the functional programming paradigm and type inference, the Kotlin language helps to build more expressive and concise code, which makes developing applications easier
- **Interoperability**: Kotlin is 100% compatible with all Java-based frameworks, which lets us stay in the same technology stack and make the most of the benefits offered by the modern JVM-based language
- **Scalability**: Kotlin's coroutines feature helps us to build server-side applications that can scale to a massive number of clients with minimal hardware requirements

Servlets

Servlets are the core of web-application development. A servlet is a Java program that runs on the server side, either on a web server or an application server. Servlets acts as a middle layer between an HTTP server and a web client, typically a web browser. The client can either be an HTTP client or a service that runs on an HTTP server. The servlet technology is the underlying technology behind JSP, which is used to create UI pages using HTML. JSP is compiled to a servlet. When a request is made by a web client, the servlet container loads the servlet. The servlet accepts the request, processes it, and returns the response to the servlet container. The servlet container in turn sends the response to the web client that issued the request. The servlet remains in memory to serve subsequent requests and the servlet gets removed from the container when it is no longer needed or the servlet container restarts.

The life cycle of a servlet

A servlet's life cycle has three phases. These are depicted in the following diagram:

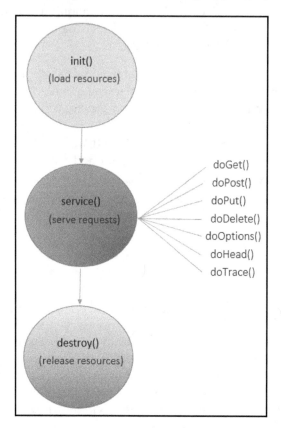

Let's look at each phase of the servlet life cycle:

- **Initialization**: The first phase in the Servlet's life cycle is initialization. In this phase, the resources that a servlet needs to serve the request are created and initialized. The Servlet classes implement the contract of the `javax.servlet.Servlet` interface, and the `javax.servlet.Servlet` interface declares the `init()` method that represents the initialization. When the servlet is loaded by the container, it invokes the `init()` method to create and initialize the resources. This `init()` method is invoked only once during the servlet's life cycle after the servlet has been loaded into the container.

- **Service**: The service phase in the servlet's life cycle represents the interaction between the servlet and the client. Whenever the server receives a request from the client for a servlet, it creates a new servlet and invokes the `service()` method. The Servlet interface declares the `service()` method, which takes the request (`ServletRequest`) and response (`ServletResponse`) objects. The `ServletRequest` object represents a client's request for a dynamic resource, and the `ServletResponse` object represents the servlet's response to the client. The `service()` method implementation checks for the HTTP request type, which could be something such as `GET`, `POST`, `PUT`, or `DELETE`, and invokes an appropriate method, such as `doGet()`, `doPost()`, `doPut()`, or `doDelete()`.

- **Destruction**: Destruction is the last phase in the servlet's life cycle. In the servlet's destruction phase, it gets removed from the container that it was loaded by during its initialization phase. The `Servlet` interface declares the `destroy()` method and the container invokes this method just before the servlet gets removed from the container. This allows the servlet to clean up resources and gracefully terminate them.

To summarize, once a servlet has been loaded into the container, it creates and initializes resources in its initialization phase. In its service phase, it serves a request from the client; in its destruction phase, however the resources gets cleaned up and the servlet get removed from the container.

Creating a simple servlet application

Let's take a look at how to create a simple servlet application using Maven and the Kotlin runtime. Follow these steps:

1. Click on **File | New | Project.**
2. In the **New Project** window, select **Maven** and enable **Create from archetype.**

3. Select **org.apache.maven.archetypes:maven-archetype-webapp** as the archetype and click on **Next**:

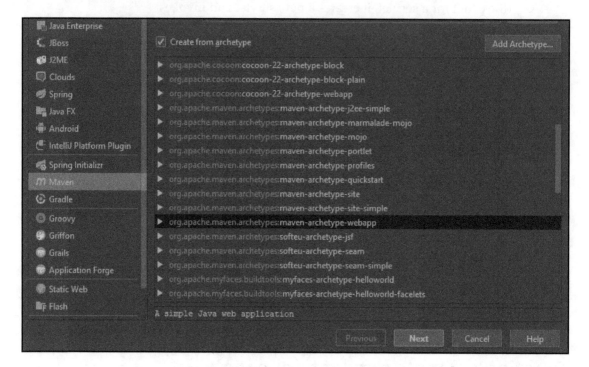

4. Enter the **GroupId**, **ArtifactId**, and **Version** for the Maven project and click on **Next**.

5. Verify the project's name and click on **Finish.** This has created a maven web app project with the following structure:

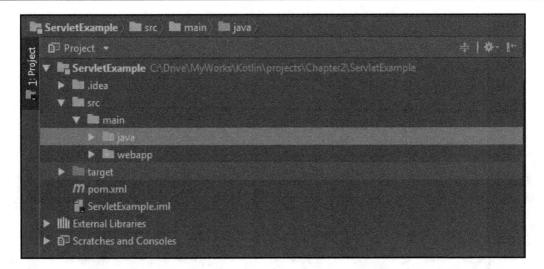

Let's write a simple login form and a welcome page.

We need to include the following dependencies so that we can use HTTP servlets in a Kotlin runtime environment:

```
<dependency>
    <groupId>javax</groupId>
    <artifactId>javaee-api</artifactId>
    <version>${javax.javaee-api.version}</version>
</dependency>
<dependency>
    <groupId>org.jetbrains.kotlin</groupId>
    <artifactId>kotlin-runtime</artifactId>
    <version>${org.jetbrains.kotlin.kotlin-runtime}</version>
</dependency>
```

We will be creating a WAR file that we specify via packaging properties. Now that we have added the required dependencies to create a servlet app, let's add a controller that receives a request and serves the response:

```
@WebServlet(name="home",value="/home")
Class HomeController:HttpServlet(){
    Override fun
doPost(request:HttpServletRequest,response:HttpServletResponse){
response.writer.write("<html><body><h2>Welcome${request.getParameter("login
Id")}</h2></body></html>")
    }
}
```

Build the application in the terminal using the `mvn clean install` command. To deploy it, configure Tomcat in the IDE and perform the following steps:

1. Go to **Edit configuration** and select any web server. We use Tomcat here for demonstration purposes.
2. Click on Configure and select Tomcat Directory.
3. Click on **Deployment**, select the artifact, and click on the **OK** button:

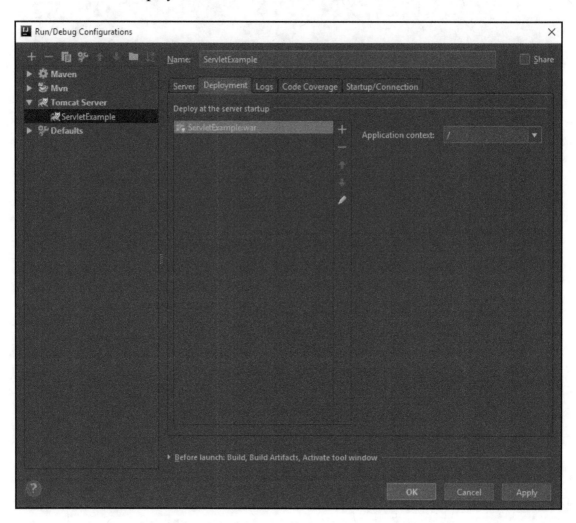

Now that we are using the run configuration, deploy the application and enter `http://localhost:8080/` in the browser.

We will then see the index page that we defined, which has a login form. Enter the details and hit `Login`:

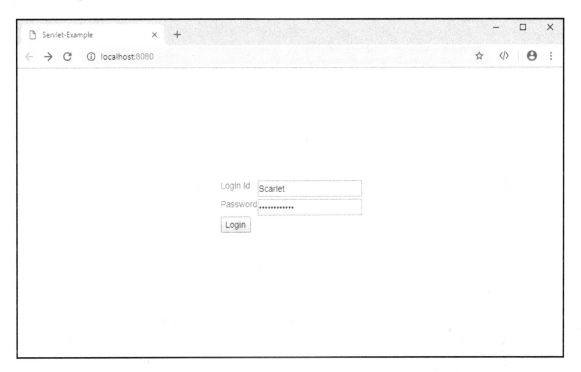

This takes us to the following screen:

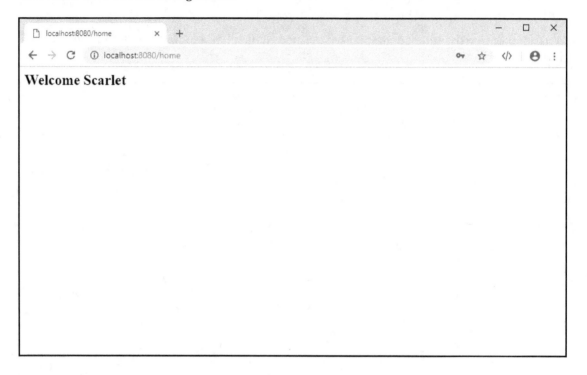

In this example, we created a simple servlet application that responds to a login request. We used the Kotlin runtime and the controller logic that we wrote in Kotlin.

 JSPs cannot contain scriptlets written in Kotlin. They can, however, contain scriptlets written in Java, and scriptlets written in Java can easily call Kotlin classes because of Kotlin's interoperability with Java. JSP's **Expression Language** (**EL**) expressions can refer to DTOs written in Kotlin.

In this section, we learned the role of a servlet in a web application, and we created and deployed a servlet to respond to a request from a web client using Kotlin.

In the next section, we will discuss the Enterprise JavaBean.

Kotlin and EJB

As we discussed earlier, Kotlin is fully interoperable with Java. It can be used with any Java-based framework; one such technology that Kotlin can work with is **Enterprise Java Beans (EJBs)**.

An overview of EJBs

An application or a service comprises different components that interact with each other. Each component implements a contract defined by the interfaces to achieve a functionality. These components exist in the runtime environment of the system and use the services in the system environment.

An enterprise bean is a server-side component. These beans implement the business logic of an enterprise application and comply with the rules of the EJB architecture. These beans live in an EJB container and the EJB container provides different services to them.

The purpose of EJBs is to provide a framework for the components of the service or an application that may be plugged into a server, thereby extending that server's functionality. EJBs provide an architecture to develop and deploy component-based enterprise applications with a high level of scalability, good performance, and robustness.

Advantages of EJBs

The advantages of EJBs are as follows:

- EJBs make it easier to develop large, distributed enterprise applications.The EJB container offers services to EJBs that include security, logging, and transactional aspects. The container is also responsible for managing the life cycle of the beans.
- The EJBs are portable application components that contain business logic.

The EJB component model

As a component model, EJB defines three bean types:

- **Session Bean**: The session bean stores the data of a particular user's session. The lifetime of a session bean is limited to the duration of the interaction between the client and the bean. The client normally creates a session bean and invokes the functions. The EJB container removes the bean when it is no longer required. Session beans can be further classified into the following three types:
  - **Stateless Bean**: The state information between the client and bean is not maintained in a stateless bean. When a function of a stateless bean is invoked by a client, the instance variables of the beans may have some client-specific state information. This information exists only during the invocation of that function. When the function finishes its execution, the client-specific state will not be saved. A stateless session bean is shared between the different clients.
  - **Stateful Bean**: The EJB container maintains the state information of the bean and the client in a stateful bean. A stateful session bean is created only for a specific client and it is not shared among the clients.
    - **Singleton Bean**: A singleton bean is instantiated only once in the application and exists throughout its life cycle. A singleton bean is shared among the different clients and can be accessed simultaneously. Singleton beans are instantiated during the start of the application and are removed before the application goes down. Singleton classes are suitable for cases in which we need to initialize or clean up resources at an application level.

- **Entity Bean**: Entity beans store the data in a data store, which is usually a relational database. Entity beans are often referred to as data-persistent units as they store the data that they carry. Entity beans have attributes and functions. Attributes are used to store data in a secondary store and functions perform operations on them. Entity beans are always shared among the clients. The EJB specifications define two entity bean models:
  - **Bean-managed Persistence**: In this model, a bean is responsible for managing the data persistence of the bean's state information. When creating the bean, we must implement details such as connecting to a database and interacting with the database to store the information.

- **Container-managed Persistence**: In this model, the EJB container manages the data-persistence aspects. The container is responsible for connecting to the database and storing state interaction between the client and the bean in the database.

- **Message-driven Bean**: A message-driven bean listens to messages that flow in an asynchronous fashion. When an EJB-based application needs to receive messages asynchronously from other systems, we can use message-driven beans. These message-driven beans are activated by the container when a message is received and it is not directly accessible to the clients. The clients subscribe to a topic or to a queue and interact with these EJBs by sending messages to the queues or topics.

Let's enhance the project that we created using servlets to include a stateless bean that will have business logic. We will write a stateless bean that accepts a name and returns a greeting message:

```
@Stateless
open class StatelessEjb {
    fun hello(name:String):String{
        return"Hello $name"
    }
}
```

Let's modify `AuthController` to make it use the stateless bean that we created:

```
@WebServlet(name = "home", value = "/home")
class HomeController: HttpServlet() {
private var statelessEjb: StatelessEjb = StatelessEjb()
    override fun doPost(request: HttpServletRequest, response:
HttpServletResponse) {
        statelessEjb.hello(request.getParameter("loginId"))
response.writer.write("<html><body><h2>${statelessEjb.hello(request.getPara
meter("loginId"))}</h2>         </body></html>")
    }
}
```

Deploy the WAR file and enter the details:

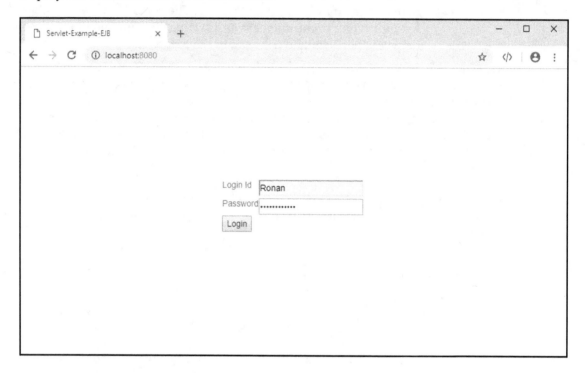

The output we get is as follows:

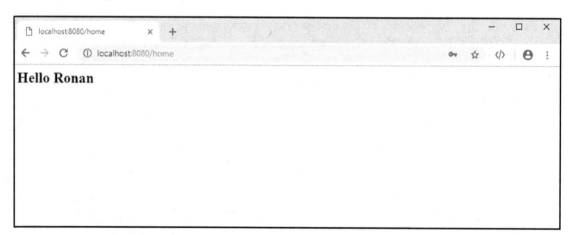

Here, we used a stateless EJB to display a greeting message in the controller.

Bean validation

Data validation is very important in enterprise applications to ensure data integrity. It allows us to check for possible data manipulation between the request made by the user and that received on the server side.

Let's take a look at an example of validating a Bean and writing a unit test to verify it. First, create a maven project:

1. Create a bean named `Person` that takes `name`, `emailId`, and `preferredLanguage` in its constructor. This is shown in the following code:

```
class Person(@field:NotBlank private val name:String,
             @field:Email private val emailId:String,
             @field:NotNull private val preferredLanguage:String)
```

Let's analyze what we have written for the `Person` bean. Take a look at how simple this class is. All we have is a `Person` class with a constructor that takes `name`, `emailId`, and `preferredLanguage` as parameters to initialize the class. We used three annotations from the `javax(javaee-api)` library: `@Email`, `@NotBlank`, and `@NonNull`:

- The `@Email` annotation ensures the `emailId` field accepts a String in the proper `emailId` format.
- The `@NotBlank` annotation ensures the field name accepts a non-null value or a String that is not empty.
- The `@NotNull` annotation ensures the `preferredLanguage` field accepts a non-null value.

2. Write a Junit test to verify this, as follows:

```
class PersonTest {

    @Test
    fun validUser() {
        val person = Person(
                "Raghavendra Rao",
                "kraghavendrarao1@gmail.com",
                "en-us")

        val validationErrors = PersonTest.validator
                                    .validate(person)
        Assert.assertTrue(validationErrors.isEmpty())
    }
```

```
@Test
fun invalidName() {
    val person = Person(
            "",
            "kraghavendrarao1@gmail.com",
            "en-us")

    val validationErrors = PersonTest.validator
                                    .validate(person)
    Assert.assertEquals(1, validationErrors.size.toLong())
}

@Test
fun invalidEmailId() {
    val person = Person(
            "Raghavendra Rao",
            "kraghavendrarao1",
            "en-us")

    val validationErrors = PersonTest.validator
                                    .validate(person)
    Assert.assertEquals(1, validationErrors.size.toLong())
}

companion object {
    private val validator: Validator =
Validation.buildDefaultValidatorFactory()
                                        .validator

    }
}
```

`PersonTest.kt` is a simple Junit test class to verify the data-validation constraints defined in the Person bean class.

We are using a `Validator` class to validate the Person bean. The `PersonTest.kt` test class initializes the Person object and it verifies that the properties of the `Person.kt` class are valid.

In this section, we learned how to carry out bean validation using the `javaee-api` library. We also wrote a unit test to verify the data.

Summary

In this chapter, we looked at the following:

- An overview of Java EE.
- Application servers and containers and their types in Java EE.
- The Java EE architecture and what's new in Java EE 8.
- Various plugins that are useful when writing Java EE applications using Kotlin. These included the all-open compiler plugin, the no-arg compiler plugin, the Kotlin-spring compiler plugin, and the Kotlin-jpa plugin.
- How to create a servlet application using Kotlin.
- Enterprise Java beans and their different types.
- How to create an application with EJB and Kotlin and an example of bean validation.

Kotlin with JSF and CDI

4

Just as Kotlin is fully interoperable with Java, the same is true for Java-based frameworks that are used in the development of enterprise applications. Frameworks such as **Java Server Faces (JSF)** and **Context Dependency Injection (CDI)** also work seamlessly with Kotlin:

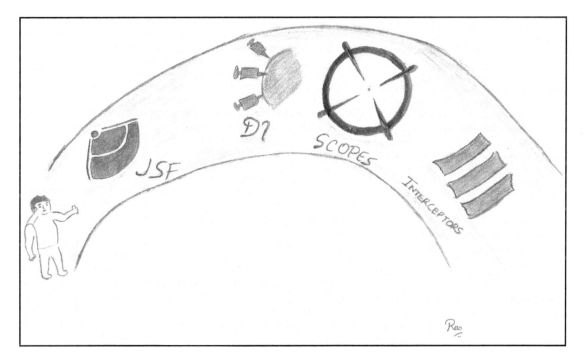

The following topics will be covered in this chapter:

- JSFs and using Kotlin to create a simple JSF application
- CDI for injecting the dependencies in an enterprise application
- Qualifiers, producers, different CDI scopes, and domain events

Technical requirements

Knowledge of the MVC framework will make it easier to understand JSF.
Similarly, familiarity with the **Inversion of Control** (**IoC**) principle will help you to
understand the concepts behind CDI.

Introduction to JSF

JSF is a component-based, server-side Java framework for developing user interfaces. It is
the primary web framework in Java EE and includes the MVC model and the template
framework.

It aims to simplify the frontend aspect of Java Enterprise applications and accelerate user
interface development. It uses a component-based model to build the user interface.
It defines a UI component model, which is bound to a well-defined request processing
model, a **POJO** (**Plain Old Java Object**), in an enterprise application. This allows
JSP custom libraries to handle those UI components and provides a mechanism to extend
the standard UI components.

JSF saves the state information of the UI components and repopulates them during the
display, since the state of the components lives beyond the lifespan of the HTTP request.

JSF operates by providing functionalities such as data conversion and component
rendering. JSF doesn't change the basic page life cycle, in which a client makes
an HTTP request and the server responds with a dynamically generated HTML page.

JSF is a standard framework for building presentation tiers for web applications. It provides
a set of presentations and user interface components. It also provides an event model for
wiring the interactions between the UI and the application objects.

Using JSF, we can build reusable components with Facelets. We can also use standard APIs,
such as Bean validation, CDIs, and tag libraries.

JSF also supports HTML 5 and Ajax calls. It additionally has Faces Flow, which allows us to
create business workflows, wizards, and sets of pages.

JSF architecture

The architecture of JSF is based on the MVC2 model, which can be represented as **Model**, **View**, and **Controller** layers. This is shown in the following diagram:

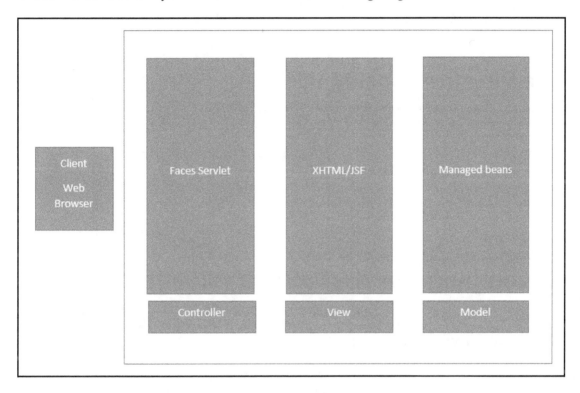

Let's look at each of these blocks in detail:

- **Controller**: The controller layer is represented by the `FacesServlet` of the JSF framework. It is responsible for dispatching the request and the page navigation. It creates a `FacesContext` object that contains information required for request processing. `FacesServlet` also initiates the JSF `Lifecycle` object by invoking it and passing the `FacesContext` object to it. The JSF `Lifecycle` object handles the JSF request processing life cycle.
- **View**: The view layer renders the pages using JSF technology, typically Facelets XHTML. This layer defines the content that is to be presented to the end user and includes page layout and other navigational components.

- **Model**: The model is represented by managed beans. JSF-managed beans are normal POJOs that conform to the JavaBeans naming conventions and are mapped to JSF pages in the view layer. JSF-managed beans have to be registered in the configuration file either using annotations in the bean class, or in the `faces-config.xml` file. The beans will have defined scopes, such as the request scope, the session, the application, or the flow.

The Benefits of using JSF

JSF reduces the amount of effort required to create and maintain applications that run on the Java application server and that render the application UI on a target client.

JSF eases the development of the web application with its reusable UI components. JSF facilitates easy data transfer between these components and manages the state of the UI across multiple server requests. It also enables the implementation of custom UI components and takes care of wiring the client-side events to the server-side application code.

Developing our first JSF application

We will create a simple Maven web application to demonstrate how to use JSF with Kotlin. The application will have a JSF page that simply displays a greeting message. Perform the following steps to develop the JSF application:

1. In IntelliJ IDEA, go to **New,** and then click on **Project**.
2. Select **maven-archetype-webapp** and create the web app project.
3. This will create the project structure, as follows:

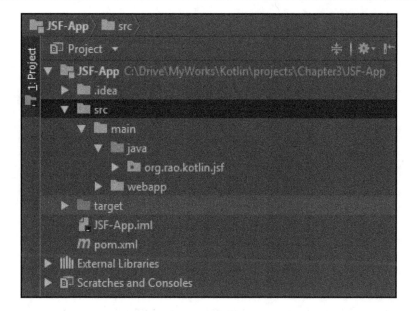

4. Next, we need to add the following Maven dependencies to the project:

```
<dependency>
    <groupId>javax.servlet</groupId>
    <artifactId>javax.servlet-api</artifactId>
    <version>${javax.servlet-api}</version>
    <scope>provided</scope>
</dependency>
<dependency>
    <groupId>com.sun.faces</groupId>
    <artifactId>jsf-api</artifactId>
    <version>${com.sun.faces.jsf-api}</version>
</dependency>
<dependency>
    <groupId>com.sun.faces</groupId>
    <artifactId>jsf-impl</artifactId>
    <version>${com.sun.faces.jsf-impl}</version>
</dependency>
```

5. Create a managed bean called `Person.kt`. This is shown in the following code:

```
@ManagedBean(name = "person")
class Person {
    val name: String
    get() = "Mathur"
}
```

6. Create a `jsf` file with an `xhtml` extension:

```
<?xml version="1.0" encoding="UTF-8"?>
<!DOCTYPE html PUBLIC "-//W3C//DTD XHTML 1.0 Transitional//EN"
         "http://www.w3.org/TR/xhtml1/DTD/xhtml1-transitional.dtd">
<html xmlns="http://www.w3.org/1999/xhtml"
      xmlns:h="http://xmlns.jcp.org/jsf/html"
      xmlns:ui="http://xmlns.jcp.org/jsf/facelets"
      xmlns:f="http://xmlns.jcp.org/jsf/core">
<f:view>
    <h:outputLabel value="JSF-App example"/>
</f:view>

<body>
<h3>
Welcome #{person.getName()}
</h3>
</body>
</html>
```

7. Mention the `index.xhtml` page in the deployment descriptor to load it following the startup of the app:

```
<welcome-file-list>
  <welcome-file>index.jsf</welcome-file>
</welcome-file-list>
```

8. Now, build the application and deploy it on the Tomcat server. The output is as follows:

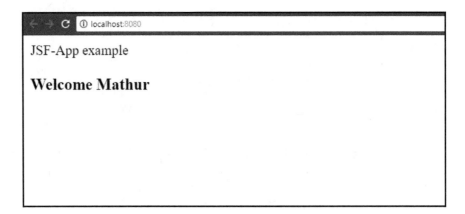

Kotlin and CDI

The IoC and dependency injection patterns are very important design principles that decouple the code from dependent objects. If we have two objects that are related to each other, one might be dependent on the other. The idea of the IoC and dependency injection patterns is to decouple this dependency so that the two objects are not tied to one another.

The Java frameworks that implement the IoC principle are Seam and Spring. Seam is a set of utilities used for web development that was integrated in the Java EE specification in order to provide dependency injection. Spring has implemented IoC and is represented by the Spring IoC container (`ApplicationContext`). The Spring container is responsible for instantiating, configuring, and assembling the required objects, which are known as beans. The Spring container manages the life cycle of the beans.

CDI is the central specification and the dependency injection framework that is built into Java EE. CDI frameworks allow us to inject the required dependencies without instantiating them manually in the code, thus simplifying the dependency injection in Java EE applications. It's a modern, extremely type-safe, and easy-to-use standard API for dependency injection. With CDI, the life cycle of the beans is managed by the Java EE container, as demonstrated in the following diagram:

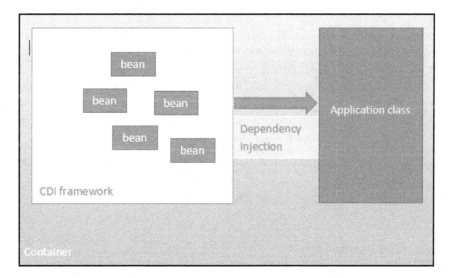

CDI was added to the Java EE specification in Java EE 6. Java EE 8 includes a new version of CDI, which has new features such as asynchronous events and event ordering. CDI unifies the **Enterprise Java beans** (**EJB**) and JSF programming models. It provides several advantages, such as allowing any JavaBean with a name and referring to it as a JSF-managed bean. This includes stateless and stateful session beans. It gives us the flexibility to inject various types of components in a loosely coupled manner with type safety.

 Session beans can be injected in CDI, but not entity beans or message-driven beans, as they are non-contextual.

The Difference between EJB and CDI-managed beans

Classes are annotated with @Stateless, @Stateful, or @Singleton to make them EJBs. These beans are managed by the container or application server and already implements a number of cross-cutting concerns, such as transactions, monitoring, pooling, and more. Stateless beans doesn't maintain the state interaction between the client and the server. The instances of the beans that are annotated with @Stateless are actually pooled. There will be several instances of these beans. The server manages them and we can configure this if we want to. If we access an instance of these beans, we get an instance that might have been created previously from the pool. After using it, it is returned to the pool. Stateful beans maintain the interaction between the client and the server.The instances of the beans that are annotated with @Stateful are not pooled. These beans are created for a particular user's session and remain associated with that session till the session is active. For Singleton beans, only one instance is maintained in the application.

CDI-managed beans are typically POJOs that are injected. These beans don't come with any cross-cutting concerns, such as transaction, monitoring, and pooling. If we need these, we can add annotations to the CDI-managed beans, such as @Transactional.

Injecting the beans

@Inject is used to inject the required dependencies. For example, let's say there are two classes—IdGenerator and Identity. IdGenerator has to be injected into the Identity class. We can use @Inject for this without having to instantiate the IdGenerator inside the Identity class.

This is shown in the following code:

```
class Identity {
    @Inject
    private lateinit var idGenerator: IdGenerator
}
```

Producers

CDI producers comes with the `@Produces` annotation. It is useful when we need to have complete control over the instantiation of the bean, with some custom code execution, before actually creating the instance.

Let's write an `IdentityCreator` class. It has a function called `createPerson()`, which takes `inputData` as an argument. If the person has preferred choice of language, it is represented by the `preferredLanguage` attribute. If `preferredLanguage` is not given in `inputData`, we will have to create a `person` instance with `defaultPreferredLanguage`. This is shown in the following code:

```
class IdentityCreator {
    private lateinit var defaultPreferredLanguage:PreferredLanguage

    fun createPerson(inputData: InputData): Person {
        val person = Person()
        if (inputData.preferredLangauge == null)
          person.preferredLangauge = defaultPreferredLanguage
        else
          inputData.preferredLangauge
    }
}
```

Let's say that creating `defaultPreferredLanguage` is not the concern of the `IdentityCreator` class and we want to inject this default property from outside using `@Inject`:

```
@Inject
private lateinit var defaultPreferredLanguage:PreferredLanguage
```

However, `PreferredLanguage` is an enum:

```
enum class PreferredLanguage (val preferredLanguage: String) {
    EN_US("en-us"), EN_UK("en-gb")
}
```

Wiring `defaultPreferredLanguage` to the `IdentityCreator` class is not possible, since `PreferredLanguage` is not a managed bean.

We need to create producers to achieve this. This is done with the following code:

```
class PreferredLanguageProducer {

    @Produces
    fun exposeDefaultPreferredLanguage(): PreferredLanguage {
        return PreferredLanguage.EN_US
    }
}
```

We can now inject this `defaultPreferredLanguage` in the `IdentityCreator` class, as shown here:

```
@Inject
private lateinit var defaultPreferredLanguage: PreferredLanguage
```

The `PreferredLanguage` type is now injectable as we specify the `Producer`. `defaultPreferredLanguage` is injected in the `IdentityCreator` class and we can use it further in the `IdentityCreator` class.

We can also specify the `@Produces` annotation at the field level. This can be done as shown in the following code:

```
class PreferredLanguageProducer {
    @Produces
    private val defaultPreferredLanguage: PreferredLanguage
}
```

Within the scope of the `PreferredLanguageProducer` bean class, we can set the value for `defaultPreferredLanguage`. When the bean is injected by CDI, the value set to `defaultPreferredLanguage` will be injected in the `IdentityCreator` class.

Qualifiers

Qualifiers are required in some cases to resolve conflicts during dependency injection by identifying the correct bean with a qualified name. In the last section, we discussed injecting the dependencies. We injected `defaultPreferredLanguage` in the `IdentityCreator` class that was produced by the `Producer` function of the `PreferredLanguageProducer` class. If we want to inject another field of the same type, we then have a problem. If we have another function that produces a bean of the `PreferredLanguage` type, the CDI wouldn't know which one to consider and inject. In order to solve this, we can specify qualifiers, such as the `@Named` annotation.

`@Named` is a qualifier that is shipped by the CDI. It is annotated with `@Qualifier` and can qualify string values for instances to be injected.

Let's say that we want to have several `preferredLanguage` types, based on a context such as `NativeEnglishSpeaker`. In this case, we would need to specify `@Named` with the `native-english-speaker` string value. This is shown in the following code:

```
class IdentityCreator {
    @Inject
    @Named("native-english-speaker")
    private lateinit var defaultPreferredLanguage: PreferredLanguage

    fun createPerson(inputData: InputData): Person {
        val person = Person()
        person.preferredLanguage = if (inputData.preferredLanguage == null)
            defaultPreferredLanguage
        else
            inputData.preferredLanguage
        return person
    }
}
```

In order to know which function or which producer is the correct one, we have to specify the `Named` annotation on the `Producer` function as well:

```
class PreferredLanguageProducer {
    @Produces
    @Named("native-english-speaker")
    fun exposeDefaultPreferredLanguage(): PreferredLanguage {
        return PreferredLanguage.EN_US
    }
}
```

We can also specify another `preferredLanguage` to be injected in the `IdentityCreator` class that comes from another producer and has a different qualifier:

```
class PreferredLanguageProducer {
    @Produces
    @Named("hindi")
    fun exposeDefaultPreferredLanguage(): PreferredLanguage {
        return PreferredLanguage.HI
    }
}
```

This can be injected as follows:

```
@Inject
@Named("hindi")
```

> These qualifiers are not only annotated on producer functions; they can also be annotated directly on beans, as follows:
> ```
> @Named("hindi")
> class PreferredLanguageProducer {
>   @Produces
>   fun exposeDefaultPreferredLanguage(): PreferredLanguage
> {
>     return PreferredLanguage.HI
>   }
> }
> ```

The `Named` qualifier with strings works fine, but this is not the best approach as it is not type safe. In this case, we are just relying on the string. If we make a typo, we don't get a warning until the application starts up. This means that we cannot just use the `Named` qualifier that comes with the string, but we can also use type-safe qualifiers if we define them in our application.

Let's say we want to have a `@NativeEnglishSpeaker` qualifier that itself is an annotation. We create a new annotation that we can use while creating `Person`:

```
@Qualifier
@Retention(RetentionPolicy.RUNTIME)
@Documented
annotation class NativeEnglishSpeaker
```

These qualifiers are annotations that are annotated with `@Qualifier` from the CDI. An annotation in the Java EE world has to have a retention runtime policy so that it is visible at runtime.

Qualifiers need to be specified at the producer function. We can then inject `PreferredLanguage` in the `IdentityCreator` class in a type-safe way. Consider the following code:

```
class PreferredLanguageProducer {

    @Produces
    @NativeEnglishSpeaker
    fun exposeDefaultPreferredLanguage(): PreferredLanguage {
        return PreferredLanguage.EN_US
    }
}
```

Here, we specified a producer function, `exposeDefaultPreferredLanguage()`, which is annotated with `@Produces` and a qualifier annotation, `@NativeEnglishSpeaker`. Now, in the `IdentityCreator` class, we annotate the `defaultPreferredLanguage` field with the `@NativeEnglishSpeaker` and `@Inject` annotations so that a `preferredLanguage` created in the producer function gets injected in it:

```
class IdentityCreator {
    @Inject
    @NativeEnglishSpeaker
    private lateinit var defaultPreferredLanguage: PreferredLanguage

    fun createPerson(inputData: InputData): Person {
        val person = Person()
        person.preferredLanguage = if (inputData.preferredLanguage == null)
            defaultPreferredLanguage
        else
            inputData.preferredLanguage
        return person
    }
}
```

We can now implement the custom qualifier types that can be used to specify at the injection point. We can use CDI to manage these beans.

We can now specify as many qualifiers as we want for all the custom qualifier types we are using if the types themselves are not sufficient to uniquely identify the injected instances. These qualifiers are handy in combination with the producers.

Scopes

CDI has a number of scope annotations. Every managed bean either explicitly or implicitly defines the scope, and the scope specifies the life cycle of all the instances of the beans. For example, we have an EJB session bean of an application with a stateless scope, as shown in the following code:

```kotlin
@Stateless
class App {
    @Inject
    private lateinit var identityCreator: IdentityCreator
    @Inject
    private lateinit var identityRepository: IdentityRepository

    fun createIdentity(inputData: InputData): Identity {
        val person = identityCreator.createPerson(inputData)
        identityRepository.store(person)
        return person

    }
}
```

Stateless beans are pooled by the application server. We have several instances of the bean, which is the concern of the application server. When we want to invoke a business function such as createPerson(), we receive an instance of the bean, execute the function, and the instance is returned back into the pool. We must not store any states in these instances as we don't know which instance we will get each time.

There are also other instance scopes, such as @Stateful. Stateful session beans are bound to a user's HTTP session. All the business functions we invoke will be invoked on the same instance. We could, therefore, store some state information in these instances. These are not shared with other users' sessions. An example of a stateful bean is shown here:

```kotlin
@Stateful
class App {
    @Inject
    private lateinit var identityCreator: IdentityCreator
    @Inject
    private lateinit var identityRepository: IdentityRepository

    fun createResource(inputData: InputData): Identity {
        val person = identityCreator.createPerson(inputData)
        identityRepository.store(person)
        return person
    }
}
```

There is a third scope, the `@Singleton` EJB scope. A singleton EJB is a bean that exists only once within a Java EE application. All invocations of the business functions will be invoked on the same instance, as shown in the following code:

```
@Singleton
class App {
    //..
}
```

Context-managed beans, or CDI-managed beans, also have scopes. For example, `IdentityCreator` and `IdentityRepository` are CDI-managed beans and they don't have any annotations, as shown in the following code:

```
package org.rao.kotlin.cdi

class IdentityCreator {
    //..
}
package org.rao.kotlin.cdi

class IdentityRepository {
    //..
}
```

CDI actually defines several scopes, more than the EJB. By default, CDI-managed beans have the `@Dependent` scope, even if we don't specify the `@Dependent` annotation:

```
@Dependent
class IdentityCreator {
    @Inject
    @NativeEnglishSpeaker
    private lateinit var defaultPreferredLanguage: PreferredLanguage

    fun createPerson(inputData: InputData): Person {
        val person = Person()
        person.preferredLanguage = if (inputData.preferredLanguage == null)
            defaultPreferredLanguage
        else
            inputData.preferredLanguage
        return person
    }
}
```

Beans annotated with `@Dependent` are the same as if we don't specify any annotation. By default, beans are dependent-scoped.

This means that the life cycle of these beans depends on the injection point at which the beans are injected. This is demonstrated in the following code:

```kotlin
@Stateless
class App {
    @Inject
    private lateinit var identityCreator: IdentityCreator
    @Inject
    private lateinit var identityRepository: IdentityRepository

    fun createResource(inputData: InputData): Identity {
        val person = resourceCreator.createPerson(inputData)
        resourceRepository.store(person)
        return person

    }
}
```

Here, for the stateless EJB, we want to inject CDI-managed beans. This EJB instance will get one dedicated `IdentityCreator` bean and one dedicated `IdentityRepository` bean, which are active during the life cycle of EJB beans. These beans are not shared with any other managed beans. This means that the `IdentityCreator` class and the `IdentityRepository` bean are dependent on the EJB bean `App`.

In this case, the life cycle of the `identityCreator` class and the `identityRepository` bean is decided by the EJB bean `App`. As it is stateless, its life cycle lasts until the instance is returned to the pool. In the case of the stateful bean, the life cycle lasts for the duration of the particular HTTP session of the requesting client.

Similarly, we could define the CDI-managed bean that itself injects other dependent CDI beans. If we have all the dependent beans, the first one will specify the life cycle for the dependent objects.

An `@ApplicationScoped` CDI bean is similar to singleton EJBs—only one instance of the bean exists within the whole application. This means we only have one instance and everything will be invoked on the same instance of the bean. Consider the following code:

```kotlin
@ApplicationScoped
class IdentityCreator {
    @Inject
    @NativeEnglishSpeaker
    private lateinit var defaultPreferredLanguage: PreferredLanguage
    //..
}
```

There are two more CDI beans—@RequestScoped and @SessionScoped. A RequestScoped CDI bean has a life cycle that is limited to a particular request. A SessionScoped CDI bean, on the other hand, has a life cycle that lasts for the duration of the active HTTP session and is managed by the CDI.

We can use different scopes within a Java EE application. The overall platform will make sure everything works as expected. We can define a bean with a larger scope and inject a smaller scoped bean in it. We can have, for example, a stateful session bean, into which we can then inject other stateless EJBs. This is possible because although we don't directly hold a reference to an IdentityCreator dependent bean, the reference to its proxy object and the framework will take care of managing the beans.

CDI and domain events

In this section, we will look at how to build a model of the domain events using CDI events. Let's say that our application specifies an event, such as a person being created. We will define an event. This event is modeled as part of the domain. We will define a listener listening to the event. The event will be fired at some point during the execution of the business logic.

Defining an event

PersonCreationEvent is an entity that resides in an entity package, more specifically a domain event. Let's say this event specifies some event information, such as identifying which person has been created:

```
class PersonCreationEvent(val identifier: UUID)
```

Now, the event can be created as part of our business logic. In the createIdentity() function, we will create a new event, the PersonCreationEvent class, indicating that a new person record has been created:

```
@Stateless
class App {
    @Inject
    private lateinit var identityCreator: IdentityCreator
    @Inject
    private lateinit var identityRepository: IdentityRepository

    fun createIdentity(inputData: InputData): Identity {
```

```
            val person = identityCreator.createPerson(inputData)
            identityRepository.store(person)
            PersonCreationEvent(person.identifier)
            return person
        }
    }
```

In the preceding code, we just created an event using the identifier of the resource being created. We can specify this new event within the execution of our domain logic.

Listening to the event

Now, the application has to specify a component that listens to this event and executes some further logic. We need to define an event listener. We can do this as part of a new managed bean, such as `PersonCreationEventListener`. This managed bean will define an observer function. An observer function comes with the signature `void`. It is important to specify a parameter, which is actually the event that we fire. The event is annotated with the `@Observes` annotation. We then execute some logic on the event parameter of the event listener, as follows:

```
class PersonCreationEventListener {
    fun onPersonCreation(@Observes event: PersonCreationEvent) {
        println("new person created with id " + event.identifier)
    }
}
```

Firing the event

Now we need to fire the event that we created. We can use CDI events for firing the event, which will loosely couple the event and the listener components. In order to do this, we need to inject a type that comes from the CDI—the `Event` type. This is shown in the following code:

```
@Stateless
class App {
    @Inject
    private lateinit var identityCreator: IdentityCreator
    @Inject
    private lateinit var identityRepository: IdentityRepository
    @Inject
    private lateinit var event: Event<PersonCreationEvent>


    fun createIdentity(inputData: InputData): Identity {
```

```
        val person = identityCreator.createPerson(inputData)
        identityRepository.store(person)
        event.fire(PersonCreationEvent(person.identifier))
        return person
    }
}
```

The `PersonCreationEvent` type is used to fire a new event. Events that are fired will be listened to by an observer function in the application.

 By default, the event handling mechanism runs synchronously. This means that once the event is fired and listened to by the listener, our business logic continues the execution.

Interceptors

In an enterprise application, it's common to have several cross-cutting concerns that are common across different components. As a rule of thumb, this common code should be kept separate from the actual business logic and shouldn't be bound to the core business logic of the component.

We will now take a look at the interceptors, including what they are, how we can utilize them to deal with cross-cutting concerns, and how to bind and activate them. We will also look at how to intercept functions that contain business logic and how to use CDI-provided annotations for this.

Interceptor

An interceptor is a component that intercepts the invocation of functions and life cycle events, such as instance creation/destruction of the associated business classes. Generally, interceptors are used for handing cross-cutting concerns, such as logging, auditing, and security.

Implementing the interceptor

Let's consider the example that we wrote earlier, where we created a person identity. Let's say we want to invoke some functionality around this identity creation function and that we don't necessarily want to mix this logic with the existing business function.

For instance, let's say we want to add audit functionality, which is a common cross-cutting concern. We can use interceptors to write a function to add audit messages, which will be invoked around the execution of the business function. We use the @Interceptors annotation to do this and then we can provide one or more interceptors for common application concerns:

```
@Stateless
@Interceptors(AuditInterceptor.class)
class App {
    @Inject
    private lateinit var identityCreator: IdentityCreator
    @Inject
    private lateinit var identityRepository: IdentityRepository

    fun createIdentity(inputData: InputData): Identity {
        val person = identityCreator.createPerson(inputData)
        identityRepository.store(person)
        return person
    }
}
```

We will create an AuditInterceptor class in the interceptor package that is annotated with the @Interceptor annotation.

This interceptor will specify a handle function that is annotated with @AroundInvoke. The @AroundInvoke annotation declares the handle() function to be invoked around our business functionality.

By injecting the InvocationContext, we can simply use the context.proceed() function to proceed with our business functionality, as follows:

```
@Interceptor
public class AuditInterceptor {
    @AroundInvoke
    fun handle(context: InvocationContext){
        context.proceed()
    }
}
```

When the createIdentity() function is called, the handler function will be invoked by intercepting the invocation of the createIdentity() function call.

We can now include a CDI-managed bean, namely the `Auditor`. This class has a single `audit()` function that simply prints a message to the console once the function has been invoked:

```
class Auditor {
    fun audit(message: String) {
        println(message)
    }
}
```

Let's inject the `Auditor` bean in the `AuditInterceptor` class and call the `audit()` function from `handle()`:

```
@Interceptor
class AuditInterceptor {
    @Inject
    private lateinit var auditor: Auditor

    fun handle(context: InvocationContext) {
        auditor.audit("message")
        context.proceed()
    }
}
```

Now, the interceptor's `handle()` function has been invoked around the business logic of creating a person.

> We could also use a `context` object to get some more information about the invocation intercepted, for example, arguments with which the function is invoked. An example code is shown here:

```
@Interceptor
class AuditInterceptor {
    @Inject
    private lateinit var auditor: Auditor

    fun handle(context: InvocationContext) {
        auditor.audit("message")
        context.parameters.forEach { param -> println(param) }
        context.proceed()
    }
}
```

This section has shown how we can intercept some logic in our application without binding too much of the intercepting logic to the business code. The @Interceptors annotation controls whether the interceptor is invoked. This is not tightly bound to the business logic.

Building custom interceptors

In the previous section, we used the @Interceptors annotation to intercept our business logic. We can also define and bind the custom interceptors. This means that we can define our own interceptors. In this section, we will look at how to use the interceptors' API to define @InterceptorBinding annotations, and how we can activate the custom interceptors.

Defining a custom interceptor

Let's create a custom annotation, such as Auditable, to audit a business function in an application:

```
@InterceptorBinding
@Retention(RetentionPolicy.RUNTIME)
@Documented
annotation class Auditable
```

The Auditable annotation is itself annotated with @InterceptorBinding and has a runtime retention policy to make the annotation visible at runtime.

We can use Auditable in business functions as follows:

```
@Stateless
class App {
    @Inject
    private lateinit var identityCreator: IdentityCreator
    @Inject
    private lateinit var identityRepository: IdentityRepository

    @Auditable
    fun createIdentity(inputData: InputData): Identity {
        val person = identityCreator.createPerson(inputData)
        identityRepository.store(person)
        return person
    }
}
```

Enhancing the auditable interceptor

We can also specify types of audit messages. We can choose to intercept the request based on its type:

```
@InterceptorBinding
@Retention(RetentionPolicy.RUNTIME)
@Documented
annotation class Auditable(val value: Auditor.AuditType)
```

The `AuditType` is defined in the `Auditor` class. We have defined CREATE, READ, UPDATE, and DELETE as audit types in this case:

```
class Auditor {
    fun audit(message: String) {
        println(message)
    }

    enum class AuditType () {
        CREATE, READ, UPDATE, DELETE
    }
}
```

We might want to use the `@Auditable` annotation in cases where we need to perform an audit event based on the type of operation.

Let's say we are going to carry out an audit on the CREATE type:

```
@Stateless
class App {
    @Inject
    private lateinit var identityCreator: IdentityCreator
    @Inject
    private lateinit var identityRepository: IdentityRepository

    @Auditable(Auditor.AuditType.CREATE)
    fun createResource(inputData: InputData): Identity {
        val person = identityCreator.createPerson(inputData)
        identityRepository.store(person)
        return person
    }
}
```

Now, in the `AuditInterceptor` class, we can define the `@Auditable` interceptor binding annotation for any type. In this case, we will do this for `CREATE`:

```
@Interceptor
@Auditable(Auditor.AuditType.CREATE)
class AuditInterceptor {
    @Inject
    private lateinit var auditor: Auditor

    @AroundInvoke
    fun handle(context: InvocationContext) {
        auditor.audit("message")
        context.proceed()
    }
}
```

The `handle()` function should always be invoked, once the `@Auditable` interceptor binding is annotated. We can also retrieve the `@Auditable` annotation from the context to get the value and do something with it. Let's say we want to use the value that comes from the annotation in the audit message that we process:

```
@Interceptor
@Auditable(Auditor.AuditType.CREATE)
class AuditInterceptor {
    @Inject
    private lateinit var auditor: Auditor

    @Inject
    private lateinit var auditProcessor: AuditProcessor

    @AroundInvoke
    fun handle(context: InvocationContext) {
        auditor.audit("message")
        auditProcessor
.processMessage(context.method.getAnnotation(Auditable::class.java).value)
        context.proceed()
    }
}
```

The `AuditProcessor` class defines a function that takes `AuditType` as argument and prints it to console. The code looks like:

```
class AuditProcessor {
    fun processMessage(type: Auditor.AuditType) {
        println("Audit message type$type")
    }
}
```

The interceptor binding can also be specified at the class:

```
@Stateless
@Auditable(Auditor.AuditType.CREATE)
class App {
    @Inject
    private lateinit var identityCreator: IdentityCreator
    @Inject
    private lateinit var identityRepository: IdentityRepository

    fun createIdentity(inputData: InputData): Identity {
        val person = identityCreator.createPerson(inputData)
        identityRepository.store(person)
        return person
    }
}
```

In this way, we can retrieve the annotations of the invocation context that has been invoked by the binding of the interceptor.

Activating the interceptor

We can now activate AuditInterceptor. One way of doing this is to specify the interceptor in the beans.xml files, as shown here:

```
<interceptors>
  <class>
      <AuditInterceptor>
  </class>
</interceptors>
```

Alternatively, we can specify this with the @Priority annotation, which indicates the interceptor's priority. For example, we can annotate the AuditInterceptor class with the @Priority annotation APPLICATION level:

```
@Interceptor
@Auditable
@Priority(Interceptor.Priority.APPLICATION)
class AuditInterceptor {
    @Inject
    private lateinit var auditor: Auditor

    @Inject
    private lateinit var auditProcessor: AuditProcessor

    @AroundInvoke
```

```
    fun handle(context: InvocationContext) {
        auditor.audit("message")
        auditProcessor
.processMessage(context.method.getAnnotation(Auditable::class.java).value)
        context.proceed()
    }
}
```

The `AuditInterceptor` class's `handle()` function is invoked at the application level, which is usually the case for the interceptor. This means that each application request is intercepted by the `AuditInterceptor` class.

Summary

In this chapter, we have discussed the following topics:

- What JSFs are
- How we can model and build core Java EE components using EJB and CDI-managed beans
- What CDI producers are and how they can be used together with qualifiers
- What the scopes of EJB and CDI-managed beans are
- How we can build and model domain events
- How we can use CDI events in order to couple logic loosely together

Kotlin with JPA and EJB

5

Data persistence is an important aspect in an enterprise application. Almost all businesses are data driven. Persisting this data, retrieving it, and processing it in order to make business decisions are common activities in an enterprise application:

The component that deals with data persistence and data retrieval is popularly known as the **object-relational mapping** (**ORM**) component. Persistence frameworks also offer ORM layers of abstraction between the application and the database. The persistence framework is responsible for converting the state of objects to entities, persisting them to a relational database, and retrieving them for processing purposes.

Java EE has an API that can be used in the ORM component of an application. This is called the **Java Persistence API** (**JPA**). This is one of the most important APIs in Java EE and the solution that Java EE uses to talk to relational databases and non-relational databases.

The following topics will be covered in this chapter:

- Data classes in Kotlin
- An introduction to JPA and its architecture
- Mapping domain entities to database tables
- Writing queries for data retrieval
- Mapping the relations between the entities
- Defining the data source and the persistence context
- JPA transactions
- Exception handling

Technical requirements

Having a knowledge of ORM will give you an advantage in this chapter, although we will go through a few basic concepts as well.

Kotlin Data Classes

When we are dealing with data layers in an application, such as inserting data or retrieving it from a data source, we need to have classes to represent this data. When we have this representation, it is easy to perform operations on the data, such as validation or manipulation.

If we are dealing with a large data set, it is good to have less code to represent the data, without affecting the required functionality. Kotlin provides us with a construct to represent the data in a cleaner way. Typically, classes marked with the `data` keyword will be created to hold the data in the application. These classes are known as data classes.

For example, consider the following code:

```
data class Person(val loginId: String) {
    lateinit var identifier: UUID
    lateinit var name: PersonName
    var preferredLanguage: PreferredLanguage? = null
}
```

Unlike common classes, data classes are created with the intention of holding the state information and don't include any functions that operate on the data. The Kotlin compiler automatically generates some of the required functions, such as equals(), hashcode(), and toString(). This makes the classes that hold the data cleaner without much boilerplate code.

Java doesn't have pure data classes. Regular Java classes can be used as data classes, but these classes may include the methods that operate on the data.

Let's compare data classes in Kotlin and Java. First, let's write a Person class in Java, which is Person.java:

```java
public class Person {

    private UUID identifier;
    private PersonName name;
    private PreferredLanguage preferredLanguage;

    public UUID getIdentifier() {
        return identifier;
    }

    public void setIdentifier(UUID identifier) {
        this.identifier = identifier;
    }

    public PersonName getName() {
        return name;
    }

    public void setName(PersonName name) {
        this.name = name;
    }

    public PreferredLanguage getPreferredLanguage() {
        return preferredLanguage;
    }

    public void setPreferredLanguage(PreferredLanguage
     preferredLanguage) {
        this.preferredLanguage = preferredLanguage;
    }

    @Override
    public String toString() {
        return "Per(" +
                "identifier=" + identifier +
```

```
                ", name=" + name +
                ", preferredLanguage=" + preferredLanguage +
                ')';
    }

    @Override
    public boolean equals(Object o) {
        if (this == o) {
            return true;
        }
        if (o == null || getClass() != o.getClass()) {
            return false;
        }
        Per per = (Per) o;
        return Objects.equals(identifier, per.identifier) &&
                Objects.equals(name, per.name) &&
                preferredLanguage == per.preferredLanguage;
    }

    @Override
    public int hashCode() {
        return Objects.hash(identifier, name, preferredLanguage);
    }
}
```

We have to declare the fields and provide getters, setters, and, optionally, override methods, such as `hashcode()`, `equals()`, and `toString()`.

In Kotlin, we can write the preceding code as follows:

```
data class Person(val loginId: String) : Identity() {
    @Id
    lateinit var identifier: UUID
    lateinit var name: PersonName

    @Enumerated(EnumType.STRING)
    var preferredLanguage: PreferredLanguage? = null
}
```

In comparison to Java, these data classes have less boilerplate code. We don't have to include getters and setters, equals, or hashcode implementations. This reduces the time required to write a large number of data classes and improves the readability of the classes.

The compiler provides a `copy` function, which is useful when we are writing immutable classes.

When we write data classes, in order for the compiler to derive the behavior of the code in a meaningful way, we have to have a primary constructor with at least a single parameter in it. This can be declared either as `var` or `val`. Data classes have to be concrete classes; they cannot be abstract. They should not be marked with `inner` or `open` keywords.

When the implementations are provided for the `equals()`, `hashcode()`, or `toString()` functions, the one provided will be used and the compiler won't generate the default implementations. We can also provide implementations for the `copy()` and `componentN()` functions. `componentN()` functions are used for decomposing a class.

The member fields declared inside the class will not be used by the compiler while generating implementations for the `equals()`, `hashcode()`, and `toString()` functions:

```
class Person(val loginId: String) : Identity() {
    @Id
    lateinit var identifier: UUID
    lateinit var name: PersonName

    @Enumerated(EnumType.STRING)
    var preferredLanguage: PreferredLanguage? = null
}
```

In our case, this means that the identifier, the name, and `preferredLanguage` will not be used by the compiler to generate these default implementations.

Sometimes, we need to copy an object to another object. The `copy()` function creates new instances rather than just keeping the references. This helps to achieve immutability. For example, let's say that for our `Person` class, we have two instances declared and we want to copy the values from one to another:

```
var person1 = Person("loginId1")
var person2: Person
```

We can now copy the values from `person1` to `person2` as follows:

```
person2 = person1.copy(loginId = "2")
```

Java Persistence API

Java EE has an API that can be used in the ORM component of an application. This is called JPA. This is one of the most important APIs in Java EE and the solution that Java EE uses to talk to relational databases and non-relational databases.

JPA offers an ORM solution based on the ORM paradigm. The framework handles the mapping of the state of the objects to the database without us having to specify many details about the mapping. All we really have to worry about is writing appropriate annotations on our POJO classes.

JPA architecture

One of the key aspects of the JPA is the entity manager API, which is responsible for providing **Create**, **Read**, **Update**, **and Delete** (**CRUD**) functionality. These are the operations that we can perform on an object that we want to persist on to the database.

Beyond this, one of the most important concepts in the persistence tier is queries. We need rich query capability at the database layer. JPA allows us to create queries in a number of different ways. One of these is **Java Persistence Query Language** (**JPQL**), which we can think of as an object-oriented version of **Structured Query Language** (**SQL**). It is just as powerful, compact, and expressive as SQL.

Another option is *criteria queries*. These are a bit different to JPQL. For criteria queries, we don't really use a **query language** (**QL**) at all. What we do instead is construct queries by writing a very object-oriented, API-style code.

Another possibility is to use native queries. This is where we can use SQL queries if we aren't using ORM constructs. We use the SQL native queries through JPA and we essentially get 80% of the benefits of JPA, even though we are using native SQL. There is also support for stored procedures.

Because JPA is such a high-level API, we can actually use it as a caching layer once we have done ORM mapping. We can cache all of the entities and the JPA has built-in support for caching.

Bootstrapping the JPA

In order to bootstrap the JPA process in a server environment, we don't have to do much. We just have to configure one XML file, which is the `persistence.xml` file under `resources/META-INF`. We define one persistence unit for a database. We can then define the JPA entities. An example of `persistence.xml` is shown here:

```
<?xml version="1.0" encoding="UTF-8"?>
<persistence version="2.1"
             xmlns="http://xmlns.jcp.org/xml/ns/persistence"
             xmlns:xsi="http://www.w3.org/2001/XMLSchema-instance"
             xsi:schemaLocation="http://xmlns.jcp.org/xml/ns/persistence
```

```
http://xmlns.jcp.org/xml/ns/persistence/persistence_2_1.xsd">
    <persistence-unit name="prod">
<provider>org.eclipse.persistence.jpa.PersistenceProvider</provider>
        <class>org.rao.kotlin.entity.Person</class>
        <class>org.rao.kotlin.entity.ContactDetails</class>
        <class>org.rao.kotlin.entity.Address</class>
        <exclude-unlisted-classes/>
        <properties>
            <property name="javax.persisteData creatednce.jdbc.driver"
                      value="org.postgresql.Driver"/>
            <property name="javax.persistence.jdbc.url"
                      value="jdbc:postgresql://localhost:5432/postgres"/>
            <property name="javax.persistence.jdbc.password"
value="********"/>
            <property name="javax.persistence.jdbc.user" value="postgres"/>
        </properties>
    </persistence-unit>
</persistence>
```

Mapping domain entities using JPA

Previously, we created a `Person` POJO class that we used to illustrate some examples using the CDI. Let's now consider the same POJO again, with some additional fields.

Let's say we want to map this class to a table in a relational database:

```
class Person : Identity() {
    var preferredLanguage: PreferredLanguage? = null
    lateinit var identifier: UUID
    lateinit var name: PersonName
    lateinit var loginId: String
    lateinit var address: Address
}
```

In order to map this POJO class to a table in the database, we need to annotate the class with `@Entity`. This makes this class identifiable to business domain entities:

```
@Entity
class Person : Identity() {
    var preferredLanguage: PreferredLanguage? = null
    lateinit var identifier: UUID
    lateinit var name: PersonName
    lateinit var loginId: String
    lateinit var address: Address
}
```

The `@Entity` annotation can only be specified at the type level; not at the field or the function level.

Each table in a database will have one or more primary keys in it to uniquely identify a record in the table. We have to specify one or more properties that act as an identifier in the entity. For this, we need to annotate the property with the `@Id` annotation. This makes our business entity identifiable.

For example, the identifier field in our `Person` entity can be marked with `@Id`, as each ID will be different in the business context. This is shown in the following code:

```
@Entity
class Person : Identity() {
    @Id
    lateinit var identifier: UUID
    lateinit var name: PersonName
    lateinit var loginId: String
    lateinit var address: Address
    var preferredLanguage: PreferredLanguage? = null
}
```

In Java, we can annotate setters and getters in the entity class.

All of the properties are automatically mapped to table columns in the database. We can also annotate other properties of the entity class as follows:

```
@Id
public void setIdentifier(UUID uuid){
    this.identifier = uuid;
}
```

In Kotlin, we don't have setters as the member fields are accessible directly.

We can also specify the table name to which our entity mapped using the `@Table` annotation. For example, let's say a `person` is a table in the database. To map the `Person` entity to this table, we can use `@Table` by specifying the `name` attribute with the table name in it, which is shown in the following code:

```
@Table(name = "person")
@Entity
class Person : Identity() {
    @Id
    lateinit var identifier: UUID
    lateinit var name: PersonName
    lateinit var loginId: String
    lateinit var address: Address
    var preferredLanguage: PreferredLanguage? = null
}
```

> If the `@Table` annotation is not mentioned in our entity class, or if it is mentioned without the name attribute supplied, the table name defaults to the name of the entity.

To interact with the database using the entity from our **data access object** (**DAO**) layer or façade, we use the functionality that comes with the JPA, called `EntityManager`.

In previous examples, we used `IdentityRepository` to store the person object. Since we now have the `EntityManager` JPA, we don't need this repository bean:

```
@Stateless
class App {
    @Inject
    private lateinit var identityCreator: IdentityCreator
    @PersistenceContext
    private lateinit var entityManager: EntityManager

    fun createIdentity(identity: Identity): Identity {
        val person = identityCreator.createPerson(identity)
        entityManager.persist(person)
        return person
    }
}
```

We acquire the `EntityManager` with the `@PersistenceContext` annotation that will be used to interact with the persistence unit of our application. We use the `persist` method of the `EntityManager` to store our entity in the database.

Our `createIdentity()` function will be executed within the transaction, which means the person data is committed to the database only after the `createIdentity()` function finishes its execution.

Queries

In the previous section, we discussed how to persist the data to the database using the entity and the entity manager of the JPA. We can also retrieve the data from the database. JPA provides APIs to query the data from the database.

Let's say we want to retrieve the person data that we created and persisted. We could either use `CreateNativeQueries`, where we can just specify the query using SQL, or we can define a `NamedQuery`. This is a database query with a specific query syntax and is defined in the entity.

The named queries can be defined as constants and used in the entity class. For example, consider the following code:

```
const val FIND_ALL_PERSON: String = "Person.findAll"

@Table
@Entity
@NamedQuery(name = FIND_ALL_PERSON, query = "select p from Person p")
class Person : Identity() {
    @Id
    lateinit var identifier: UUID
    lateinit var name: PersonName
    lateinit var loginId: String
    lateinit var address: Address
    var preferredLanguage: PreferredLanguage? = null
}
```

We have defined `NamedQuery` in the `Person` entity. It takes a name, a unique constant defined in the class, and a query, which is JPQL. `Person` mentioned in the query is an entity type, not the table name.

We write all the constants in the `Queries` class and access that constant in the `Person` entity:

```
object Queries{
        const val FIND_ALL_PERSON:String =  "Person.findAll"
    }
```

We can then use `NamedQuery` in our `findAllPerson()` function:

```
@Stateless
class App {
    @Inject
    private lateinit var identityCreator: IdentityCreator
    @PersistenceContext
    private lateinit var entityManager: EntityManager

    fun createPerson(inputData: InputData): Person {
        val person = identityCreator.createPerson(inputData)
        entityManager.persist(person)
        return person
    }

    fun findAllPerson(): List<Identity> {
        return entityManager.createNamedQuery(Queries.FIND_ALL_PERSON,
                            Person::class.java).resultList
    }
}
```

In the preceding class, we inject the required dependencies. We have two functions—`createPerson()` and `findAllPerson()`. We create a request instance of the `InputData` type and we insert the data using the entity manager. In the `findAllperson()` function, we use `NamedQueries` to retrieve the result and we get the `resultList` back using `entityManager`. This is a list of `person` entities that are persisted. This is how we retrieve the list and create the `person` record in the database.

Modeling JPA entities

Previously, we learned how to define the basic unit of persistence—an entity, using a Kotlin data class. Let's now look at how we can define and map relations to the domain entities using JPA.

Mapping entities

We can establish a mapping between the entities using JPA's `@OneToOne`, `@OneToMany`, `@ManyToOne`, and `@ManyToMany` annotations.

Let's consider `PersonEntity`:

```
@Entity
class Person : Identity() {
    @Id
    lateinit var identifier: UUID
    lateinit var name: PersonName
    lateinit var loginId: String
    var preferredLanguage: PreferredLanguage? = null
}
```

Here, `preferredLanguage` is an enum, so it can be included with the `@Enumerated` annotation within the entity:

```
@Entity
class Person : Identity() {
    @Id
    lateinit var identifier: UUID
    lateinit var name: PersonName
    lateinit var loginId: String

    @Enumerated(EnumType.STRING)
    var preferredLanguage: PreferredLanguage? = null
}
```

 By default, the value of an enum type is an implicit ordinal mapping that is resolved by the order in which the enum types are declared. This means that when we use an enum type, the ordinal value is used to represent it and the integer value of the enum type will be included in the database.

OneToMany mapping

Now, let's modify the `Person` entity to add other entities to it. Let's say that `Person` has a list of contacts, which is explained in the following code:

```
@Table
@Entity
class Person : Identity() {
    @Id
    lateinit var identifier: UUID
    lateinit var name: PersonName
    lateinit var loginId: String

    @Enumerated(EnumType.STRING)
    var preferredLanguage: PreferredLanguage? = null
```

```
    lateinit var contact: List<ContactDetails>

}
```

`ContactDetails` is another type here:

```
class ContactDetails {
    private lateinit var id: UUID
    lateinit var number: String

    private var type: ContactType? = null
}
```

Let's say `ContactDetails` has a `ContactType`, which is an enum type. A contact type might be, for example, WORK, MOBILE, or HOME:

```
enum class ContactType(val contactType: String) {
    WORK("work"), MOBILE("mobile"), HOME("home")
}
```

The `Person` type instance can now have multiple contact details. This has to be mapped to the database, which means that `ContactDetails` is also an entity and therefore has to be annotated with `@Entity`:

```
@Entity
class ContactDetails {
    @Id
    private lateinit var id: UUID
    private lateinit var number: String

    @Enumerated(EnumType.STRING)
    private var type: ContactType? = null
}
```

Let's now say that the `Person` entity also has an `Address`:

```
class Address {
    lateinit var street: String
    lateinit var city: String
    lateinit var state: String
    lateinit var country: String
}
```

Now, the `Person` entity class appears as follows:

```
class Person : Identity() {
    @Id
    lateinit var identifier: UUID
    lateinit var name: PersonName
    lateinit var loginId: String

    @Enumerated(EnumType.STRING)
    var preferredLanguage: PreferredLanguage? = null

    lateinit var contact: List<ContactDetails>
    lateinit var address: Address


}
```

The interesting thing here is that `Address` is not identifiable, as we have not marked it with the `@Entity` annotation. `ContactType`, on the other hand, is identifiable; it maps to the `contact_type` table and it has to have an ID. We are also going to map the enum as a string and then map all the values in our domain. Let's take a look at how we can do this.

The `Person` class includes a list of contacts that maps to a table called `contacts` in the database. Since we have two tables in our database, `person` and `contacts`, they have to be joined with a link.

We need to specify the JPA annotation `@OneToMany` to bind these two entities. Consider the following code:

```
@Entity
 class Person : Identity() {
    @Id
    lateinit var identifier: UUID
    lateinit var name: PersonName
    lateinit var loginId: String

    @Enumerated(EnumType.STRING)
    var preferredLanguage: PreferredLanguage? = null

    @OneToMany
    lateinit var contact: List<ContactDetails>
    lateinit var address: Address
}
```

The reason that we choose the `@OneToMany` annotation is that we have one person entity that can have multiple contact details.

JPA models these entities to the appropriate tables in the database.

Cascading

Since we have a one-to-many relationship here, this means that we can have one column in our `contacts` table that refers to a unique entry in the `person` table. Furthermore, we can specify how these entities can be bound. For example, we can perform cascading, as shown in the following code:

```
@Table(name = "person")
@Entity
class Person : Identity() {
    @Id
    lateinit var identifier: UUID
    lateinit var name: PersonName
    lateinit var loginId: String

    @Enumerated(EnumType.STRING)

    var preferredLanguage: PreferredLanguage? = null
    @OneToMany(cascade = arrayOf(CascadeType.ALL))
    lateinit var contact: List<ContactDetails>

    lateinit var address: Address
}
```

Cascading on the `Person` entity specifies that whenever we perform any operation on the `Person` entity, that operation passes down to all other entities that are bound to it. For example, if we save, update, or delete the `Person` entity, these operations are cascaded down to the `ContactDetails` entity.

Fetching strategy

We can also specify the fetching strategies of the data using the fetch type attribute. For example, we can specify that we always want to fetch the `ContactDetails` *eagerly* when loading the `Person` entity. Consider the following code:

```
@Table(name = "person")
@Entity
class Person : Identity() {
    @Id
    lateinit var identifier: UUID
    lateinit var name: PersonName
    lateinit var loginId: String

    @Enumerated(EnumType.STRING)
    var preferredLanguage: PreferredLanguage? = null
```

```
    @OneToMany(cascade = arrayOf(CascadeType.ALL), fetch =
      FetchType.EAGER)
    lateinit var contact: List<ContactDetails>
    lateinit var address: Address


}
```

Since we have to execute a joint operation, we can also load the data *lazily* when the LAZY fetch type is specified:

```
@Table(name = "person")
@Entity
class Person : Identity() {
    @Id
    lateinit var identifier: UUID
    lateinit var name: PersonName
    lateinit var loginId: String

    @Enumerated(EnumType.STRING)
    var preferredLanguage: PreferredLanguage? = null
    @OneToMany(cascade = arrayOf(CascadeType.ALL), fetch =
      FetchType.LAZY)
    lateinit var contact: List<ContactDetails>
    lateinit var address: Address


}
```

Naming a join column

Since we bind a Contact entity to a Person, we can choose to give a name to the joining column. The name that we specify here will be the foreign key reference in the target entity, which is the contacts table:

```
@Table(name = "person")
@Entity
class Person : Identity() {
    @Id
    lateinit var identifier: UUID
    lateinit var name: PersonName
    lateinit var loginId: String

    @Enumerated(EnumType.STRING)
    var preferredLanguage: PreferredLanguage? = null

    @OneToMany(cascade = arrayOf(CascadeType.ALL), fetch =
      FetchType.LAZY)
```

```
    @JoinColumn(name = "PERSON_ID")
    lateinit var contact: List<ContactDetails>
    lateinit var address: Address
}
```

As the `ContactDetails` entity always refers to the `Person` entity with the `PERSON_ID` as foreign key, we can mark it as non-nullable:

```
@JoinColumn(name = "PERSON_ID", nullable = false)
lateinit var contact: List<ContactDetails>
```

ManyToOne mapping

It is also possible to back reference from the `ContactDetails` entity to the `Person` entity using the `@ManyToOne` annotation:

```
@Table(name = "contacts")
@Entity
class ContactDetails {
    @Id
    private lateinit var id: Integer
    lateinit var number: String

    @Enumerated(EnumType.STRING)
    private var type: ContactType? = null

    @ManyToOne(cascade = arrayOf(CascadeType.ALL), fetch =
     FetchType.LAZY)
    lateinit var person: Person
}
```

In the preceding code snippets, we have illustrated an example of the `OneToMany` and `ManyToOne` annotations. Similarly, we can use the `OneToOne` and `ManyToMany` annotations.

A relationship between two classes can be one of the following:

- **Bidirectional**: Both classes hold a reference to the other
- **Unidirectional**: Only one class stores the reference of the other

Let's now move on to talk about binding `Address` to a `Person` entity. `Address` is not an entity; it is just a model object. If it were an entity, we could specify the relationship as we did for the `ContactDetails` entity, binding `Address` and `Person`. Instead, we will use the `@Embedded` annotation:

```
@Table(name = "person")
@Entity
class Person : Identity() {
    @Id
    lateinit var identifier: UUID
    lateinit var name: PersonName
    lateinit var loginId: String

    @Enumerated(EnumType.STRING)
    var preferredLanguage: PreferredLanguage? = null

    @OneToMany(cascade = arrayOf(CascadeType.ALL), fetch =
            FetchType.LAZY)
    @JoinColumn(name = "PERSON_ID", nullable = false)
    lateinit var contact: List<ContactDetails>
    @Embedded
    lateinit var address: Address
}
```

We need to mark the `Address` class with the `@Embeddable` annotation, which is shown in the following code:

```
@Embeddable
class Address {
    lateinit var street: String
    lateinit var city: String
    lateinit var state: String
    lateinit var country: String
}
```

This means that no separate table is created for `Address` as it is not an entity. All the properties of `Address` will be inserted into the `person` table.

All the fields defined in the class are mapped to the columns of a table in the database. To make JPA not persist a field, we can annotate it with the `@Transient` annotation.

For example, consider the following code:

```
@Table(name = "person")
@Entity
data class Person(val loginId: String) : Identity() {
    @Id
    lateinit var identifier: UUID
    @Transient
    late init var lastName: String
    @Enumerated(EnumType.STRING)
    var preferredLanguage: PreferredLanguage? = null
    @Embedded
    lateinit var address: Address
}
```

In this case, the `lastName` field is not mapped to a column in a `person` table.

In this section, we have discussed how to use the `@Entity` annotation for the entities of our domain. We specified the `@Embedded` annotation for model-type objects and we established the mapping between the entities and the data classes.

Data sources

We get data for processing from the data sources. We also persist data into data sources. Let's take a look at how we can configure and use data sources in our application server. We'll look at how we can use the default data source and how we can customize and configure it using persistence contexts and persistence units.

Persistence units

Persistence units are used to define different data sources and actions that will be applied to the data source when the application starts up.

Let's create a persistence unit in our persistence XML file:

```
<persistence xmlns="http://java.sun.com/xml/ns/persistence"
xmlns:xsi="http://www.w3.org/2001/XMLSchema-instance"
xsi:schemaLocation="http://java.sun.com/xml/ns/persistence
http://java.sun.com/xml/ns/persistence/persistence_2_0.xsd" version="2.0">

    <persistence-unit name="local" transaction-type="RESOURCE_LOCAL">
        <properties>
            <property name ="javax.persistence.schema-
generation.database.action" value="drop-and-create"/>
```

```
            </properties>
        </persistence-unit>
    </persistence>
```

Here, we have just specified one persistence unit in our persistence XML file that we named `local`.

The persistence unit uses the `javax.persistence.schema-generation.database.action` property. When the application server starts up, it drops and creates the database schema for the databases, depending on the JPA mapping.

We can specify the data source. If we don't, the default data source will be used.

To specify the data source, we use `jta-data-source`, as shown in the following code:

```xml
<persistence xmlns="http://java.sun.com/xml/ns/persistence"
            xmlns:xsi="http://www.w3.org/2001/XMLSchema-instance"
            xsi:schemaLocation="http://java.sun.com/xml/ns/persistence
            http://java.sun.com/xml/ns/persistence/persistence_2_0.xsd"
            version="2.0">

    <persistence-unit name="local" transaction-type="JTA">
        <jta-data-source>jdbc/local_datasource</jta-data-source>
        <properties>
            <property name="javax.persistence.schema-
            generation.database.action"
                    value="drop-and-create"/>
        </properties>
    </persistence-unit>
</persistence>
```

Here, we specified a data source that is itself configured on the application server. We could choose not to configure the URLs and credentials in the persistence XML file because we could do that in the application server and point to the data source specified. This is sufficient if we have one database in our application.

If we would like to specify several databases, we could have another persistence unit in the XML file:

```xml
<persistence xmlns="http://java.sun.com/xml/ns/persistence"
            xmlns:xsi="http://www.w3.org/2001/XMLSchema-instance"
            xsi:schemaLocation="http://java.sun.com/xml/ns/persistence
            http://java.sun.com/xml/ns/persistence/persistence_2_0.xsd"
            version="2.0">

    <persistence-unit name="local" transaction-type="JTA">
        <jta-data-source>jdbc/local_datasource</jta-data-source>
```

```
    </persistence-unit>

    <persistence-unit name="integration" transaction-type="JTA">
        <jta-data-source>jdbc/int_datasource</jta-data-source>
    </persistence-unit>

    <persistence-unit name="production" transaction-type="JTA">
        <jta-data-source>jdbc/prod_datasource</jta-data-source>
    </persistence-unit>
</persistence>
```

Persistence context

When we have multiple persistence units defined in the persistence.xml file, we need to inject the appropriate one to EntityManager using the @PersistenceContext annotation. We can point to a specific persistence unit using the PersistenceContext entity's unitName attribute.

Using @PersistenceContext on EntityManager, let's point to the integration unit:

```
@Stateless
class App {
    @Inject
    private lateinit var identityCreator: IdentityCreator
    @PersistenceContext(unitName = "integration")
    private lateinit var entityManager: EntityManager

    fun createIdentity(inputData: InputData): Person {
        val person = identityCreator.createPerson(inputData)
        entityManager.persist(person)
        return person
    }

    fun findAllPerson(): List<Identity> {
        return
         entityManager.createNamedQuery(Queries.FIND_ALL_PERSON,
                Person::class.java).resultList
    }
}
```

Using `unitName = "integration"`, we point to a persistence unit in the `integration` environment. We can point to different persistence units as follows:

```
@Stateless
class App {
    @Inject
    private lateinit var identityCreator: IdentityCreator
    @PersistenceContext(unitName = "production")
    private lateinit var entityManager: EntityManager

    fun createIdentity(inputData: InputData): Person {
        val person = identityCreator.createPerson(inputData)
        entityManager.persist(person)
        return person
    }

    fun findAllPerson(): List<Identity> {
        return
         entityManager.createNamedQuery(Queries.FIND_ALL_PERSON,
             Person::class.java).resultList
    }
}
```

 When we have only one database, we don't actually have to configure the persistence unit for entity manager injection. In this case, the default persistence unit defined in the `persistence.xml` file will be used. This is shown in the following code snippet:

```
<persistence xmlns="http://java.sun.com/xml/ns/persistence"
             xmlns:xsi="http://www.w3.org/2001/XMLSchema-instance"
             xsi:schemaLocation="http://java.sun.com/xml/ns/persistence
             http://java.sun.com/xml/ns/persistence/persistence_2_0.xsd"
             version="2.0">

    <persistence-unit name="local" transaction-type="JTA">
        <jta-data-source>jdbc/local_datasource</jta-data-source>
        <properties>
            <property name="javax.persistence.schema-
            generation.database.action" value="drop-and-create"/>
        </properties>
    </persistence-unit>
</persistence>
```

On the other hand, our application server has to be configured with the connection details for the specific data source.

In this section, we have learned how to configure our application to use the persistence context and the persistence units of the specific data sources.

Transactions

As we said earlier, data is an important part of enterprise applications. Creating and managing data is critical. It is also necessary to maintain the integrity of the data while performing operations.

Transactions are sets of operations that can be carried out on the entities. Transaction management essentially involves managing the life cycle of the entities to maintain the integrity of the data. When a transaction executes a set of operations, it will either succeed or be rolled back if there are any failures. There is no way in which half the operations will execute, leaving the data in an inconsistent state.

Let's take a look at how to handle transactions in Java EE applications. We will discuss how we can use the Java Transaction API with both EJBs and CDI-managed beans using the `@Transactional` and `@TransactionAttribute` annotations. We will also look at how the transaction lifecycle is managed and how to handle exceptions.

Consider the following EJB, which is used to create the identity of a person:

```
@Stateless
class App {
    @Inject
    private lateinit var identityCreator: IdentityCreator
    @PersistenceContext(unitName="local")
    private lateinit var entityManager: EntityManager

    fun createIdentity(inputData: InputData): Person {
        val person = identityCreator.createPerson(inputData)
        entityManager.persist(person)
        return person
    }

    fun findAllPerson(): List<Identity> {
        return
          entityManager.createNamedQuery(Queries.FIND_ALL_PERSON,
                            Person::class.java).resultList
    }
}
```

By default, the EJB business function starts new transactions. This means that both the `createIdentity()` and `findAllPerson()` functions will be executed within a transaction. Once the function completes the execution and returns it, the transaction will be committed to the database.

We could also specify a different transaction handling function using the `@TransactionAttribute` from the EJB by specifying a type that is, by default, a `REQUIRED` type. This means that a new transaction is required:

```kotlin
@Stateless
class App {
    @Inject
    private lateinit var identityCreator: IdentityCreator
    @PersistenceContext(unitName="local")
    private lateinit var entityManager: EntityManager

     @TransactionAttribute(TransactionAttributeType.REQUIRED)
    fun createIdentity(inputData: InputData): Person {

        val person = identityCreator.createPerson(inputData)
        entityManager.persist(person)
        return person
    }

    fun findAllPerson(): List<Identity> {
        return
         entityManager.createNamedQuery(Queries.FIND_ALL_PERSON,
                            Person::class.java).resultList
    }
}
```

We could also specify another attribute, `TransactionAttributeType.REQUIRES_NEW`, which requires a new transaction.

For example, let's say we have two EJBs and the second one requires a new transaction. When the second EJB's function executes, the first transaction will be suspended. Then, the second transaction will be executed. Once it is committed, the first transaction resumes and continues its execution.

We can also specify that a transaction is not supported using
`TransactionAttributeType.NOT_SUPPORTED`.

Here's an example:
```
@TransactionAttribute(TransactionAttributeType.NOT_SUPPOR
TED)
fun deleteIdentity(inputData: InputData): Person {
    //...
}
```

By default, CDI-managed beans' functions don't execute in a transaction. However, we can use the `@Transactional` annotation that comes from the Java Transaction API to specify that a transaction is required, or that a new transaction will be started. A transaction type (`TxType`) is used to specify the transaction. Consider the following code:

```
@Dependent
class IdentityCreator {
    @Inject
    private lateinit var defaultPreferredLanguage: PreferredLanguage
    @Transactional(TxType.REQUIRED)
    fun createPerson(inputData: InputData): Person {
        val person = Person()
        person.preferredLanguage = if (inputData.preferredLanguage ==
         null)

            defaultPreferredLanguage
        else
            inputData.preferredLanguage
        return person
    }
}
```

We can also specify `REQUIRES_NEW`; this requires a new subsequent transaction:

```
@Transactional(TxType.REQUIRES_NEW)
fun createPerson(inputData: InputData): Person {
    val person = Person()
    person.preferredLanguage = if (inputData.preferredLanguage ==
     null)
        defaultPreferredLanguage
    else
        inputData.preferredLanguage
    return person
}
```

When the function execution is completed and returned, the transaction will be committed.

Exception handling

Exception handling is crucial for enterprise applications. Exceptions can arise in the middle of execution, such as a `PersonCreationException` in our example. Once an exception arises somewhere within the execution, the data will either be persisted in the database or the complete transaction will be rolled back, depending on the exception.

For example, let's say our `createPerson()` function throws `PersonCreationException`:

```
public class PersonCreationException extends Exception {
 public PersonCreationException(String message) {
   super(message)
 }
}
```

Since `PersonCreationException` is a checked exception, the transaction will not be rolled back if the exception is thrown during the execution of the `createPerson()` function. These kinds of exceptions are commonly called **application exceptions**.

Application exceptions are checked exceptions that either have to be handled in a function, or declared to be thrown in the function declaration. That means that although the `createPerson()` function throws an exception, the person object would still be persisted in the database. This is shown in the following code:

```
@Stateless
class App {
    @Inject
    private lateinit var identityCreator: IdentityCreator
    @PersistenceContext(unitName="local")
    private lateinit var entityManager: EntityManager

    @TransactionAttribute(TransactionAttributeType.REQUIRED)
    fun createIdentity(inputData: InputData): Person throws
PersonCreationException {
        val person = identityCreator.createPerson(inputData)
        entityManager.persist(person)
        throw new PersonCreationException("exception occurred while
         creating the person")
        return person
    }

    fun findAllPerson(): List<Identity> {
        return
         entityManager.createNamedQuery(Queries.FIND_ALL_PERSON,
                          Person::class.java).resultList
```

```
        }
    }
}
```

If `PersonCreationException` were a runtime exception, the entire transaction would be rolled back. These exception types extend from the `RuntimeException` class and are commonly called **system exceptions**:

```
public class PersonCreationException extends RuntimeException {
    public PersonCreationException (String message) {
        super(message);
    }
}
```

> The application exception extends from the Java `Exception` class. If such an exception is thrown during the execution of EJB- or CDI-managed bean functions, the transaction will not be rolled back, as these kinds of exceptions are expected and the function either declares the exception to be thrown or it handles the exceptions.
>
> The system exceptions are child classes of the Java `RuntimeExeption` class. If such an exception is thrown during the execution of a function, the transaction will be rolled back as these kinds of exceptions are not expected at runtime.

However, if we want to roll back the transaction once an exception arises during the execution of the function, we can use the `@ApplicationException` annotation with `rollback = true`. This makes the exceptions that occur to be treated as application exceptions, which causes the transaction to roll back:

```
@ApplicationException(rollback = true)
public class PersonCreationException extends RuntimeException {
    public PersonCreationException (String message) {
        super(message)
    }
}
```

Now, if this `PersonCreationException` is thrown during the execution, the transaction will be rolled back and the person data would not be persisted into the database:

```
@TransactionAttribute(TransactionAttributeType.REQUIRED)
fun createIdentity(inputData: InputData): Person throws
PersonCreationException {
    val person = identityCreator.createPerson(inputData)
    entityManager.persist(person)
    throw new PersonCreationException("exception occurred while
```

```
creating the person")
        return person
   }
```

Similarly, for the CDI-managed beans, the CDI doesn't take the `@ApplicationException` annotation into consideration in order to roll back the transaction. These beans can, however, be configured to use the `@Transactional` annotation to roll back on a specified exception type:

```
class IdentityCreator {

    @Transactional(rollbackOn = PersonCreationException.class)

        fun createPerson(inputData: InputData): Person {
        //..
    }
}
```

Using JPA in an application

So far, we have looked at how to create EJBs and CDI-managed beans and how to inject the beans in classes. We then looked at defining entities, defining relations between entities, and mapping entities to the database tables. Let's now combine all of this information to create a simple application where we will create an identity such as a `person` object and persist it into the database. Later, we will enhance this module so that it can carry out read, update, and delete operations.

Let's create a simple JPA project using Maven with the following dependencies:

```xml
<dependencies>
    <dependency>
        <groupId>org.jetbrains.kotlin</groupId>
        <artifactId>kotlin-stdlib</artifactId>
        <version>${kotlin.version}</version>
    </dependency>
    <dependency>
        <groupId>org.jetbrains.kotlin</groupId>
        <artifactId>kotlin-test-junit</artifactId>
        <version>${kotlin.version}</version>
        <scope>test</scope>
    </dependency>
    <dependency>
        <groupId>javax.annotation</groupId>
        <artifactId>javax.annotation-api</artifactId>
        <version>${javax.annotation-api}</version>
```

```xml
    </dependency>
    <dependency>
        <groupId>javax.ejb</groupId>
        <artifactId>javax.ejb-api</artifactId>
        <version>${javax.ejb-api}</version>
    </dependency>
    <dependency>
        <groupId>javax.enterprise</groupId>
        <artifactId>cdi-api</artifactId>
        <version>${javax.enterprise.cdi.api}</version>
    </dependency>
    <dependency>
        <groupId>org.hibernate.javax.persistence</groupId>
        <artifactId>hibernate-jpa-2.1-api</artifactId>
        <version>${hibernate-jpa}</version>
    </dependency>
    <dependency>
        <groupId>org.hibernate</groupId>
        <artifactId>hibernate-core</artifactId>
        <version>${hibernate-core}</version>
    </dependency>
    <dependency>
        <groupId>org.eclipse.persistence</groupId>
        <artifactId>org.eclipse.persistence.jpa</artifactId>
        <version>${org.eclipse.persistence.jpa}</version>
    </dependency>
    <dependency>
        <groupId>postgresql</groupId>
        <artifactId>postgresql</artifactId>
        <version>${postgresql}</version>
    </dependency>

    <dependency>
        <groupId>junit</groupId>
        <artifactId>junit</artifactId>
        <version>${junit.version}</version>
        <scope>test</scope>
    </dependency>
    <dependency>
        <groupId>org.mockito</groupId>
        <artifactId>mockito-core</artifactId>
        <version>${mockito-core}</version>
        <scope>test</scope>
    </dependency>
</dependencies>
```

Create a `beans.xml` file under the `resources/META-INF` directory with `bean-discovery-mode` set to `all`, as follows:

```xml
<?xml version="1.0" encoding="UTF-8"?>

<beans xmlns="http://xmlns.jcp.org/xml/ns/javaee"
       xmlns:xsi="http://www.w3.org/2001/XMLSchema-instance"
       xsi:schemaLocation="http://xmlns.jcp.org/xml/ns/javaee
       http://xmlns.jcp.org/xml/ns/javaee/beans_1_1.xsd"
       version="1.1" bean-discovery-mode="all">
</beans>
```

Add the `persistence.xml` file, which will have the following database configurations:

```xml
<?xml version="1.0" encoding="UTF-8"?>
<persistence version="2.1"
             xmlns="http://xmlns.jcp.org/xml/ns/persistence"
             xmlns:xsi="http://www.w3.org/2001/XMLSchema-instance"
             xsi:schemaLocation="http://xmlns.jcp.org/xml/ns/persistence
             http://xmlns.jcp.org/xml/ns/persistence/persistence_2_1.xsd">
    <persistence-unit name="prod">
<provider>org.eclipse.persistence.jpa.PersistenceProvider</provider>
        <class>org.rao.kotlin.service.PersonServiceImpl</class>
        <class>org.rao.kotlin.entity.Person</class>
        <class>org.rao.kotlin.entity.ContactDetails</class>
        <class>org.rao.kotlin.entity.Address</class>
        <exclude-unlisted-classes/>
        <properties>
            <property name="javax.persisteData creatednce.jdbc.driver"
                      value="org.postgresql.Driver"/>
            <property name="javax.persistence.jdbc.url"
                      value="jdbc:postgresql://localhost:5432/postgres"/>
            <property name="javax.persistence.jdbc.user"
                      value="postgres"/>
            <property name="javax.persistence.jdbc.password"
                      value="*****"/>
        </properties>
    </persistence-unit>

</persistence>
```

Now, let's consider the `Person` entity that we wrote earlier:

```kotlin
@Table(name = "person")
@Entity
@NamedQuery(name = FIND_ALL_PERSON, query = "select p from Person p")
data class Person(val loginId: String) {
    @Id
```

```kotlin
    lateinit var identifier: String
    lateinit var name: String

    @Enumerated(EnumType.STRING)
    var preferredLanguage: PreferredLanguage? = null

    @OneToMany(cascade = arrayOf(CascadeType.ALL), fetch =
     FetchType.LAZY)
    @JoinColumn(name = "PERSON_ID", nullable = false,
     referencedColumnName = "identifier")

    lateinit var contact: List<ContactDetails>
    @Embedded
    lateinit var address: Address
}
```

Our aim is to create this person entity and insert it into the database. Let's create specific layers in the project setup. We will create dao, service, and entity packages, as demonstrated in the following screenshot:

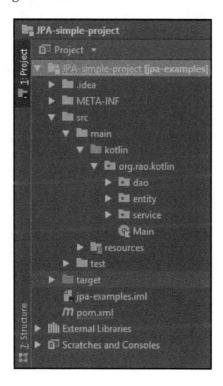

dao is used to deal with the database and is responsible for persisting the data. The dao layer talks to the database and is responsible for making the data ready for persistence. The entity package includes all the required entities in the project.

First, we will write a unit test case:

1. We will create a request in the setUp() function and mock the response:

```kotlin
@RunWith(MockitoJUnitRunner::class)
class PersonTest {
    @Mock
    private lateinit var personDao: PersonDaoImpl
    private lateinit var createPersonRequest: Person
    private lateinit var createPersonResponse: Person

    @Before
    fun setUp() {

        createPersonRequest = Person("myLoginId" +
Random().nextInt())
        createPersonRequest.name = "myName"
        val contactDetails = ContactDetails()

        contactDetails.number = "1234567891"
        contactDetails.type = ContactType.WORK
        val contactDetailsList = ArrayList<ContactDetails>()
        contactDetailsList.add(contactDetails)
        createPersonRequest.contact = contactDetailsList

        val address = Address()
        address.street = "Charles street"
        address.city = "Bengaluru"
        address.state = "Karnataka"
        address.country = "India"
        createPersonRequest.address = address

        createPersonResponse = Person("testLoginId")
        createPersonResponse.identifier =
UUID.randomUUID().toString()

    }

    @Test
    fun test() {
Mockito.`when`(personDao.createPerson(createPersonRequest)).thenRet
urn(createPersonResponse)
        createPersonRequest.preferredLanguage =
```

```
PreferredLanguage.EN_US
        val person = personDao.createPerson(createPersonRequest)
        Assert.assertNotNull(person.identifier)
    }
}
```

In this test case, we create the request object that needs to be persisted and mock the response for the `Person` class in the `setUp()` function. We also mock `personDao` and, using this, we invoke the `createPerson()` function by passing the request. We use the `Mockito when` clause to return the mock response when the call is made to the `personDao.createPerson()` function, and we assert for a non-null value of the identifier in the mock response.

2. Let's now implement the `dao` class. It has a `createPerson()` function. Create an entity manager for the context that we defined in the `persistence.xml` file:

```
@Stateless
class PersonDaoImpl : PersonDao {
    @PersistenceContext(unitName = "prod")
    private var entityManager: EntityManager = Persistence
.createEntityManagerFactory("prod")
.createEntityManager()

    override
    fun createPerson(person: Person): Person {
        entityManager.transaction.begin()
        entityManager.persist(person)
        entityManager.transaction.commit()
        return person
    }
}
```

3. Add `PersonServiceImpl`, which makes the data ready for persisting. It checks for `PreferredLanguage` and adds a unique ID to the person data:

```
@Dependent
class PersonServiceImpl : PersonService {
    @Inject
    private lateinit var personDao: PersonDao

    @Inject
    private lateinit var defaultPreferredLanguage:
PreferredLanguage

    override
```

```
    fun createPerson(createPerson: Person): Person {
        var person = createPerson

        person.preferredLanguage = if
(createPerson.preferredLanguage == null)
            defaultPreferredLanguage
        else
            person.preferredLanguage
        person.identifier = UUID.randomUUID().toString()
        return personDao.createPerson(person)
    }
}
```

4. Let's write a class that invokes `createPerson` in the service class with the `createPersonRequest` function and actually persists the data in the database. This class is a kind of integration test for the code that we have written so far:

```
object App {
    @Inject
    lateinit var personServiceImpl: PersonServiceImpl

    @JvmStatic
    fun main(args: Array<String>) {

        val createPersonRequest = Person("myLoginId" +
         Random().nextInt())
        val contactDetails = ContactDetails()

        contactDetails.number = "1234567871"
        contactDetails.type = ContactType.WORK
        val contactDetailsList = ArrayList<ContactDetails>()
        contactDetailsList.add(contactDetails)
        createPersonRequest.contact = contactDetailsList

        val address = Address()
        address.street = "Avenue Road"
        address.city = "Bengaluru"
        address.state = "Karnataka"
        address.country = "India"

        createPersonRequest.address = address
        createPersonRequest.name = "myName"
        createPersonRequest.preferredLanguage =
PreferredLanguage.EN_US
        val person =
         personServiceImpl.createPerson(createPersonRequest)
        println("Data created " + person.identifier)
```

```
  }
}
```

In this class, we create a request for the data to be created. We create
a `createPersonRequest` of the `Person` type. We instantiate this instance with
the `Person()` constructor and populate some of this test data to this instance. We
invoke the `createPerson()` function of the `service` class and, in response, it
gets the `person` entity that is being created in the database.

5. We can see that the data is actually persisted in the `person` table in the database:

6. The same `person` entry is persisted in the contact table that we mapped using
    the `OneToMany` relationship:

Summary

In this chapter, we looked at the following:

- How to represent the data using Kotlin data classes
- A brief introduction to JPA and its architecture
- How to map relations between the entities using JPA's `@OneToOne`, `@OneToMany`, `@ManyToOne`, and `@ManyToMany` annotations
- How we can retrieve data from a database using Queries
- How to define the data source
- Transaction management in JPA using `entityManager`
- Handling exceptions in JPA
- A simple JPA project to demonstrate the database operations

6
Enterprise Messaging with Kotlin

Messaging is one of the most important considerations when designing an enterprise application. Messaging systems are widely used in enterprise applications and allow us to develop scalable and reliable applications. The idea behind messaging systems is to generate messages about application events, push these messages into some kind of a queue, persist them into a datastore, and then later retrieve them from that store for further processing. A messaging framework is based on a combination of a common data model, a common command set, and a messaging infrastructure to allow different system components to communicate through a shared set of interfaces:

In this chapter, we will learn about a number of enterprise messaging techniques using the Java EE **Java Message Service** (**JMS**) API and Kotlin.

The objectives of this chapter are as follows:

- Understanding messaging domains
- Messaging queues and topics
- Building messaging services using Kotlin
- Acknowledging messages
- Transactions in messaging systems

Technical requirements

An understanding of messages and the messaging domain will help you to learn some of the techniques that we are going to discuss in this chapter. We will use GlassFish as a messaging provider, so it is necessary to install this software. Installation is covered in this chapter.

Understanding the messaging domains

Let's start by looking at what we require from a messaging system and how it works at a high level. A messaging system is characterized by the following attributes:

- The message itself
- The interaction mode
- The messaging system

The message represents the business data that is used either for further processing or for persistence.

The interaction mode can be either synchronous or asynchronous. In synchronous mode, the producer of the message and the receiver system are both in sync and have to be available simultaneously. They will be tightly coupled. In asynchronous mode, however, the interacting systems are loosely coupled, which means the applications are not tied to each other over a message interaction and they aren't aware of the existence of each other. All they need is the messaging format to be defined. The applications interact with a message provider to send and receive messages.

In a messaging system, we have producers and consumers. The producer sends out the messages and the consumer consumes the messages. The producer doesn't necessarily know whether the messages have been consumed. This is to ensure the reliability of the system. The consumer might not necessarily exist at the time the message is produced and when the consumer comes up it consumes the message. Also, if the consumer crashes for some reason while it is processing the message, when it comes back, the message will still be there for it to process. If we have multiple consumers waiting for messages, it makes sense to drop the messages into a queue and let the consumers process the messages independently. Messaging systems also have publishers and subscribers. Publishers publish messages on a topic and subscribers listen to specific topics for messages. Publishers are unaware of subscribers.

Messaging architecture

A typical messaging architecture used in enterprise applications is as follows:

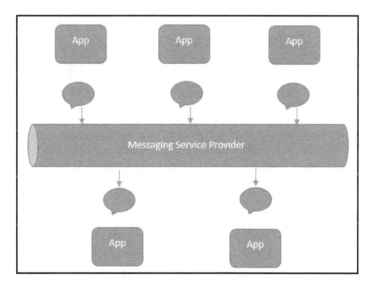

As depicted in the preceding diagram, the applications are loosely coupled and interact with the standard messaging provider to write and read messages. A known message format is defined, so that the communicating application can understand the message and derive a meaningful representation.

Messaging domains

In a typical enterprise messaging system, we can send and read messages using the messaging system. There are two different ways to do this:

- Point-to-Point messaging model
- Publish-Subscribe model

Point-to-point messaging model

In the point-to-point messaging model, one producer produces the message and one consumer receives it and further processes it. This model represents a one-to-one relationship between the producer and the consumer. If the sender wants to send the message to more than one application, it has to produce the message again and write to the provider. This is depicted in the following diagram:

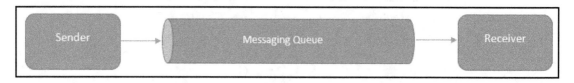

As shown in the preceding diagram, the producer sends the message to the queue and the consumer reads it from there, carries out some operations on it, and persists it if there is any persisting system configured to store the message. In this model, the messaging queue decouples the sender and the receiver of the message.

This model is suitable for an enterprise application that communicates with a single application or a set of small applications.

Publish-subscribe messaging model

In the publish-subscribe messaging model, a publisher broadcasts the message and consumers who are subscribed can consume the message and carry out some operations on it. This model represents a one-to-many relationship. Here, the messages are logically associated using topics and the subscribers register with the message provider about specific topics. Whenever the publisher sends out relevant messages, the message provider that is maintaining the list of subscribers for that topic will notify and deliver the messages.

This is shown in the following diagram:

As depicted in the preceding diagram, the publisher broadcasts the message to a topic, and the subscribed consumers can consume the messages from there and process them further.

In this model, the messaging topic decouples the publisher and the subscriber of the message.

Messaging queues and topics

Messaging queues and topics are the mechanisms by which messages are delivered from one point to another. They act as the staging area for messages. Messages are pushed onto a queue or topic and wait for the consumer to consume them.

The queue is used in the point-to-point messaging model, where the message is produced by the producer and received by a single consumer. The topic is used in the publish-subscribe messaging model, where the message is published by a publisher to a topic and is then consumed by multiple subscribers that are listening on that topic.

Java messaging System

Java messaging system is the standard Java API for the messaging systems. Any JMS implementation should expose this Java API as an interface. JMS focuses on the messaging API and its underlying messaging framework can be provided by different JMS providers.

There are different JMS implementations available, including OpenMQ, RabbitMQ, WebSphere MQ, and WildFly. We can choose any of these JMS providers for our application; we are going to use GlassFish, which is a reference implementation of the JMS specification and is open source.

Let's look at how to install the GlassFish server, which acts as a JMS provider. We will use GlassFish 5, which is the latest version of GlassFish at the time of writing this book.

Installing GlassFish

The GlassFish server can be downloaded using the following URL: `https://javaee.github.io/glassfish/download`.

The following screenshot shows the main screen:

Select **GlassFish 5.0 - Full Platform** and download it. Once it is downloaded, unzip the file and go to the `glassfish-5.0\glassfish5\glassfish\bin` directory. Start the server using `startserv`. This will bring up the GlassFish server on its default port, `4848`. In the browser, head over to `http://localhost:4848/`. This URL takes us to the GlassFish server console. This is shown in the following screenshot:

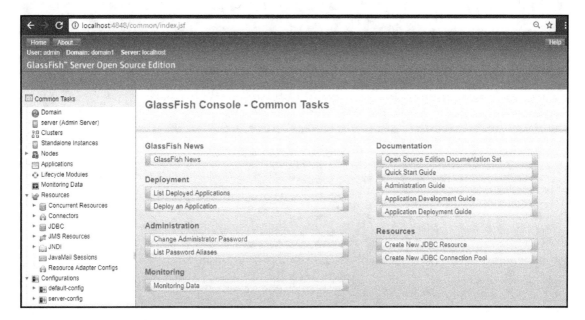

Now, we need to create the resources for messaging. By default, the GlassFish server has a JMS resource defined for us, which is `jms/__connectionFactory`. We will use this connection factory to create a JMS context:

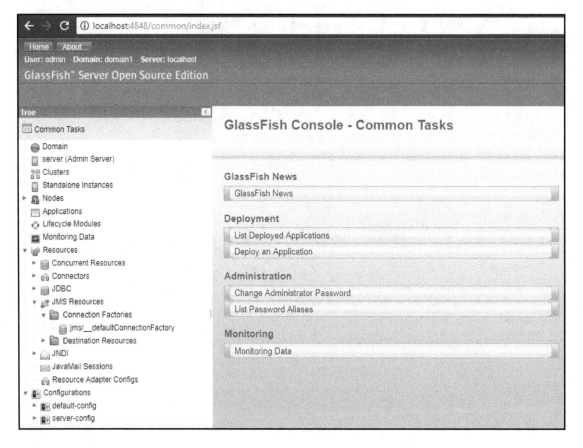

This is all it takes to install the GlassFish server. We will use this JMS provider in the following sections.

Configuring GlassFish

We have installed the GlassFish server. Let's now take a look at how to initialize our JMS provider, before we actually write some code to send and receive messages.

First, we define some resources in the GlassFish server, which are called **administered objects**. These have names, which we can use to access the resources in our application code. The first admin object is `connectionFactory`. By default, the server has a `connectionFactory` called `__defaultConnectionFactory`. This is used for bootstrapping in the messaging model. We can use a **Java Naming and Directory Interface (JNDI)** lookup by passing the name of the factory. This gives an object in return, which represents the `ConnectionFactory`.

We then use the `connectionFactory` to create the `JMSContext`. This can be used to create queues and topics, and send messages to them.

 In JMS, in order to implement the point-to-point model, we use queues. To implement the publish-subscribe model, we use topics. We look up these resources using JNDI in our code. The GlassFish server defines a default connection factory, `__defaultConnectionFactory`. This factory, the queues, and topics are registered as part of the JNDI setup inside the GlassFish server.

Finally, let's create something called destination resources. These destination resources serve as the message stores. We can create queues and topics as message stores. To create a resource, click on **Destination Resource**, select **New**, and define the resource. We provide a JNDI name, which will be used for looking up the resource, and a physical name. We also need to select the type of resource, either queue or topic. This is shown in the following screenshot:

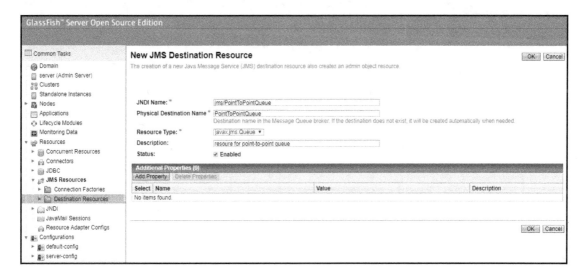

Here, we created a queue called `jms/PointToPointQueue`. Similarly, we can create a topic as follows:

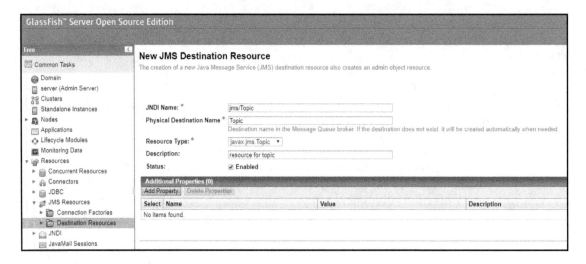

We have now created two destination resources—a messaging queue called `PointToPointQueue` and a messaging topic called `Topic`. This is shown in the following screenshot:

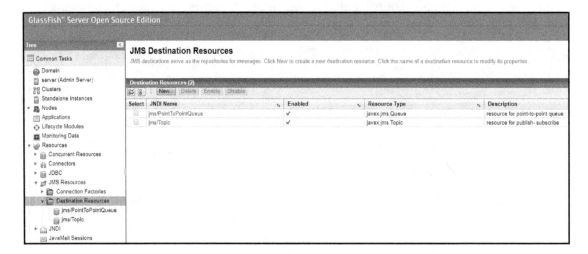

We are now all set with the administration objects required to demonstrate the point-to-point and publish-subscribe models. Let's write some code to demonstrate these models.

Building a messaging service using Kotlin

As discussed, Java messaging service has defined the following two modes of operation for exchanging messages:

- Point-to-Point messaging
- Publish-Subscribe messaging

In the point-to-point messaging model, a sender sends the message over a messaging service provider and a consumer consumes the message. In this model, we use a queue as a messaging service provider. In the publish-subscribe model, a publisher publishes the message and the subscribers will receive the messages. In this model, we use a topic as a messaging service provider.

In this section, we will demonstrate these two models and discuss some of the messaging types that can be used in these programming models.

Point-to-point messaging

Let's create a Maven project to demonstrate what it takes to write a point-to-point messaging model.

We need to add the following dependencies to the project. We will use Kotlin and a few other dependencies such as the **GlassFish Message Queue (glassfishmq)** library and `weld-se-core` library to initialize the container:

```
<dependencies>
  <dependency>
    <groupId>org.jetbrains.kotlin</groupId>
    <artifactId>kotlin-stdlib</artifactId>
    <version>${kotlin.version}</version>
  </dependency>
  <dependency>
    <groupId>org.jetbrains.kotlin</groupId>
    <artifactId>kotlin-test-junit</artifactId>
    <version>${kotlin.version}</version>
    <scope>test</scope>
  </dependency>
  <dependency>
    <groupId>org.glassfish.main.appclient</groupId>
    <artifactId>gf-client</artifactId>
    <version>${gf-client}</version>
  </dependency>
  <dependency>
```

```
      <groupId>org.glassfish.mq</groupId>
      <artifactId>imqjmsra</artifactId>
      <version>${imqjmsra}</version>
  </dependency>
  <dependency>
      <groupId>org.jboss.weld.se</groupId>
      <artifactId>weld-se-core</artifactId>
      <version>${weld-se-core}</version>
  </dependency>
  <dependency>
      <groupId>junit</groupId>
      <artifactId>junit</artifactId>
      <version>${junit}</version>
    <scope>test</scope>
  </dependency>
 </dependencies>
```

Writing a producer class

After creating the Maven project with these dependencies, we will create a message
`Producer` class:

```
class Producer{
}
```

We need to initialize `InitialContext` here. `InitialContext` bootstraps the context and
provides the entry point for the resolution of the named resources that we created in the
GlassFish server.

We will inject `InitialContext` through **Context Dependency Injection** (**CDI**) as follows:

```
class Producer {
 @Inject
 private lateinit var initialContext: InitialContext
}
```

As we said earlier, queues are used in the point-to-point messaging model. We look for a
queue using a JNDI lookup and this will return a reference object to a queue. This queue
will be used to send messages by the producer and to read messages by the consumer.

We also need to look up the `ConnectionFactory` using JNDI. We use this `connectionFactory` to create the `JMSContext`, using which we can send messages to the queue:

```
val queue = initialContext.lookup("jms/PointToPointQueue") as Queue
val connectionFactory =
initialContext.lookup("jms/__defaultConnectionFactory") as
ConnectionFactory
```

We will create a producer using `JMSContext`. The `createContext()` function returns an instance of `JMSContext`. This is shown in the following code:

```
connectionFactory.createContext()
                 .createProducer()
                 .send(queue, message)
```

Our `Producer` class looks as follows:

```
class Producer {
    @Inject
    private lateinit var initialContext: InitialContext

    fun sendMessage(message: String): String {
        try {
            val queue = initialContext.lookup("jms/PointToPointQueue") as
Queue
            val connectionFactory =
initialContext.lookup("jms/__defaultConnectionFactory") as
                                        ConnectionFactory
            connectionFactory.createContext()
                    .createProducer()
                    .send(queue, message)
            println("Message sent")
            return "Message sent"
        }catch ( e: NamingException){
            println("unable to load a resource "+e.message)
            return "Unable to deliver a message"
        }
    }
}
```

A quick comparison to Java code

Let's take a moment to write the same class in Java and see the differences provided by Kotlin:

```java
public class Producer {
    @Inject
    InitialContext initialContext;

    public String sendMessage(String message) {
      try {
            Queue queue =
(Queue)initialContext.lookup("jms/PointToPointQueue");
            ConnectionFactory connectionFactory = (ConnectionFactory)
             initialContext.lookup("jms/__defaultConnectionFactory");
            JMSContext jmsContext = connectionFactory.createContext();
            jmsContext.createProducer()
                        .send(queue, message);
            jmsContext.close();
        }catch (NamingException e) {
            e.printStackTrace();
        }
        return "Message sent";
    }
}
```

Note how the code in Kotlin looks more expressive compared to Java. We don't need the type declaration, we just use either `val` or `var` and the type is inferred from the context. This means that no explicit type casting is required; Kotlin provides us with an elegant syntax to express the type.

Also, note that the `initialContext` can be null. If we are not injecting `initialContext`, we end up with a `NullPointerException`. We then add the null check in the code. If we forget to add the null check and the context is not initialized, the compiler won't complain but the code will fail at runtime.

Kotlin code is more mature in this respect. The compiler forces us to add null checks using `?.` before accessing a variable that is declared as `null`:

```kotlin
@Inject
private var initialContext: InitialContext? = null
```

Let's say we are trying to use this `initialContext` directly without the value being injected, as follows:

```kotlin
val queue = initialContext.lookup("jms/PointToPointQueue") as Queue
```

This code fails to compile and gives the following error:

```
Error:(15, 39) Kotlin: Only safe (?.) or non-null asserted (!!.) calls are
allowed on a nullable receiver of type InitialContext?
```

Before using `initialContext`, the compiler forces us to add a null check or to initialize the variable. This way, type safety is guaranteed and possible runtime errors are reduced.

Writing a Consumer class

Let's now write the `Consumer` class to receive the message from the queue. On the `Consumer` side, we still need the `JMSContext` to retrieve the messages from the queue. The code looks similar to that which we wrote for the producer:

```kotlin
class Consumer {
    @Inject
    private lateinit var initialContext: InitialContext

    fun receiveMessage(): String {
        val queue = initialContext.lookup("jms/PointToPointQueue") as Queue
        val connectionFactory =
initialContext.lookup("jms/__defaultConnectionFactory") as
                                ConnectionFactory
        val message = connectionFactory
                .createContext()
                .createConsumer(queue)
                .receiveBody(String::class.java)

        println("Message received $message")
        return message
    }
}
```

We looked up the queue using a JNDI lookup and we loaded the `defaultConnectionFactory`. Then, we created `JMSContext` using the `createContext()` function invoked on `connectionFactory`. We created the consumer, passed the queue that we looked up, and invoked the `receiveBody()` function to retrieve the message sent by the producer.

Writing a test case for the Point-to-point messaging model

Let's write a test case to see this code in action.

We are actually going to write two test cases: one for the `Producer` class, which sends a message to the queue, and another one for the `Consumer` class, which retrieves the message from the queue.

First, let's write a test case for the `Producer` to simulate the `sendMessage()` function:

```
class ProducerTest {

    @Test
    fun sendMessageTest() {

        val seContainerInitializer = SeContainerInitializer.newInstance()
        val producer = seContainerInitializer.initialize()
                .select(Producer::class.java)
                .get()

        Assert.assertNotNull(producer)
        val message = producer.sendMessage("TEST MESSAGE")
        Assert.assertEquals("Message sent", message)
    }
}
```

When this test is executed, it pushes a TEST MESSAGE to the queue. The message waits in the queue for a consumer to consume it.

Let's now write a test for the `Consumer` to test the `receiveMessage()` function:

```
class ConsumerTest {

    @Test
    fun receiveMessageTest() {

        val seContainerInitializer = SeContainerInitializer.newInstance()
        val consumer = seContainerInitializer.initialize()
                .select(Consumer::class.java)
                .get()
        Assert.assertNotNull(consumer)
        val message = consumer.receiveMessage()
        Assert.assertNotNull(message)
    }
}
```

If we run these test cases, we can see that the `sendMessage()` function in the `Producer` class produces the message and pushes it into the queue. The `receiveMessage()` function in the `Consumer` class has consumed the message from the producer.

Publish-subscribe model

Creating a publish-subscribe model is similar to creating a point-to-point model as the API used to send messages is similar. The context is what will change; we will load a topic here instead of a queue. We use the same dependencies that we used in the point-to-point messaging model.

Writing a Publisher class

We write a `Publisher` class to publish a message to the topic:

```
class Publisher {
    @Inject
    private lateinit var initialContext: InitialContext

    fun publishMessage(message: String) {
        val topic = initialContext.lookup("jms/Topic") as Topic
        val connectionFactory =
initialContext.lookup("jms/__defaultConnectionFactory")
                                    as ConnectionFactory

        connectionFactory.createContext()
                .createProducer()
                .send(topic, message)
    }
}
```

Again, this is similar to what we wrote in the `Producer` class.

We inject `InitialContext` using CDI, we look up the topic using JNDI, and we load `connectionFactory`. We then create `JMSContext` by invoking the `createContext()` function on the `connectionFactory` obtained. Using `JMSContext`, we create the producer instance and we invoke the send function by passing the message and the topic as the destination resource.

Writing a Subscriber class

The `Subscriber` class is again similar to the `Consumer` class that we wrote earlier:

```
class Subscriber {
    @Inject
    private lateinit var initialContext: InitialContext

    @Throws(NamingException::class)
```

```
fun listenToMessage(): String? {
    val topic = initialContext.lookup("jms/Topic") as Topic
    val connectionFactory =
initialContext.lookup("jms/__defaultConnectionFactory")
                            as ConnectionFactory
    var messageResponse = connectionFactory.createContext()
            .createConsumer(topic)
            .receiveBody(String::class.java)
    return messageResponse
    }
}
```

We load the `topic` and `connectionFactory` and we create `JMSContext`, using which we create a consumer by passing a topic to listen to. When the message is published by the publisher, this subscriber will receive the message.

Writing a test case for the publish-subscribe model

Let's write test cases to check the `publishMessage()` and `listenToMessage()` functions.

We can write a `PublisherTest` as follows:

```
class PublisherTest {

    @Test
    fun testPublishMessage() {
        val seContainerInitializer = SeContainerInitializer.newInstance()
        val seContainer = seContainerInitializer.initialize()
        val publisherInstance = seContainer.select(Publisher::class.java)

        val publisher = publisherInstance.get()
        Assert.assertNotNull(publisher)
        val message = "Test messgage for topic111"
        publisher.publishMessage(message)
    }
}
```

We initialize the container to inject the dependencies. We get an instance of `Publisher` and invoke the `publishMessage()` function by passing the message. This message will be published to the topic.

Let's write a `SubscriberTest` to check the `Subscriber`:

```kotlin
class SubscriberTest {
    private lateinit var executorService: ExecutorService
    private lateinit var countDownLatch: CountDownLatch

    @Before
    fun setUp() {
        countDownLatch = CountDownLatch(10)
        executorService = Executors.newFixedThreadPool(4)
    }

    @Test
    @Throws(NamingException::class)
    fun receiveMessageTest() {
        val seContainerInitializer = SeContainerInitializer.newInstance()

        val subscriber = seContainerInitializer.initialize()
                .select(Subscriber::class.java)
                .get()
        Assert.assertNotNull(subscriber)
        val runnableTask = {
            var msgResponse: String? = null
            try {
                msgResponse = subscriber.listenToMessage()
            } catch (e: NamingException) {
                e.printStackTrace()
            }
            if (msgResponse != null) {
                println("Yay--- message received $msgResponse")
            }
        }
        for (i in 0..3) {
            executorService.submit(runnableTask)
        }
        countDownLatch.await(120, TimeUnit.SECONDS)
    }
}
```

In the `SubscriberTest` class, we created four threads, which we subscribed to in order to listen to the topic that we created. This is similar to having four different applications subscribed and listening to the topic. We span the threads using the `Executor` framework.

The subscriber's `listenToMessage()` function is a blocking call. When `SubscriberTest` invokes the `listenToMessage()` functions in four different threads, the threads start listening to the topic.

In the preceding test case, the thread in execution waits for the publisher to publish the message for two minutes (120 seconds). After that, the thread exits gracefully. This code can be inside a `while...` loop, meaning the subscriber will always listen to the topic:

```
while(true) {
  val runnableTask = {
  var messageResponse = subscriber.listenToMessage()
  if (messageResponse != null) {
     println("Yay--- message received $messageResponse")
  }
 }
}
```

Whenever the messages are published, the messages will be received by the subscribers listening on the topic. When the publisher publishes the message, these four threads will receive the message.

As we have seen, the APIs of both the point-to-point and the publish-subscribe models are syntactically similar. Both the queue and the topic derive from the `Destination` interface. These messaging models have the following steps in common:

1. We load the messaging service providers using a JNDI lookup
2. We load `connectionFactory` using a JNDI lookup
3. We initialize `JMSContext` using the factory
4. We send the messages to and receive the messages from the queue or topic

In the examples that we have seen so far, we have just passed string messages. We can actually pass messages of any type that is serializable. The message itself can include information such as the message identifier or the destination type.

Messages have the following structure:

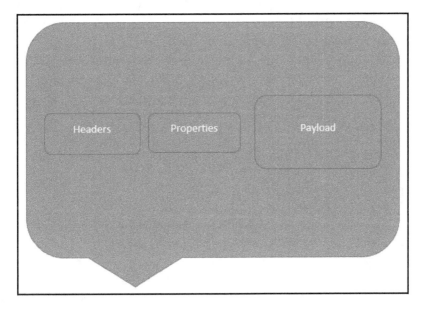

Messages will have headers, properties, and payload.

There are different headers that we can apply to the messages, as listed here:

- `Identity`: Each `MessageType` has a `uniqueId` represented by `JMSMessageId`. This can be used to identify a and refer to the message.
- `Priority`: Messages can be given a priority. `JMSPriority` is used to set the priority. When the priority message arrives, the messaging provider will deliver it in the order of priority. Priority is an integer value from 0-9, 0 being the least priority and 9 being the highest.
- `Durability`: We can set a message as durable using the `JMSDeliveryMode` property. This tells the messaging provider to store the messages in a way that is durable. This means that even if the service provider restarts or recovers from a crash, the messages will still be available to consume. Non-durable messages are stored in memory and are subject to loss when the provider is restarted. Durable messages, however, are stored on hardware. `JMSDeliveryMode` can either be `DeliveryMode.NON_PERSISTENT` or `DeliveryMode.PERSISTENT`.

- `Expiration`: We can define the expiry time using the `JMSExpiration` property. When messages with the `JMSExpiration` property are sent to the provider, the provider discards the messages once the amount of time indicated has elapsed, whether or not the messages are durable.
- `DestinationType`: We can set the destination resource to which the messages are delivered using the `JMSDestination` property. This value can be either a `queue` or a `topic`.

There are also properties that we can set for the message. These include the following:

- **Messaging provider properties**: The messaging provider can set some properties, which are meaningful in the context of that provider. `JMS` is usually prefixed to any property of this kind.
- **Application properties**: The running application can set properties on the message before it gets delivered to the queue or topic. These properties can be used during the handshake between the applications that produce and receive messages.
- **Standard properties**: These properties are prefixed with `JMSX` and are defined in the JMS specification. The messaging provider can choose to support some or all of these properties in the implementation. These properties will be set by the messaging provider when the message is delivered.

JMS has different types that can be used while sending or receiving the messages. It has a message interface and a set of classes that implement the message interface. These include `TextMessage`, `ObjectMessage`, `MapMessage`, `BytesMessage`, `StreamMessage`, and so on. We can set the properties while sending the message. `TextMessage` is used to pass simple text messages along with the other properties. `ObjectMessage` can be used to pass any object that is serializable. `MapMessage` can be used to send the type of `Map`, while `BytesMessage` takes an array of bytes.

Let's enhance our point-to-point messaging model to send and receive messages of the `TextMessage` type. Instead of `String`, we use `TextMessage` in the producer. The consumer in this case receives the `Message` type instead of `String`:

```
class Producer {
    @Inject
    private lateinit var initialContext: InitialContext

    fun sendMessage(message: String): String {
        try {
            val queue = initialContext.lookup("jms/PointToPointQueue") as
Queue
```

```
        val connectionFactory =
initialContext.lookup("jms/__defaultConnectionFactory")
                                    as ConnectionFactory
        val jmsContext = connectionFactory.createContext()
        val textMessage = jmsContext.createTextMessage(message)

        jmsContext.createProducer()
                .send(queue, textMessage)
        return "Message sent"
    } catch (e: NamingException) {
        return "Unable to deliver a message"
    }
  }
}
```

Consider the following code for the `Consumer` class. It is very similar to that which we wrote earlier, but here the consumer receives a `TextMessage` instead of a string message:

```
class Consumer {
    @Inject
    private lateinit var initialContext: InitialContext

    fun receiveMessage(): Message {

        val queue = initialContext.lookup("jms/PointToPointQueue") as Queue
        val connectionFactory =
initialContext.lookup("jms/__defaultConnectionFactory")
                                    as ConnectionFactory
        val textMessage = connectionFactory
                .createContext()
                .createConsumer(queue)
                .receive()
        return textMessage
    }
}
```

The `ProducerTest` class remains the same, as shown in the following code:

```
class ProducerTest {
    @Test
    fun sendMessageTest() {
        val seContainerInitializer = SeContainerInitializer.newInstance()
        val producer = seContainerInitializer.initialize()
                .select(Producer::class.java)
                .get()

        Assert.assertNotNull(producer)
```

```
        val message = producer.sendMessage("TEST MESSAGE")
        Assert.assertEquals("Message sent", message)

    }
}
```

The `ConsumerTest` class also remains the same; we just add an extra line to assert the type of the message. This is shown in the following code:

```
class ConsumerTest {

    @Test
    fun receiveMessageTest() {
        val seContainerInitializer = SeContainerInitializer.newInstance()
        val consumer = seContainerInitializer.initialize()
                .select(Consumer::class.java)
                .get()
        Assert.assertNotNull(consumer)

        val message = consumer.receiveMessage()
        Assert.assertNotNull(message)
        Assert.assertTrue(message is TextMessage)
    }
}
```

Here, if we look at the message type and its properties, we can see that we have used a text message in place of the string message. We can then carry out appropriate processing based on the message and the context.

Message acknowledgement

So far, we have learned how messages can be delivered from one point to another. We have used queues and topics to send the messages. Once the messages are consumed by the consumer, the messages will be removed from the messaging provider. Once the message is processed by the consumer, it can send an acknowledgement back to the messaging provider, so that the provider takes the messages off the queue or the topics. There are different ways to send this acknowledgement:

- **Auto acknowledge**: In auto acknowledgement, when the message is received by the client, the message will be removed from the JMS provider. The message will be automatically removed from the queue or the topic once it is processed by the consumer.
- **Duplicates OK**: In duplicates OK mode, the consumer can receive duplicate messages.

- **Client acknowledgment**: In client acknowledgment mode, the client or the consumer has to acknowledge the message once it is received. Until then, the message won't be removed from the queue or topic. The provider will resend the message until it receives acknowledgement from the consumer that it has received the message.

Let's see this in action. We previously created the point-to-point messaging model. Consider this module again. Here, we have the `Producer` class, which produces a message for the queue:

```
class Producer {
    fun sendMessage(message: String): String {
     //...
    }
}
```

The `Consumer` class consumes the message from the queue:

```
class Consumer {
        fun receiveMessage(): Message {
        //....
    }
}
```

We had test cases to invoke each of these classes to produce and consume the messages:

```
class ProducerTest {
    @Test
    fun sendMessageTest() {
        //...
        val message = producer.sendMessage("TEST MESSAGE")
        Assert.assertEquals("Message sent", message)
    }
}
// Consumes the messages
class ConsumerTest {
    @Test
    fun receiveMessageTest() {
            //..
        val message = consumer.receiveMessage()
        Assert.assertNotNull(message)
        Assert.assertTrue(message is TextMessage)
    }
}
```

By default, when we create a `JMSContext` using `ConnectionFactory`, `sessionMode` is set to `AUTO_ACKNOWLEDGE`:

```
connectionFactory.createContext(JMSContext.AUTO_ACKNOWLEDGE)
```

This means that once a message is produced by a producer and consumed by a consumer, it is automatically acknowledged to the messaging provider and the message will be removed from the queue.

If we re-run our `ConsumerTest` alone, it will wait for the message until there is a message in the queue:

When the producer produces the message, the message will be consumed by the consumer and the message will be removed from the queue. When the consumer starts processing the message, it is automatically acknowledged and will be removed from the queue.

Let's now change `JMSContext` to `DUPS_OK_ACKNOWLEDGE` and see what happens. We will run `ProducerTest` and `ConsumerTest` once again. Notice that the message will be consumed by the receiver and the tests will pass.

Let's now re-run the `ConsumerTest` alone. The output will be as follows:

This time, the `ConsumerTest` didn't block. It got the message and the test passed. If we run it again, the consumer would still receive the message as the `sessionMode` is set to `duplicates_ok`. Until the receiver sends acknowledgement, the provider keeps the message in the queue.

If we add the acknowledgement in the code once the message has been processed, after the consumer consumes the message, it will be removed from the queue. If we execute `ConsumerTest` again, it will wait for the next message to be produced in the queue.

In client acknowledgement, the message receiving party has to send acknowledgement after it processes the message. After acknowledgement, the message will be removed from the queue or the topic. Acknowledging the message tells the provider that it has processed the message and not to send it again. If we don't acknowledge the message, it will be there in the provider until we acknowledge it:

```
class Consumer {
    @Inject
    private lateinit var initialContext: InitialContext

    fun receiveMessage(): Message {
        val queue = initialContext.lookup("jms/PointToPointQueue") as Queue
        val connectionFactory =
initialContext.lookup("jms/__defaultConnectionFactory")
                                    as ConnectionFactory
        val jmsContext =
connectionFactory.createContext(JMSContext.CLIENT_ACKNOWLEDGE)
        val textMessage = jmsContext.createConsumer(queue)
                                    .receive()
        return textMessage
    }
}
```

 In this case, acknowledging the message after processing it is the responsibility of the receiver. We created `sessionMode` as `CLIENT_ACKNOWLEDGE` only in the `Consumer` class.

Transactions

As you may know, transactions are sets of indivisible operations that either succeed or roll back. Transactions in a messaging system are used to group the messages logically. When we send a group of messages in a transaction to a queue or topic, we either commit them or we roll them back. This means that the messages are either all delivered in one go or they are rolled back. On the consumer or receiver side, the messages are all either consumed and acknowledged or rolled back.

Let's take a closer look. When messages are sent in a transaction, the messages are not sent to the messaging provider, in our case the GlassFish server queue/topic, until we invoke the `commit()` function on the `jmsContext` as shown in the following diagram:

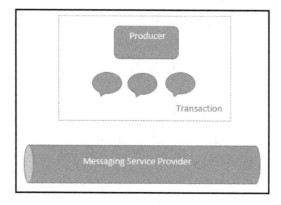

On the consuming side, when transactions are enabled, the messages will be removed from the queue or topic only when they are committed or rolled back. Until the `commit()` function is called, the message stays in the messaging provider service. This is shown in the following diagram:

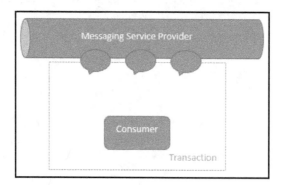

Let's take a look at some code to understand these concepts further.

Enabling transactions in the point-to-point messaging model

Consider the point-to-point messaging model that we created earlier with the `Message` type. We can enable transactions in the `Producer` class with `JMSContext.SESSION_TRANSACTED` as follows:

```
val jmsContext = connectionFactory
                    .createContext(JMSContext.SESSION_TRANSACTED)
```

Our message `Producer` class looks as follows:

```
class Producer {
    @Inject
    private lateinit var initialContext: InitialContext

    fun sendMessage(message: String): String {
        try {
            val queue = initialContext
                            .lookup("jms/PointToPointQueue") as Queue
            val connectionFactory = initialContext
                            .lookup("jms/__defaultConnectionFactory")
                                as ConnectionFactory
            val jmsContext = connectionFactory
                            .createContext(JMSContext.SESSION_TRANSACTED)
            val textMessage = jmsContext.createTextMessage(message)
            jmsContext.createProducer()
                        .send(queue, textMessage)
            return "Message sent"
        } catch (e: NamingException) {
            println("unable to load a resource " + e.message)
            return "Unable to deliver a message"
        }
    }
}
```

Note that we have created the context in transaction mode but we are not committing the message. This means the message has not yet reached the messaging provider, so our `ConsumerTest` blocks while waiting for the message.

This is shown in the following screenshot:

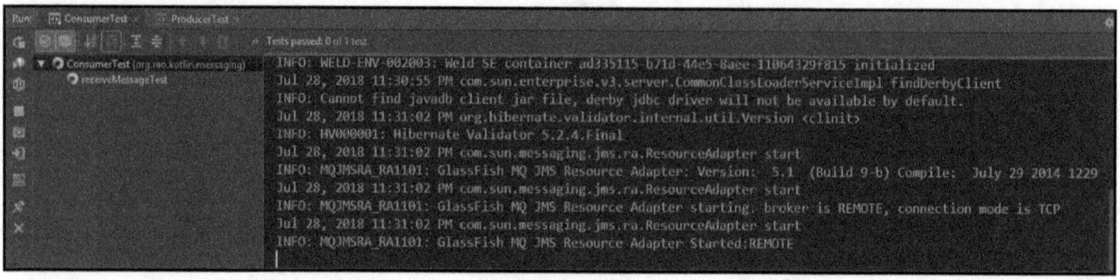

Let's invoke the `commit()` function in the `Producer` class, as follows:

```
jmsContext.commit()
```

The `ConsumerTest` class, which was waiting for the message, has now received the message:

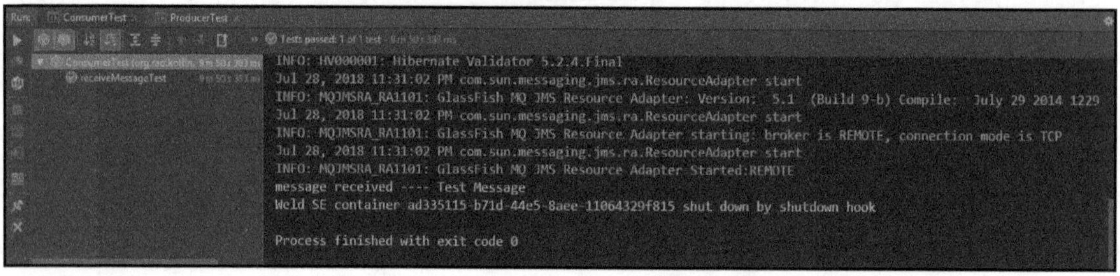

We'll also take a look at the `Consumer` class:

```kotlin
class Consumer {
    @Inject
    private lateinit var initialContext: InitialContext
    fun receiveMessage(): Message {

        val queue = initialContext
                    .lookup("jms/PointToPointQueue") as Queue
        val connectionFactory = initialContext
                    .lookup("jms/__defaultConnectionFactory") as
         ConnectionFactory
        val jmsContext = connectionFactory
                    .createContext(JMSContext.SESSION_TRANSACTED)
        val textMessage = jmsContext.createConsumer(queue)
                                 .receive()
        return textMessage
    }
}
```

Note that we have again created the context with the transaction enabled, and we are not committing the message. This means that we are not acknowledging the messaging provider after processing the message. As a result, the message will continue to exist in the provider. If we run `ConsumerTest` again, we continue to get the following result until we acknowledge the message:

Let's invoke `commit()` after receiving the message:

```kotlin
class Consumer {
    @Inject
    private lateinit var initialContext: InitialContext

    fun receiveMessage(): Message {

        val queue = initialContext
                      .lookup("jms/PointToPointQueue") as Queue
        val connectionFactory = initialContext
                      .lookup("jms/__defaultConnectionFactory")
                          as ConnectionFactory
        val jmsContext = connectionFactory
                      .createContext(JMSContext.SESSION_TRANSACTED)
        val textMessage = jmsContext.createConsumer(queue)
                                .receive()
        jmsContext.commit()
        return textMessage
    }
}
```

Run the `ConsumerTest` class again and notice that this time, the `commit()` function sends an acknowledgement to the provider that the message has been received. Any further calls on `ConsumerTest` will block and wait for the message to be produced:

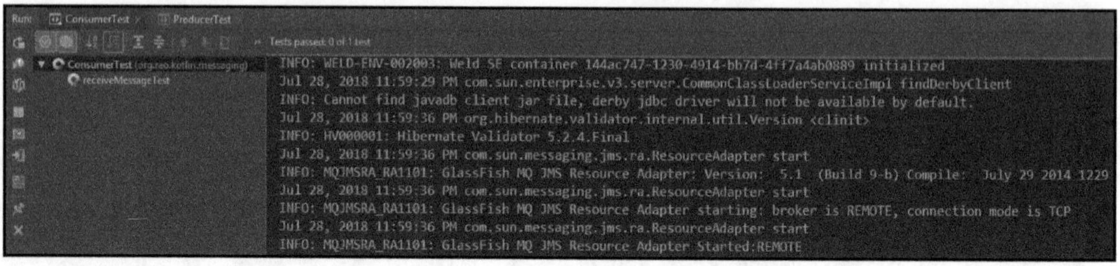

Enabling transactions in the publish-subscribe messaging model

We demonstrated the transactions in the point-to-point messaging model. The same can be enabled in the publish-subscribe model, as shown here:

```kotlin
class Publisher {
    @Inject
    private lateinit var initialContext: InitialContext

    fun publishMessage(message: String) {
        val topic = initialContext
                    .lookup("jms/Topic") as Topic
        val connectionFactory = initialContext
                    .lookup("jms/__defaultConnectionFactory")
                        as ConnectionFactory

        val jmsContext = connectionFactory
                    .createContext(JMSContext.SESSION_TRANSACTED)
        jmsContext.createProducer()
                .send(topic, message)
        jmsContext.commit()
    }
}
```

The `Subscriber` model is as follows:

```
class Subscriber {
    @Inject
    private lateinit var initialContext: InitialContext

    @Throws(NamingException::class)
    fun listenToMessage(): String? {
        val topic = initialContext
                        .lookup("jms/Topic") as Topic
        val connectionFactory = initialContext
                        .lookup("jms/__defaultConnectionFactory")
                            as ConnectionFactory
        val jmsContext = connectionFactory
                            .createContext(JMSContext.SESSION_TRANSACTED)
        var messageResponse = jmsContext.createConsumer(topic)
                                .receiveBody(String::class.java)
        return messageResponse
    }
}
```

The behavior is the same when we enable the transactions in the publish-subscribe model. Messages are not sent to the provider until the `commit()` function is invoked by the producer class and the message stays in the provider until `commit()` is called by the consumer class.

Summary

In this chapter, we covered the following:

- A brief introduction to messaging domains. We learned about different messaging models, point-to-point and publish-subscribe. We also looked at topics and queues and how they are used in these models.
- An introduction to JMS. We looked at installing and configuring GlassFish, which is a reference implementation of JMS.
- An implementation of a point-to-point model and a publish-subscribe model using Kotlin and GlassFish. We also looked at different message types and message properties.
- Different ways of acknowledging the messages to the messaging provider.
- Transactions to group the messages in a logical order.

7
Developing RESTful Services with JAX-RS

Modern-world enterprise applications are designed and developed to be interoperable, to involve interaction between the applications, and to be delivered over a network. Applications of different underlying platforms communicate with each other over the internet and understand the data produced by these applications:

The following topics will be covered in this chapter:

- Web services
- Implementing a RESTful Web service with Kotlin
- Understanding different terminologies of the REST world
- Developing web services using JAX-RS

Technical requirements

It is beneficial to have a good understanding of **Representational State Transfer** (**REST**), but we will cover the basics of this in the chapter. Furthermore, having an understanding of how to use the **Client for URLs** (**cURL**) command as a REST client to invoke web services is a plus.

Web services

A web service is an interoperable application that can be delivered over the web. These are also commonly known as **application services**. Characteristics of web services include the interoperable nature between the applications over a network, and the ability to communicate with other services, as depicted in the following diagram:

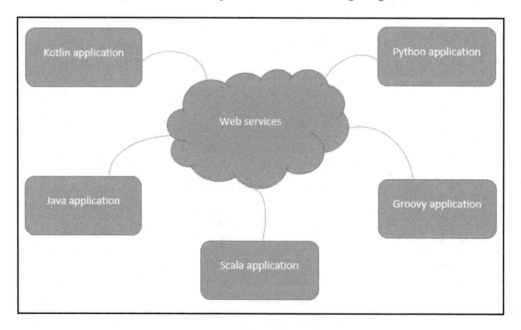

These applications can interact with each other, irrespective of the underlying technology used for building them. These application services provide the output that other applications can understand, and the output of an application is consumable by another application.

In short, a service is referred to as a web service when it is platform independent, involves interaction with other services, and communicates over the web.

Working model of the web service

The web service is based on the *request-response* model. When services interact with each other, one passes an input to the other. The service accepts the input in a particular format, processes the input, and returns the response in a format that the receiving client can understand, as shown in the following diagram:

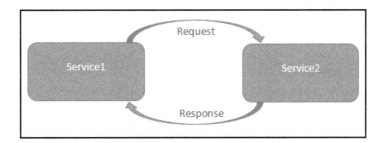

Let's say we have a web service that takes input data and returns output data in exchange. The data that we input to a web service is called the request and the data that we get in exchange for an input from the web service is the response. When an application wants to consume the web service, it has to send an input, or trigger a call, in order to start consuming the web service.

Typically, the application sends a request in a standard format that the web service can understand for processing. When a web service returns the response, it sends it in a standard exchange format that the application that sent the request can understand.

 The standard format of request and response is what makes web services platform independent. This is how a Python-based application can talk to a Java or Kotlin application.

In the web services world, there are two standard formats for request and response:

- **JSON: JavaScript Object Notation (JSON)** data is what JavaScript represents as an object. For example, a sample JSON payload looks like this:

  ```
  {
    "loginId":"john@abc.org",
    "name":"John",
    "city":"Bengaluru"
  }
  ```

  This example defines a JSON object with a comma-separated list of name-value pairs. A JSON object is surrounded by curly braces, { and }. A name-value pair consists of a field name (in double quotes), followed by a colon (:), followed by the field value.

  JSON is easy to read, write, and parse while processing the request.

- **XML: Extensible Markup Language (XML)** is yet another way to represent structured information. For example, a sample XML payload looks like this:

  ```
  <person>
    <loginId>john@abc.org</loginId>
    <name>John</name>
    <city>Bengaluru</city>
  </person>
  ```

The JSON and XML data formats are supported by most of the web services of different platforms. These are common in modern applications. This is how web services became independent; by making the request and response independent of the platform.

Once we have the common format for data exchange, we can look at how to define the request structure and how to interpret the response from the web service. Each web service will have a service definition that talks about what a web service can offer.

A service definition specifies the standard request-response format that is used, whether this is JSON or XML. It specifies the structure of the request, how a consuming application can create a request, and what a request format would look like. This also defines the response structure, which is the structure of the response returned by the service. In addition, the service definition specifies the endpoint with which a service can be invoked.

There are other alternatives to JSON/XML for data exchange between the services, such as BSON (short for Binary JSON), MessagePack, and YAML (short for YAML Ain't Markup Language). BSON is a binary-encoded format of JSON-like data. It also contains extensions to JSON to represent the data types that are not part of the JSON specification. MessagePack is also a binary-encoded JSON-like data exchange format. BSON and MessagePack are binary encoded and not human readable. YAML is a unicode-based data exchange format and is in human-readable format.

RESTful web services

REST is an architectural style for managing the state information. REST specifies the uniform interface, and when applied to the services makes them interoperable over the web. The RESTful architecture is based on HTTP 1.1 and aims to make best use of the **HTTP (Hyper Text Transfer Protocol)**. The REST style is used mostly for web-based applications. It provides an easy way to exchange data, irrespective of the underlying platform of the services.

REST is a style, not a standard. REST embraces the ideas of HTTP, as well as defining the best way to use HTTP protocol to build distributed systems. REST is very intuitive in nature and embraces simplicity in its system architecture style when applied.

REST builds on top of HTTP protocol and derives HTTP verbs, such as request methods, headers, status code, request-response models, negotiation for data to be represented (content negotiation), and so on. This enforces the stateless distribution mechanism for developing interoperable systems.

These are the REST service principles:

- It should be stateless.
- It should access all the resources from the server using a **Uniform Resource Identifier (URI)**.
- It does not have inbuilt encryption.
- It does not have sessions.
- It uses HTTP protocol.
- For performing CRUD operations, it should use HTTP verbs such as GET, POST, PUT, and DELETE.
- It should return the result only in the standard data exchange form, such as JSON or XML, BSON, atom, or **Open Data Protocol (OData)**.

Understanding REST verbs

HTTP is a widely used application protocol for data exchange within the **World Wide Web** (**WWW**). This defines how the messages are formatted, how they can be transferred over the web, and the verbs or actions that the client or server has to do for data communication. REST verbs are derived from standard HTTP. Let's familiarize ourselves with these verbs.

Resources

A resource is a fundamental concept in the world of REST. This can be anything that can be accessed and processed over the web. It can also be a simple HTML file, identity data, an image, a video, a text file, or a CSV file. These resources are uniquely identified by URI on the web. The client makes a request using this uniquely identifiable resource on the server, and the server responds with the resource in return.

In REST, we use some of the standard HTTP verbs to map to the CRUD operations of the services. The HTTP verbs themselves are varied. These include HTTP GET, HTTP POST, HTTP PUT, and HTTP DELETE.

HTTP GET is the most extensively used HTTP method on the web. If we load any website in a browser, the browser accordingly makes a GET request to the service hosted. GET is used to retrieve the information from the server, but is more commonly used to read the data. If we want to retrieve a record of an identity (let's say a person's record), the GET request will look as follows:

```
GET {{host-service}}/person/10
```

We specify the *hostname,* a *path,* /person in this case, and a unique identifier for the person.

GET is considered to be a safe method as this call doesn't modify anything on the server. GET calls are not expected to have any side effects as they don't modify anything on the server. For this reason, a GET operation is known as a non-idempotent operation. The server issues the same response no matter how many times a GET request is made.

The POST method is used to create the data on the server side. A HTTP POST call requests that the resource be created and it is enclosed inside the request. Consider the following code:

```
POST /person
{
"loginId":"user1@ymail.com",
"name":"username"
}
```

Typically, an endpoint is exposed to receive a POST call that accepts the request body. Here, we pass the resource to be created in the request body, the server processes the request, does the basic validation of this request (if there is one), creates the resource, and then signals to the client that a new record has been created. Upon resource creation, the server responds with a 201 status code that indicates the creation of a new resource on the server side and a location header of the newly created resource.

Sending a location header is just a convention in REST. There is no hard and fast rule that the endpoint creating the resource must include a location header. Some service implementations choose to send the location header, using which the resource can be referenced later. Other service implementations may choose not to include the location header. This is because the service may expose another endpoint, which takes the input using which the resource is created earlier in order to get the unique ID or the reference of the resource that is created on the server side.

We can use POST to both create a new record, as well as updating an existing one.

HTTP PUT is typically used to update a resource. This takes the request body, which is the data to be updated, and the reference ID or the URI of the resource that the request was made to update, as shown by the following code:

```
PUT {{host-service}}/person/10
{
"name":"username"
}
```

HTTP PUT can also be used to create a resource. PUT is conventionally used for updating the existing resources in the web services.

Preferably, PUT is used for resources that we already know exist on the server, and it is referenced with a URI that we received after the creation.

HTTP `DELETE` is used to delete a resource on the server. The service defines what delete means to it; it can be a soft delete or a hard delete of the resources. We pass an identifier, or reference of the resource, to be deleted for the delete operation. The HTTP `DELETE` method requests the server to delete the referenced resource. If the server deletes the resource, it returns a 204 status code and empty response body like this:

```
DELETE person/10
```

When we call a `DELETE` operation with a reference to the resource to be removed, this call actually translates to finding that particular referenced entity on the data source and performing a delete operation on it.

> The HTTP `POST` and `PUT` and `DELETE` operations are known as idempotent operations. These requests modify the resources on the server side.

HTTP status codes

A status code is a way of conveying the status of the operation performed on the resources. These status codes are set on the server side and sent to the client who made a request on the resources. Based on the status code, the client gets to know whether the requested operation is fulfilled or not. Status codes also indicate that if there was an error on the server side while processing the request, the input supplied from the client itself is invalid, and so on.

As in HTTP, REST also has response status codes of different ranges, which are used to indicate the status of the operation that was requested. Status codes are three digit numbers that range from 100 to 599. Each series indicates the following:

- **100-199 series**: The general information in the response
- **200-299 series**: The requested operation is completed on the server
- **300-399 series**: The request needs to be redirected to another resource in order for the request to be completed
- **400-499 series**: Something in the request is incorrect
- **500-599 series**: Errors on the server side

> The status code is used for conveying the response to the server's attempt to fulfill a client's request.

Let's try to understand the status codes and when they can be used in the following sections.

The 100 series

The 100 series is used for conveying informational messages to the client. It is very uncommon to see this series, but possible to send the information status like this:

- **100 Continue**: This status code indicates that the server has received the request headers and is ready to accept the payload that the client wants to send. The client first makes a request to the server; if the server responds with 100 Continue in response header, the client then sends the request body for further processing. The server can choose to respond with 417 Expectation Failed status if it is not ready to accept the request.
- **101 Switching Protocols**: This status code indicates that the server is fine for switching the protocol that the client is requesting.
- **102 Processing**: This status code indicates that the server is processing the request and it may take a long time for this to complete. This prevents a client from being timed out when waiting for the response.
- **103 Early Hints**: This status code is used to indicate that the server is likely to send a final informational response to the client. It is common for servers to send HTTP responses that contain links to external resources that need to be processed before consuming the actual response; for example, rendering an HTML file or an image by a web browser. Sending early hints helps to prepare the clients to process the response.

Status codes 104-199 are unassigned and have no defined meaning.

The 200 series

The 200 series is used for indicating the success of the operation requested by the client. This tells the client that the request has been processed successfully, the necessary changes have been made to the resource, and a successful response has been issued to the client:

- **200 OK**: This status code indicates that the request processing is successful and the server responds with the success response body.
- **201 Created**: This status code indicates that the server processed the request successfully and a new resource is created on the server.

- **202 Accepted:** This status is used to indicate that the server has accepted the request. Generally this status code is used when the server takes longer time to process the request. When the server accepts the request, it sends the 202 status code to the client indicating that it has accepted the request and takes time to complete the processing of the request.

- **203 Non-Authoritative Information**: This status code used to indicate that the server(origin) has processed the request successfully but the enclosed response is modified from that of origin server's original response. Sometimes the HTTP proxy which is in between the client and the server can modify the response coming from the server.
  The HTTP proxy changes the status code to 203 if it modifies the response. 203 status code is a *Non-Authoritative Information* and indicates the transformation applied on the original response from the server. It changes the original HTTP status code and there is no way to check what was the original status code from the server.
  As an alternative to 203 HTTP status code, RFC suggest to use a *warning header* set to **214 Transformation applied**. In case of this warning header, the original status code from the origin will not be modified once the proxy applies any transformation on the response.

- **204 No Content**: This status code indicates that the request processing is successful and the server responds with an empty response body. Usually, the 204 No Content status code is used for a successful delete operation on a resource.

The 300 series

The 300 series is used for indicating that the resource requested has been moved to a different location and the client has to redirect its request to a new resource:

- **304 Not Modified**: This status code indicates that the resource has not been modified since it was last accessed.

The 400 series

The 400 series indicates that the request that the client sending is invalid and not in a format that the server can process:

- **400 Bad Request**: This status code indicates that the server is unable to process the request as either the syntax is incorrect, or the value doesn't match the condition that server has defined.

- **401 Unauthorized**: This status code indicates that authentication is required to access the requested resource.
- **403 Forbidden**: This status code is indicates to the client that it either lacks the required authorization to access the resource, or the server refuses to process the request though the request is valid. The reason will be listed in the response body.
- **404 Not Found**: This status code indicates that the requested resource is not found on the server at the location specified in the request.
- **405 Method Not Allowed**: This status code indicates that the HTTP method specified in the request is not allowed on the resource identified by the URI.
- **408 Request Timeout**: This status code indicates that the client failed to respond within the elapsed time set on the server side.
- **409 Conflict**: This status code indicates that the request cannot be processed or completed as it conflicts with the constraints defined on the resources in the server. For example, a resource creation request that already exists can return 409 Conflict, indicating that the resource is already present on the server side.

The 500 series

The 500 series indicates that something went wrong while processing the request on the server side. These may possibly arise when exceptions are not handled properly, when the server ends up in a run-time exception, or with any other errors, such as out of memory. This indicates that the request cannot be fulfilled.

The 500 series status code informs us that there is something wrong with the execution of the action performed in the given resource:

- **500 Internal Server Error**: This status code indicates that the requested action has not been processed successfully by the server. This occurs when the server encounters an error while processing the request and the server returns the 500 status code.
- **503 Service Unavailable**: This status code indicates that the server is not available to process the request or when it is down.
- **504 Gateway Timeout**: This status code indicates that the request is sent to the server but the response was not received on time.

Introduction to JAX-RS

JAX-RS stands for **Java API extension for RESTful Web services**. JAX-RS is a specification that defines a set of APIs for developing web services in REST architecture style. This has become very popular in the past few years and is commonly used to build microservices. As previously discussed, RESTful services are interoperable services that interact with each other over the network, and JAX-RS helps us to build these services.

JAX-RS is Java's implementation for the REST style of architecture. This is a collection of Java annotations and interfaces that aid in developing RESTful web services. Here, there are both client- and server-side APIs, which are designed to do REST-based development in Java EE. JAX-RS specification was standardized in Java EE 6, the JAX-RS version was updated to JAX-RS 2.0 in Java EE 7, and this was improved in Java EE 8.

JAX-RS provides support for developing and consuming RESTful web services. JAX-RS is a set of **Plain Old Java Object** (**POJO**) based resource classes with some standard annotations on it, and this is designed to use a stateless communication model, such as HTTP. It specifies how to create an endpoint using POJOs as resources using the HTTP protocol, and uses either XML or JSON to represent the data.

JAX-RS annotations

JAX-RS is an annotation-driven model for creating the web services. The annotations are applied on the classes to expose them as resources or RESTful APIs. Here, there are different annotations, such as `@PATH` , `@GET` ,`@POST` , `@PUT`, and `@DELETE`. These annotations correspond to HTTP verbs and CRUD operations in general. The classes will be annotated with `@PATH` annotation to represent the root of the resource, and each function will be annotated in correspondence with the HTTP verbs in order to respond to the HTTP requests. There are also the `@QueryParam` and `@PathParam` annotations, which are intended for data retrieval, and the `@Produces` and `@Consumes` annotations for binding and unbinding data to the classes.

Furthermore, there are annotations that we can use for validation, such as `@Email` and `@NotNull`.

Let's take a look at these annotations in detail:

- @Path: When a class is annotated with @Path , that class becomes a resource. This means it can be accessible using a URI from outside. Let's say we have a class called Controller. We use the @Path annotation on this Controller class to mark it as a resource as follows:

```
@Path("/home")
public class Controller{
}
```

This resource can now be accessed using a URI such as https://{{hostname}}/home.

Now that we have defined a resource, we need to add a function that responds to the request. These functions can be annotated with @GET, @POST, @PUT, or @DELETE, and so on, based on the action that the resource needs to perform. These annotations correspond to the HTTP verbs that we discussed and have the same meaning.

- @GET: The @GET annotation is used for reading a resource. When @GET is applied to a function, a resource can be read on it. Consider the following example:

```
@Path("/home")
public class Controller{
  @GET
  public String login(){
    return "login.html"
  }
}
```

Similarly, we can define functions with @POST, @DELETE, and @PUT as follows:

```
@POST
public String create(){
//..
}
@PUT
public String update(){
//..
}
@DELETE
public void delete(){
//..
}
```

Once we define the resources and functions, we also need to specify the MIME type through which data is exchanged in the specified format. Different MIME types that we can use include `application/xml`, `application/json`, `image/png`, and `text/plain`.

To specify the MIME type, we use the `@Produces` and `@Consumes` annotations.

- `@Produces`: This is used to specify what type of data is returned to the client who is invoking the function via an HTTP request, as shown by the following code:

```
@Produces("application/json")
@POST
public String create(){
   //..
}
```

- `@Consumes`: This is used to specify what type of data is acceptable for the function that processes the HTTP request, as shown by the following code:

```
@Consumes("application/json")
@PUT
public String create(){
   //..
}
```

- `@PathParam`: This is used to map the query parameter to the parameter in a function for processing the request further. Now, `@PathParam` is usually used to retrieve the data by providing the input. This input is what gets mapped to the parameter of the function, which will then be used to pull the required data from the data source that the web service is tied to, as follows:

```
@Produces("application/json")
@GET
public getPerson(@PathParam("loginId") String loginId) {
}
```

Now let's take a look at how JAX-RS is actually implemented in an application.

Implementing a RESTful service using Jersey

So far, we have discussed what web services are, how to implement them in a REST style, and the different HTTP methods and status codes. Now that we're familiar with these, let's take a look at the RESTful services in action.

We use Jersey to implement a RESTful web service. **Jersey RESTful Web Services** is an open source framework for developing RESTful web services. It is a reference implementation of JAX-RS and it provides support for JAX-RS APIs. It adds some of its own features and APIs that extend from the JAX-RS toolkit for the simplification of web service development.

We will create a Maven web project, add the Jersey dependency, and define resources and functions in order to respond to the HTTP request.

Create a Maven web project and add the dependencies as follows:

```
<dependency>
    <groupId>com.sun.jersey</groupId>
    <artifactId>jersey-server</artifactId>
    <version>${jersey.version}</version>
</dependency>

<dependency>
    <groupId>com.sun.jersey</groupId>
    <artifactId>jersey-json</artifactId>
    <version>>${jersey.version}</version>
</dependency>

<dependency>
    <groupId>com.sun.jersey</groupId>
    <artifactId>jersey-client</artifactId>
    <version>>${jersey.version}</version>
</dependency>

<dependency>
    <groupId>org.jetbrains.kotlin</groupId>
    <artifactId>kotlin-stdlib</artifactId>
    <version>${kotlin.version}</version>
</dependency>
```

Let's write a really simple resource to start with. We will define a resource with a `@GET` annotation that returns a string as follows:

```
@Path("/home")
public class Controller {
    @GET
    fun home(): String {
        return "hello"
    }
}
```

Here we have defined a resource, `/home`, and a function, `home()`, that just return a string. Build this application and deploy it on a server.

We have deployed the service developed on Tomcat on port `8080`. When we access `localhost:8080/home`, the browser sends a `GET` request and the endpoint, `/home`, is mapped to the `home()` function, which returns the string message. The following screenshot depicts this:

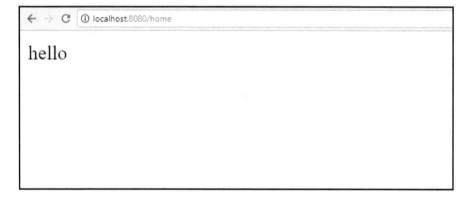

Similarly, let's add another resource called `/greet` like this:

```
@Path("/greet")
public class HelloWorld {

    @GET
    @Path("{parameter}")
    fun greet(@PathParam("parameter") name: String): Response {
        val response = "Hello : $name"
        return Response.status(200)
                        .entity(response)
                        .build()
    }
}
```

This resource is accessible via `localhost:8080/greet/{{name}}`. Once we invoke this resource, we get a greet message back. Consider the following screenshot:

We have now created a simple application to illustrate RESTful web services.

Implementing Real-World RESTful Web Services

Notice that we didn't configure, or use, any databases while implementing the web service using Jersey in the preceding section. Instead, we simply demonstrated how to map a request and return a response back using REST verbs. Real-world web services save the data in a data store and read it from there.

Let's add a `POST` function to create a record in the database and a `GET` function to read it. Let's say we want to create an application that allows us to manage identities where we create organizations, groups, users, and so on. To start with, let's create an organization. We will enhance this application in the following chapters.

Defining the layers

We will create different layers in the application to process the request and take that request to the database in order to create that entry in it.

Consider the following diagram:

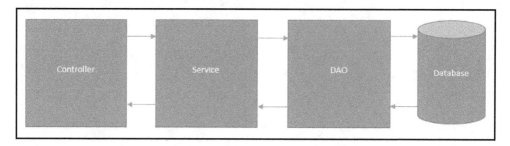

We have a **Controller** layer that accepts the request, does the validation (if there is any validation logic there) and passes the request to the **Service** layer. The **Service** layer maps the request object to entities and passes the request to the **Data Access Object** (**DAO**) layer. The **DAO** layer separates the business logic from the persistence logic. It has the logic to connect to the database, thus creating this organization record in the table in our example.

Create a simple Maven web project with Jersey, which we discussed earlier, and other JPA dependencies that we described in Chapter 5, *Kotlin with JPA and EJB*.

Add different packages, such as controller, service, dao, and so on. Take a look at the following screenshot:

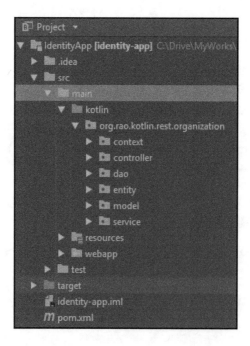

Writing a POST function for a create operation

An endpoint, /organization, is exposed in the OrganizationController class using the @Path annotation as follows:

```
@Path("/organization")
public class OrganizationController {

}
```

In order to process the request in controller class, the POST function looks like this:

```
@POST
@Consumes(MediaType.APPLICATION_JSON)
@Produces(MediaType.APPLICATION_JSON)
fun createOrganization(organizationRequest: OrganizationRequest)
        : Response {
    val response = "Created : ${organizationRequest.orgName}"
    var orgId =
organizationService.createOrganization(organizationRequest)
    return Response.status(201)
            .location(URI(orgId))
            .entity(response).build()
}
```

This function accepts organizationRequest and processes it for validation (if there is any validation logic). The request is then passed to the service layer. After processing the request, the service layer returns orgId, which gets wrapped around the standard response object and returned to the client that issued the HTTP request.

The service class instance is injected through CDI using the @Inject annotation to the controller like this:

```
@Inject
private lateinit var organizationService: OrganizaionService
```

The service class implementation for mapping the create org request to the org entity looks like this:

```
fun createOrganization(organizationRequest: OrganizationRequest) {
    var orgId:String = UUID.randomUUID().toString();
    var organizationEntity:OrganizationEntity =
                OrganizationEntity(orgId)
    organizationEntity.orgName = organizationRequest.orgName
```

```
        organizationEntity.description = organizationRequest.description

        organizationDao.createOrganization(organizationEntity)
        return orgId
    }
```

With the `createOrganization()` function in the service layer, we create a UUID and an entity by passing the UUID. The UUID then gets mapped to the primary key column of a table (organization table) in a database. We then map the request contents to the entity instance that we created and pass that entity to the `dao` layer.

There are various libraries available for mapping the objects of a desired type. Since we are dealing with simple mapping, we are directly mapping to the entity here.

`organizationDao` is injected to the service class as follows:

```
@Inject
private lateinit var organizationDao: OrganizationDao
```

The `createOrganization()` function in the `dao` class looks like this:

```
fun createOrganization(organizationEntity: OrganizationEntity):{
    entityManager.transaction.begin()
    entityManager.persist(organizationEntity)
    entityManager.transaction.commit()
}
```

The `createOrganization()` function accepts the entity (`organizationEntity`) and uses the `entityManger` that we described in Chapter 5, *Kotlin with JPA and EJB*, to connect to a database and persist that entity. An `org` entry will then be created in the `organization` table of the database.

So, we developed a create organization API. Now let's build and deploy this RESTful service on the Tomcat Server.

Invoking the create organization API using cURL

Once the service is up and running, we can make a cURL request to the web service to create the `organization` as follows:

```
curl -X POST \
  http://localhost:8080/organization \
  -H 'Accept: application/json' \
  -H 'Content-Type: application/json' \
```

```
-d '{
        "orgName": "TestOrg",
        "description": "this is test org"
}'
```

This will return the location header, which is a URI that can be used to refer to the resource later. It will also return a 201 status code, indicating that a new resource has been created, as shown in the following screenshot:

```
Connected to localhost (::1) port 8080 (#0)
POST /organization HTTP/1.1
User-Agent: curl/7.38.0
Host: localhost:8080
Accept: application/json
Content-Type: application/json
Content-Length: 60

[data not shown]
upload completely sent off: 60 out of 60 bytes
HTTP/1.1 201
Location: http://localhost:8080/organization/4c118afd-eccb-4ac7-bcfc-15e47f10770a
Content-Type: application/json
```

We can see that entry in the database by querying it directly, as shown in the following screenshot:

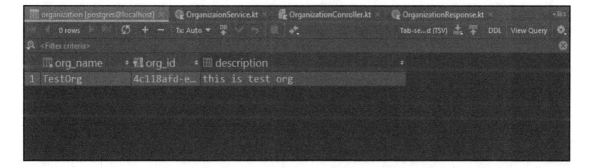

Writing a GET function for a read operation

Now let's retrieve the organization using the GET function. We will start by defining a resource to accept a path parameter, which is orgId in this example.

The `retrieveOrganization()` function in controller can be written to accept a path parameter, which happens to be an `orgId` that was returned when the identity was created. The `retrieveOrganization()` function returns the `org` object that is wrapped in a standard response in the JSON format, as seen in the following code:

```
@Path("/{orgId}")
@GET
@Produces(MediaType.APPLICATION_JSON)
fun retrieveOrganization(@PathParam("orgId") orgId: String): Response {
    var organizationResponse: OrganizationResponse =
    organizationService.retrieveOrganization(orgId)
    return Response.status(200)
            .entity(organizationResponse)
            .build()
}
```

The service class function takes `orgId` and passes the request to `dao` layer, as seen in the following code:

```
fun retrieveOrganization(orgId: String): OrganizationResponse {
    var organizationEntity: OrganizationEntity =
    organizationDao.retrieveOrganization(orgId)

    var organizationResponse: OrganizationResponse =
                    OrganizationResponse()
    organizationResponse.orgId = organizationEntity.orgId
    organizationResponse.orgName = organizationEntity.orgName
    organizationResponse.description = organizationEntity.description
    return organizationResponse
}
```

Once we get the response from the database after invoking the `retrieveOrganization()` function on the `organizationDao` instance, we map the entity object to the response class. The response class is similar to a request, but it is used for returning the response from the server side. The `OrganizationResponse` class is as follows:

```
class OrganizationResponse {
    var orgId: String?= null
    var orgName: String? = null
    var description: String? = null

    override fun toString(): String {
        return "Organization [orgId=$orgId, orgName=$orgName,
                    description=$description]"
    }
}
```

The `retrieveOrganization()` function implementation in `dao` layer is as follows:

```
fun retrieveOrganization(orgId: String): OrganizationEntity {
    entityManager.transaction.begin()
    var organizationEntity: OrganizationEntity =
    entityManager.find(OrganizationEntity::class.java, orgId)
    entityManager.transaction.commit()
    return organizationEntity
}
```

This uses the `find()` function to retrieve the desired entity given the unique identifier, which is `orgId`, and returns the `OrganizationEntity` that is being loaded from the database.

So, we created a get organization API. Now, once again, build and deploy this RESTful service on the Tomcat Server.

Invoking the get organization API using cURL

Using the cURL request to retrieve an organization given its UUID is done as follows:

```
curl -X GET \
  http://localhost:8080/organization/4c118afd-eccb-4ac7-bcfc-15e47f10770a \
  -H 'Accept: application/json' \
  -H 'Content-Type: application/json' \
```

When we invoke the cURL request, we get the organization that we created, shown in the following screenshot:

```
Connected to localhost (::1) port 8080 (#0)
GET /organization/4c118afd-eccb-4ac7-bcfc-15e47f10770a HTTP/1.1
User-Agent: curl/7.38.0
Host: localhost:8080
Accept: application/json
Content-Type: application/json

HTTP/1.1 200
Content-Type: application/json
Transfer-Encoding: chunked
Date: Tue, 14 Aug 2018 11:05:19 GMT

[data not shown]
00   101    0   101    0     0   1086     0 --:--:-- --:--:-- --:--:-- 1294{"description":"this is test org","orgId":"4c118afd-e
cb-4ac7-bcfc-15e47f10770a","orgName":"TestOrg"}
```

Similarly, we can implement the PUT and DELETE functions.

Summary

In this chapter, we discussed the following:

- What web services are and how they interact with each other over a network, irrespective of the underlying platform
- How to make a web service RESTful
- Different terms in the REST world, such as resources, HTTP methods, and HTTP status codes
- JAX-RS, a Java implementation of REST style
- JAX-RS annotations such as `@PATH`, `@GET`, `@POST`, `@PUT`, and `@DELETE`
- A simple RESTful web service implementation using Jersey
- A demonstration of a real RESTful web service with `POST` and `GET` examples

8

Securing JAVA EE Applications with Kotlin

Security is a very important consideration for enterprise applications, microservices, and cloud-based services. Applications should only be accessible to authorized clients, and this is a very common aspect for almost all modern enterprise applications:

In this chapter, we will focus on how to secure an application and how to protect it by providing a secure way of accessing the resources on the server.

We will also discuss the following:

- How to use the identity store to store user details
- The different authentication and authorization mechanisms that Java EE provides
- Implementing an API in Kotlin to secure the application and JWT support

Technical requirements

When it comes to applications, security is a common concern. Having a basic understanding of authentication and authorization concepts will be beneficial. Being familiar with the **Lightweight Directory Access Protocol** (**LDAP**)—or any active directory—will be an advantage when progressing through this chapter.

Introduction to security API

The Security 1.0 API is a brand new API specification in Java EE 8 that provides a new programming model for securing enterprise applications. The security API version 1.0 is a reference implementation of JSR 375, the Java EE Security API specification. This specification is aimed at simplifying and supporting new security aspects for platform services, standardizing the way that we secure applications. The security API is annotation-driven and uses a lot of CDI and **Expression Language** (**EL**) to make the implementation easier.

The key features of the security API implementation include the following:

- The `IdentityStore` mechanism
- `HttpAuthenticationMechanism`
- The `SecurityContext` interface

`IdentityStore` provides an implementation for storing user details, but other implementations are also out there, such as an embedded store, a database store, and the LDAP implementation.

The authentication mechanism is a way of validating the user details provided against `IdentityStore`. The `SecurityContext` interface is geared toward a programmatic way of granting or denying access (authorization) to the resources. There is also a hashing mechanism provided in the specification that can be used for securing passwords, as well as other sensitive information.

We will take a look at some of these points and illustrate them using examples in the further sections of this chapter.

> The Java EE Security (JSR 375) reference implementation is named Soteria and is currently maintained by the Eclipse-ee4j community.

The IdentityStore mechanism

`IdentityStore` is where we can store user details such as user ID, secrets, and other information associated with that particular identity. The `IdentityStore` API in Java EE 8 is an interface that is used to interact with the identity stores in order to validate the user credentials against the identity store. The API takes in the credentials, validates the data in the identity store, and returns the validation result. The idea of this abstraction is to ease the use of identity stores for user authentication and authorization mechanisms. The `IdentityStore` mechanism operates as follows:

The user's credentials can consist of a **userID** and **Password**, or an OAuth token, depending on the data store implementation in the application. The `IdentityStore` API validates this information by locating this data in the data store, and returns a status to indicate whether or not the authentication is successful. The API can be implemented to return other membership details, such as the group or role association of the identity.

There are multiple `IdentityStore` implementations available, including embedded identity store implementations, and database and LDAP implementations. These built-in `IdentityStore` implementations can easily be configured through annotations, and can also be made available for use in the application for authenticating identities.

EmbeddedIdentityStoreDefinition

`@EmbeddedIdentityStoreDefinition` is an in-memory data store implementation. This is used for any proof of concept or testing, as the user credentials are directly specified upon annotation. It's easy to configure `EmbeddedIdentityStore` in an application; we just have to specify the annotation on the configuration class and provide the identity information in the annotation itself. For example, consider the following code:

```
@EmbeddedIdentityStoreDefinition(
        Credentials(callerName = "user1", password = "secret1", groups =
arrayOf("user")),
        Credentials(callerName = "user2", password = "secret2", groups =
arrayOf("admin")))
@DeclareRoles("user", "admin")
@ApplicationPath("home")
@ApplicationScoped
class ApplicationConfig : Application() {
    override fun getClasses(): Set<Class<*>> {
        val classes = HashSet<Class<*>>()
        classes.add(Controller::class.java)
        return classes
    }
}
```

Here, we specified `user1` as a normal user, and `user2` as an admin user, with their credentials and group membership.

DatabaseIdentityStoreDefinition

`@DatabaseIdentityStoreDefinition` annotation is used for a database that stores the user identity information. Applications can be configured to use a database to store the identity, and queries will be specified, one for retrieving user information, and the other for group identity information.

For example, if we add this annotation and specify the lookup name and queries, it will then be used for validating the request:

```
@DatabaseIdentityStoreDefinition(
        dataSourceLookup = "java:comp/env/jdbc/identityDS",
        callerQuery = "select password from user where user_id = ?",
        groupsQuery = "select group_name from groups where user_id = ?")
@ApplicationPath("home")
@ApplicationScoped
class ApplicationConfig : Application() {
    override fun getClasses(): Set<Class<*>> {
        val classes = HashSet<Class<*>>()
        classes.add(Controller::class.java)
        return classes
    }
}
```

LdapIdentityStoreDefinition

`@LdapIdentityStoreDefinition` is used with any active directory servers that store the identity information.

Here, we provide the LDAP queries to retrieve the user information:

```
@LdapIdentityStoreDefinition(
        url = "ldap://localhost:8090",
        callerBaseDn = "ou=org,dc=testdata,dc=org",
        groupSearchBase = "ou=group,dc=test,dc=org",
        groupSearchFilter = "((member=%s)(objectClass=groupOfNames))")

@ApplicationScoped
class ApplicationConfig : Application() {
    override fun getClasses(): Set<Class<*>> {
        val classes = HashSet<Class<*>>()
        classes.add(Controller::class.java)
        return classes
    }
}
```

We've discussed how to configure `@EmbeddedIdentityStoreDefinition`, `@DataBaseIdentityStoreDefinition`, and `@LdapIdentityStoreDefinition`. With these identity stores, we can write code for application security by configuring these identity store implementations in the code.

HttpAuthenticationMechanism

Once we have `IdentityStore` implementation, we can use it in our application code for security. In Java EE 8, there is an API that can achieve this element of security—`HttpAuthenticationMechanism`. This can be used to secure servlets, and equally, to secure any frameworks based on them. `HttpAuthenticationMechanism` is used to validate the user identity information. `HttpAuthenticationMechanism`, together with the `IdentityStore`, enables the application to control the identity stores that it uses for authentication in a portable manner.

The `HttpAuthenticationMechanism` validates the request and checks the authentication status. It then uses the identity store to validate the identity information that it has received from the incoming request. After this, it passes the request information to the identity store. Based on the validation result, it either grants access or denies it. The following diagram depicts this:

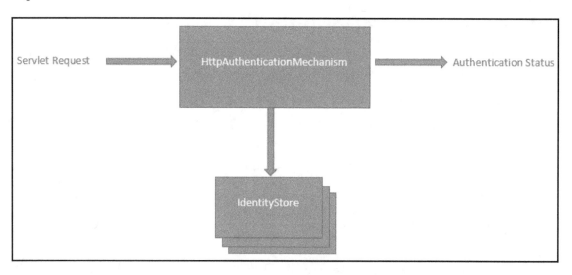

`HttpAuthenticationMechanism` can be configured to use multiple identity stores, as shown in the preceding diagram, and can use `IdentityStoreHandler` to manage these identity stores. `IdentityStoreHandler` groups the `IdentityStore` implementations together. The handler can be injected using CDI into an `HttpAuthenticationMechanism` implementation.

`HttpAuthenticationMechanism` is an interface. There are default implementations available for this.

BasicAuthenticationMechanismDefinition

`BasicAuthenticationMechanismDefinition` will trigger the browser of the client to prompt for a username and password, which maps to the HTTP basic authentication mechanism that isn't very widely used any more. The following code is an example of this:

```
@BasicAuthenticationMechanismDefinition(
        realmName = "top-level-realm")
@ApplicationScoped
class ApplicationConfig : Application() {
    override fun getClasses(): Set<Class<*>> {
        val classes = HashSet<Class<*>>()
        classes.add(Controller::class.java)
        return classes
    }
}
```

The request has to specify the user ID and password in Base 64-encoded format, such as `Basic {{userId:secret}}`. It must then pass it to the authorization header.

> For browser-based clients, the server sends a `WWW-Authenticate:` `Basic realm=top-level-realm` header when the request is made for the first time. The browser prompts the client to enter the credentials.

FormAuthenticationMechanismDefinition

The `FormAuthenticationMechanismDefinition` will present the user with a web form for credentials. We can specify the login page to be displayed for user authentication, as well as an error page, in case an error arises. Alternatively, default pages can be used. The following code is an example of this:

```
@FormAuthenticationMechanismDefinition(
        loginToContinue = LoginToContinue(
                loginPage = "/login.html",
                errorPage = "/error.html"))
@ApplicationScoped
class ApplicationConfig : Application() {
    override fun getClasses(): Set<Class<*>> {
        val classes = HashSet<Class<*>>()
        classes.add(Controller::class.java)
        return classes
    }
}
```

Custom form-based HTTP authentication

Using the `@CustomFormAuthenticationMechanismDefinition` annotation, the application can be configured to use a custom form for authentication. Here, we can specify the custom login page and an implementation for validating the credentials, as follows:

```
@CustomFormAuthenticationMechanismDefinition(
        loginToContinue = LoginToContinue(loginPage = "/login.jsf"))
@ApplicationScoped
class ApplicationConfig : Application() {
    override fun getClasses(): Set<Class<*>> {
        val classes = HashSet<Class<*>>()
        classes.add(Controller::class.java)
        return classes
    }
}
```

We can also implement the `HttpAuthenticationMechanism` interface and provide the custom authentication mechanism.

The `HttpAuthenticationMechanism` defines three functions, as follows:

```
AuthenticationStatus validateRequest(HttpServletRequest request,
HttpServletResponse response, HttpMessageContext httpMessageContext) throws
AuthenticationException;

    default AuthenticationStatus secureResponse(HttpServletRequest request,
HttpServletResponse response, HttpMessageContext httpMessageContext) throws
AuthenticationException {
        return AuthenticationStatus.SUCCESS;
    }

    default void cleanSubject(HttpServletRequest request, HttpServletResponse
response, HttpMessageContext httpMessageContext) {
        httpMessageContext.cleanClientSubject();
    }
```

Note that the `validateRequest()` function is abstract, and default implementations are provided for the other two functions.

We need to implement the `validateRequest()` function and use an `IdentityStore` implementation to validate the credentials that we received from the request:

```
override fun validateRequest (
        req:HttpServletRequest,
        res:HttpServletResponse,
        context:HttpMessageContext):AuthenticationStatus {
```

```
val result = myIdentityStore.validate(
  UsernamePasswordCredential(
    req.getHeader("name"),
    req.getHeader("password")))
    //...
}
```

The SecurityContext API

As we mentioned earlier, the `SecurityContext` API provides programmatic security. The `IdentityStore` and authentication mechanisms are like declarative modes for handling security, whereas the `SecurityContext` API is geared toward more programmatic control for the authentication and authorization mechanisms in the application. This new `SecurityContext` interface unifies many different security APIs that were scattered across individual Java EE technology specifications.

The `SecurityContext` object represents all security information that has been gathered on the user who made the current request. An implementation of the `SecurityContext` API should be provided at runtime as a CDI-managed bean. We can inject `SecurityContext` to our application code via CDI as follows:

```
@Inject
lateinit var securityContext:SecurityContext
```

At this point, we can authenticate the user, check the user's role/group membership, and grant or deny access to the resource. We can then use this context object in our code to make security decisions. The `SecurityContext` interface declares five methods:

```
public interface SecurityContext {
  Principal getCallerPrincipal ();

  <T extends Principal> Set<T> getPrincipalsByType (Class<T> type);

  boolean isCallerInRole (String role);

  boolean hasAccessToWebResource (String resource, String... methods);

  AuthenticationStatus authenticate (
      HttpServletRequest httpServletRequest,
      HttpServletResponse httpServletResponse,
      AuthenticationParameters authParameteres);
}
```

Let's understand what these methods are:

- The first method is the `getCallerPrincipal()`. When invoked, this method returns the `Principal` type object that represents the current user who issued the request.
- Implementations of the security API can also provide their specialized `Principal` types. We should use `getPrincipalsByType()` by passing the desired type to get the principal object of that type.
- The `isCallerInRole()` method can be used to find out the roles of the users in the current request.
- There is also the `hasAccessToWebResource()` method, which is used to check the permission of the user as regards access to the resource residing on the server side. The authenticate method then triggers re-authentication for the user in the current request scope.

> With applications, we will generally mostly be using the `getCallerPrincipal()` and `isCallerInRole()` methods.
>
> We can also use the `SecurityContext` and `getCallerPrincipal()` methods in place of the old `HttpServletRequest.getUserPrincipal()` and `EJBContext.getCallerPrincipal()` method implementations.

This is an overview of the Security 1.0 API. The very first version of the specification has standardized the security model in Java EE and is packed with the powerful features required for a modern enterprise applications. Next, we will demonstrate securing the resources using `IdentityStore` and `AuthenticationMechanism`.

Implementing security API using Kotlin

In this section, we will discuss how to protect a REST resource by implementing the security API using Kotlin. We created a resource to create and read an organization as an identity data in the previous chapter. In this chapter, we will add a security layer to this RESTful service by implementing custom `HttpAuthenticationMechanism` and `IdentityStore` mechanisms.

We will add the following security-related dependencies to the existing dependencies:

```
<dependency>
    <groupId>org.glassfish.soteria</groupId>
    <artifactId>javax.security.enterprise</artifactId>
    <version>${org.glassfish.soteria}</version>
</dependency>
<dependency>
    <groupId>javax.servlet</groupId>
    <artifactId>javax.servlet-api</artifactId>
    <version>${javax.servlet-api}</version>
</dependency>
<dependency>
    <groupId>org.glassfish</groupId>
    <artifactId>javax.security.auth.message</artifactId>
    <version>${javax.security.auth.message}</version>
</dependency>
```

Now, let's implement our custom `IdentityStore`. For demonstration purposes, we store the user details in the store implementation itself.

We implement the `IdentityStore` interface and override the `validate()` function, as shown in the following code:

```
@ApplicationScoped
@ManagedBean
class MyIdentityStore : IdentityStore {
    override fun validate(userCredential: Credential):
                CredentialValidationResult {
        return if (userCredential is UsernamePasswordCredential
                userCredential.compareTo("testUser", "testUserPass")) {
            CredentialValidationResult("admin",
                    HashSet(asList("user")))
        } else CredentialValidationResult.INVALID_RESULT
    }
}
```

We also write our own custom `AuthenticationMechanism` by implementing the `HttpAuthenticationMechanism` interface and overriding the `validateRequest()` function. Consider the following code for this:

```
@ApplicationScoped
class MyAuthMechanism : HttpAuthenticationMechanism {
    @Inject
    internal var myIdentityStore = MyIdentityStore()

    override fun validateRequest(req: HttpServletRequest,
```

```
                                    res: HttpServletResponse,
                                    context: HttpMessageContext):
AuthenticationStatus {
     val result = myIdentityStore.validate(
            UsernamePasswordCredential(
                    req.getHeader("UserId"),
                    req.getHeader("Password")))
     return if (result.status == VALID) {
        AuthenticationStatus.SUCCESS
     } else {
        AuthenticationStatus.SEND_FAILURE
     }
   }
 }
```

With the `validateRequest()` function, we extract the user's credentials from the `UserId` and `Password` headers and construct an instance of the `UsernamePasswordCredential` type, which holds the user ID and password. We then invoke our custom `IdentityStore` instance's `validate()` function by passing the credentials.

Our request now includes two new headers—`UserId` and `Password`. When the request is made, the `validateRequest()` function will be invoked. In turn, this invokes the store's `validate()` function and checks for the credentials passed in the header. If the credentials are valid, the organization response will be returned, with `200` as the status code. If not, the `401` status code is returned, indicating unauthorized access.

Let's verify this by making a REST call using the following commands:

```
curl -X GET \
http://localhost:8080/organization/4c118afd-eccb-4ac7-bcfc-15e47f10770a\
  -H 'Accept: application/json' \
  -H 'Content-Type: application/json' \
  -H 'Password: testUserPass' \
  -H 'UserId: testUser' \
```

When we invoke the REST endpoint using the `curl` command, we get the `org` response, as we passed the correct credentials:

```
Trying ::1...
Connected to localhost (::1) port 8080 (#0)
GET /organization/4c118afd-eccb-4ac7-bcfc-15e47f10770a HTTP/1.1
User-Agent: curl/7.38.0
Host: localhost:8080
Accept: application/json
Content-Type: application/json
Password:
UserId: testUser

HTTP/1.1 200
Content-Type: application/json
Transfer-Encoding: chunked
Date: Tue, 21 Aug 2018 11:31:31 GMT

[data not shown]
00   101    0   101    0     0   1074      0 --:--:-- --:--:-- --:--:--    1278{"
escription":"this is test org","orgName":"TestOrg","orgId":"4c118afd-eccb-4ac7-
cfc-15e47f10770a"}
```

Let's make a call with an `invalid` password. Here, we expect to receive the `401` status code:

```
curl -X GET \
http://localhost:8080/organization/4c118afd-eccb-4ac7-bcfc-15e47f10770a\
   -H 'Accept: application/json' \
   -H 'Content-Type: application/json' \
   -H 'Password: invalid' \
   -H 'UserId: testUser' \
```

The following screenshot shows the output:

```
GET /organization/4c118afd-eccb-4ac7-bcfc-15e47f10770a HTTP/1.1
User-Agent: curl/7.38.0
Host: localhost:8080
Accept: application/json
Content-Type: application/json
Password: invalid
UserId: testUser

HTTP/1.1 401
Content-Type: text/html;charset=utf-8
Content-Language: en
Content-Length: 1033
Date: Tue, 21 Aug 2018 11:38:18 GMT

[data not shown]
00  1033 100  1033    0     0  10989      0 --:--:-- --:--:-- --:--:-- 13243<!doctype html><html lang="en"><head><title>HTTP Status 401 – Una
thorized</title><style type="text/css">h1 {font-family:Tahoma,Arial,sans-serif;color:white;background-color:#525D76;font-size:22px;} h2 {font-
amily:Tahoma,Arial,sans-serif;color:white;background-color:#525D76;font-size:16px;} h3 {font-family:Tahoma,Arial,sans-serif;color:white;backgr
und-color:#525D76;font-size:14px;} body {font-family:Tahoma,Arial,sans-serif;color:black;background-color:white;} b {font-family:Tahoma,Arial,
ans-serif;color:white;background-color:#525D76;} p {font-family:Tahoma,Arial,sans-serif;background:white;color:black;font-size:12px;} a {color
black;} a.name {color:black;} .line {height:1px;background-color:#525D76;border:none;}</style></head><body><h1>HTTP Status 401 – Unauthorized<
h1><hr class="line" /><p><b>Type</b> Status Report</p><p><b>Description</b> The request has not been applied because it lacks valid authentica
ion credentials for the target resource.</p><hr class="line" /><h3>Apache Tomcat/9.0.2</h3></body></html>
 Connection #0 to host localhost left intact
```

As expected, the `401` Unauthorized status code is returned.

This example is a simple demonstration of how the security layer can be implemented using Kotlin and Java EE Security API.

Securing JAX-RS APIs with JWT

Token-based authentication is more common in the modern enterprise applications because it is stateless, unmodifiable, and of course, secure in nature. JWT is one of the most popular token-based authentication mechanisms.

A **JSON Web Token** (**JWT**) is a JSON object representation in an encoded format. This is used for authentication and authorization and is based on the RFC 7519 standard. This is a compact JSON model used for managing stateless authentication and claiming verification over the web interactions. In a JWT, the claims are encoded as a JSON object in the payload part of the token. This is digitally signed and secured through the interaction of two parties; for example, this could be the client and the server.

Once the user is authenticated against the server, the `JWT` token is digitally signed and trustable. It carries a sufficient amount of information about the user.

A service can take this token in the request as part of the existing `auth` interaction it had in the first place, and this time, it doesn't look in any LDAP/databases for authentication. This means that once the user is authenticated, the subsequent request need not contain the client credentials. Instead, the client can just pass the token obtained as part of the request, and the server looks at the token and grants the access to the resources based on the token validation.

The `JWT` token can either be passed in the request header or the request parameter, as it is in an encoded format.

The structure of JWT

A JWT consists of three parts—the header, payload, and signature.

Header

The first part of the token is the header. This provides information, such as which algorithm is being used for signing the token, and the nature of the token. For example, consider the following code:

```
{
    "alg": "HS256",
    "typ": "JWT"
}
```

Note that the header is represented as a JSON object. Here, `alg` represents the algorithm used, and `typ` indicates the type of token. In this case, this is JWT. Different algorithms, such as `HS256`, `HS384`, `RS256`, and `ES512` can be used to sign the token. The type is open for extensibility to support other token types in future.

Payload

The second part of the `JWT` token is the payload. Here, we have a set of claims that are again represented as a JSON object:

```
{
    "sub": "testuserid",
    "name": "Test User",
    "aud": [
        "https://myserver.com/jwt_token",
        "http://localhost/jwt_token"
    ],
    "iat": 1534935981,
    "exp": 1534937448
}
```

Here, the `sub`—the subject of the claim—is an identifier. The claim can have a `name` value, and `iat` is the timestamp that shows at which point the token is issued. The `exp` is the timestamp, indicating at which point the token will expire. The timestamps are shown in epoch format.

`aud` is the audience claim that identifies the recipients that the JWT is intended for. Generally, the `aud` value is an array of case-sensitive strings, each containing a string or URI value. The interpretation of audience values is generally application-specific.

Signature

The third part of the token is the signature, which is a signed version of the previous two elements. This is shown as follows:

```
HMACSHA256(base64UrlEncode(header)+"."+base64urlEncode(payload), secret)
```

Here, we create an `HMACSHA256` signed token. We use the `base64UrlEncoding` of the header, followed by a period, then a `base64UrlEncode` of the payload, which is the collection of the claims and an HMAC secret.

Depending on the algorithm used, this step of signing the token may vary. However, the idea here is to encode and sign the token with a secret. This becomes the third part of the `JWT` token.

So, our `JWT` token is in a format like this:

```
Base64UrlEncode(header).base64Encode(payload).HMACSHA256(base64UrlEncode(he
ader)+"."+base64urlEncode(payload), secret)
```

An example value of the JWT is shown as follows:

```
eyJhbGciOiJIUzI1NiIsInR5cCI6IkpXVCJ9
.eyJzdWIiOiJ0ZXN0dXNlcmlkIiwibmFtZSI6IlRlc3QgVXNlciIsImlhdCI6MTUzNDkzNzQ0OH
0
._mPNoWWCq3dYjN7cU3lemI23Ft_uEyA9woY_dJpu9l0
```

Note that the three parts of the token are separated by the period (`.`) character. The JWT of this sort will be passed in the request while making a call to the resource on the server. This `JWT` token can be passed as an authorization header, as a `Bearer` token, or a query parameter; whichever form that the server's resource can understand.

One final note about the JWT is that the claims that we use, such as `aud`, `iat`, `exp`, and `sub`, are registered with the IANA (`https://www.iana.org/assignments/jwt/jwt.xhtml`), the organization that manages these sorts of names used when generating the JWT token information. We can register the new name with the IANA. But this already has a set of reusable claims that are sufficient for the web/REST resource authentication and authorization.

As we have seen, a JWT is a compact, stateless, digitally signed token that we can use for authentication and authorization mechanisms.

We will implement a simple example of generating a JWT and validating it to see how to protect a REST endpoint using JWT.

Implementing JWT

Let's consider the identity app once again. We implemented `IdentityStore` and `AuthMechanism` to authenticate the user, and then provided access to the user to invoke the `/organization` endpoint.

We will modify this project to demonstrate the JWT. We will also add a new `/login` resource, which takes the user ID and password in the header, and validates it against `IdentityStore`, as explained earlier. Let's write this sequence to understand what we intend to do:

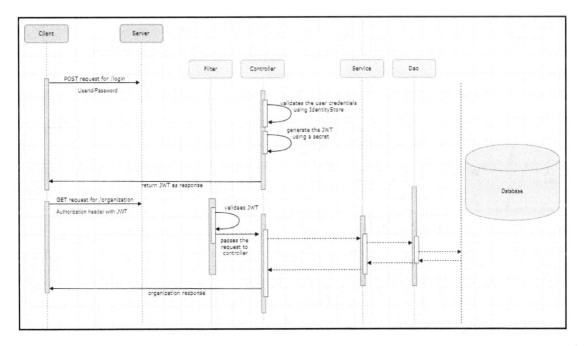

As shown in the preceding sequence diagram, `/login` is the entry point that takes the user's credentials, which we then validate using the `IdentityStore`, before generating the JWT token and returning it as a response. The end user passes this JWT to invoke the `/organization` API.

Let's take a look at these steps in detail:

Once the user is authenticated against our custom identity store, we will invoke the createJWT() function, as follows:

```
public fun createJwt(id: String, issuer: String, subject: String,
                 expiryTime: Long): String {
    val signatureAlgorithm = SignatureAlgorithm.HS256
    val currentTimeInMillis = System.currentTimeMillis()
    val date = Date(currentTimeInMillis)
    val apiKeySecretBytes = DatatypeConverter.parseBase64Binary(SECRET)
    val signingKey = SecretKeySpec(apiKeySecretBytes,
                        signatureAlgorithm.getJcaName())

    val builder = Jwts.builder()
                    .setId(id)
                    .setIssuedAt(date)
                    .setSubject(subject)
                    .setIssuer(issuer)
                    .setAudience(AUDIENCE)
                    .signWith(signatureAlgorithm, signingKey)

    if (expiryTime >= 0) {
        val expMillis = currentTimeInMillis + expiryTime
        val exp = Date(expMillis)
        builder.setExpiration(exp)
    }
    return builder.compact()
}
```

This function takes an ID, jwtId, an issuer, a subject, and expiryTime as input arguments. We use the HMACSHA256 algorithm and a defined secret to generate the JWT, and use the Jwts.builder() method from the jjwt library to create the token. We will return this token in response to the /login API.

Let's invoke a curl command for the /login API with valid credentials, as follows:

```
curl -X POST \
  http://localhost:8080/login \
  -H 'Accept: application/json' \
  -H 'Content-Type: application/json' \
  -H 'UserId: testUser'
  -H 'Password: testUserPass' \
```

The output of the preceding REST API call is as follows:

```
Connected to localhost (::1) port 8080 (#0)
POST /login HTTP/1.1
User-Agent: curl/7.38.0
Host: localhost:8080
Accept: application/json
Content-Type: application/json
UserId: testUser
Password:

0     0    0     0     0     0      0      0 --:--:-- 0:00:01 --:--:--      0< HTTP/1.1 200
Content-Length: 202
Date: Thu, 23 Aug 2018 05:05:15 GMT

[data not shown]
00    202 100   202     0     0    106      0 0:00:01 0:00:01 --:--:--    107 JWT:eyJhbGciOiJIUzI1NiJ9.eyJqdGkiOiIxMjMOIiwiaWFOIjo
NTM1MDAwNzEzLCJzdWIiOiJzdWIiXMjMiLCJpc3MiOiJsb2NhbGhvc3QiLCJhdWQiOiIvandOdG9yZW4iLCJleHAiOjElMzUwMDE2MTN9.1ZWJlw4zj3xGTghq9Q36GYpy_
cxYCbCN-QJhJ1s_Lk
```

The `/login` API returns a JWT token, valid for 15 minutes. We passed the expiry time of fifteen minutes when generating the token.

Now let's try to invoke the `GET` organization API with an invalid authorization header and see what happens:

```
curl -X GET \
    http://localhost:8080/organization/4c118afd-eccb-4ac7-bcfc-15e47f10770a \
    -H 'Accept: application/json' \
    -H 'Authorization: Bearer 123' \
    -H 'Content-Type: application/json'
```

The output of the preceding REST invocation is as follows:

```
Connected to localhost (::1) port 8080 (#0)
GET /organization/4c118afd-eccb-4ac7-bcfc-15e47f10770a HTTP/1.1
User-Agent: curl/7.38.0
Host: localhost:8080
Accept: application/json
Authorization: Bearer 123
Content-Type: application/json

HTTP/1.1 403
Content-Type: text/html;charset=utf-8
Content-Language: en
Content-Length: 982
Date: Thu, 23 Aug 2018 05:10:35 GMT
```

An invalid authorization header resulted in a `403` response.

Now, let's pass the valid JWT that we obtained in the authorization header, as follows:

```
curl -X GET \
http://localhost:8080/organization/4c118afd-eccb-4ac7-bcfc-15e47f10770a\
  -H 'Accept: application/json' \
  -H 'Authorization: Bearer
eyJhbGciOiJIUzI1NiJ9.eyJqdGkiOiIxMjM0IiwiaWF0IjoxNTM1MDAwNzEzLCJzdWIiOiJzdW
IxMjMiLCJpc3MiOiJsb2NhbGhvc3QiLCJhdWQiOiIvand0dG9rZW4iLCJleHAiOjE1MzUwMDE2M
TN9.1ZWJlw4zj3xGTghq9Q36GYpy_7cxYCbCN-QJhJ1s_Lk' \
  -H 'Content-Type: application/json'
```

The output of the preceding REST call is as follows:

```
curl -X GET \
http://localhost:8080/organization/4c118afd-eccb-4ac7-bcfc-15e47f10770a \
 -H 'Accept: application/json' \
 -H 'Authorization: Bearer eyJhbGciOiJIUzI1NiJ9.eyJqdGkiOiIxMjM0IiwiaWF0IjoxNTM1MDAwNzEzLCJzdWIiOiJzdWIxMjMiLCJpc3MiOiJsb2NhbGhv
3QiLCJhdWQiOiIvand0dG9rZW4iLCJleHAiOjE1MzUwMDE2MTN9.1ZWJlw4zj3xGTghq9Q36GYpy_7cxYCbCN-QJhJ1s_Lk' \
 -H 'Content-Type: application/json'
% Total    % Received % Xferd  Average Speed   Time    Time     Time  Current
                               Dload  Upload   Total   Spent    Left  Speed
00  101    0   101    0     0   1074      0 --:--:-- --:--:-- --:--:--  1074{"description":"this is test org","orgName":"TestOrg"
"orgId":"4c118afd-eccb-4ac7-bcfc-15e47f10770a"}
```

Now, the `GET` organization API returns the organization details in response.

So, we have looked at how a REST API can be secured with JWT with a simple use case. In real-world applications, the complexity can be increased by using private and public keys while generating and verifying the JWT.

Summary

In this chapter, we discussed the following:

- A brief introduction to the Security 1.0 API. Here, we described the key features of the API, including the `IdentityStore` mechanism, `HttpAuthenticationMechanism`, and the `SecurityContext` interface.
- Different implementations of `IdentityStore`, including embedded identity stores, database identity stores, and LDAP stores.
- Authentication mechanisms and their different implementations, including basic authentication, form-based authentication, and custom form-based `auth` mechanisms.
- The implementation of Security API using Kotlin to secure a REST API through simple authentication.
- A brief introduction to JWT and the method for securing a REST API with a JWT-based authentication.

Implementing Microservices with Kotlin

9

In the modern, cloud-based application era, the idea of a monolith application that manages all tasks no longer exists. The application is designed in small pieces, each handling a single business responsibility. Microservices is an architectural style in which a large complex application is composed of multiple, smaller services:

This style loosely couples the system being developed and each service can be developed independently. With Kotlin, it is much easier to write the microservices in order to experience the benefits of this architectural style of developing software.

In this chapter, we will discuss the following:

- Microservices and their architecture
- Breaking a monolith application into smaller microservices
- The benefits of the microservices architecture style
- How to test microservices

Technical requirements

Having a decent understanding of monoliths and microservices is a good way to start this chapter. We will enhance the application that we developed in the previous chapter using microservices architectural principles.

Introduction to microservices

Microservices is a software methodology for designing and developing software. It is an architectural style that structures an application to be composed of multiple smaller services. Each service exposes its operation via well-defined interfaces and is responsible for a single business requirement.

These services are independent of each other and this style of architecture consequently makes the application a collection of loosely-coupled services. The concept of microservices is aimed at developing an application that is loosely coupled, easily scalable, easily testable, and delivers the piece of software in a shorter interval of time.

Different microservices work together to form a larger application as a whole. They also communicate via unified, standard, well-defined interfaces.

 Like the REST principles, the microservices architecture is a way of designing the enterprise software. There are no hard and fast rules defined for this architectural principle. Its main motive is to sufficiently decompose the application in order to facilitate application development and deployment in agile fashion, and they must also be easily testable and scalable.

The **microservices architecture** (**MSA**) is designed to separate the application into small, independent services, each one performing a specific functionality. These services are stateless and communicate with each other over the REST, regardless of the underlying platform it is developed in. The services are highly resilient, which means services are designed to be easily recoverable, which assume a high load or a failure.

Microservices has proven to be the capable model for developing a loosely-coupled system that is scalable, easily testable, and reduces the development cycle compared to single, large monolith applications. With Kotlin, it is much easier to develop such services and maintain such code bases.

To design microservices, we need to identify and design small services, each service performing one specific task. These smaller services form the building blocks of the microservices. For them to communicate, we need to define and choose the interface types so that the consuming service won't be tightly coupled to the other services. In addition, when interfaces are used, these services can be developed simultaneously; the services don't have to worry about the other service implementations, and they can have an independent life cycle from development up until deployment.

Advantages of microservices

Some of the advantages of microservices are as follows:

- As each service focuses on one responsibility, the code becomes clearer, easier to test, and has a more controlled flow.
- Services can be independently deployable by an automated deployment process.
- Unlike monolith services, it doesn't suffer from the single point of failure. All the services are deployed separately and talk to different data stores.
- Any change or upgrade can be easier with microservices. Unlike the monolith, making an upgrade won't results in downtime for the system as a whole. Only the required system will be upgraded.
- We can have smaller code bases with the microservices, and maintaining such code bases becomes easier.
- When it comes to scalability, the service that is getting more requests can be scaled easily, leading to better resource utilization and better system performance.

The microservices style of architecture may not be employed for every use case. Although it offers several advantages, it also has some side-effects. If the number of smaller services increases, deploying and managing can be overhead sometimes. Communication between services might contribute to the latency.

Breaking the monolith into microservices

Traditionally, enterprise applications were built as single, large, monolith applications. They were also sometimes built on database-driven systems that stored all logic, from UI to business, and data. Typically, a monolith application looks something like the following:

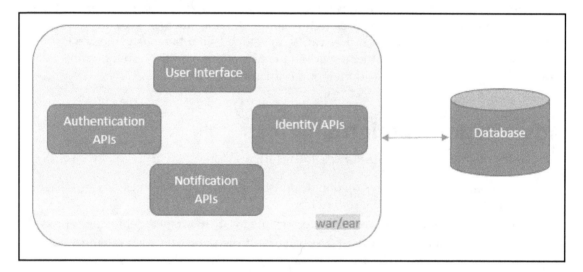

The problem with the monolith service architecture is that any failure in the system will halt the entire system and a small problem can bring down the entire application. When any code change or new implementation has to be applied, this would result in rebuilding and redeploying the whole system.

Since there is a code change, the system has to go through the entire verification process. Any library upgrade is a nightmare. When the system becomes bulky, it is very difficult to maintain.

Any code refactoring to improve the code quality or performance will take a lot more time and, if there are no sufficient test cases, this process would be really challenging. For a mission-critical system, these kinds of quality issues and delivery delays are not acceptable and the system becomes unpredictable.

Microservices architecture (MSA)

The MSA aims to solve the problems that were present in the monolith design. A microservice is an efficient and flexible approach to building an application. This splits the application being developed into small services that can exist independently, and each service has its own life cycle. Each microservice is responsible for a single functionality only. Consequently, the service's focus is only on doing this and doing it well.

A typical MSA looks like the following:

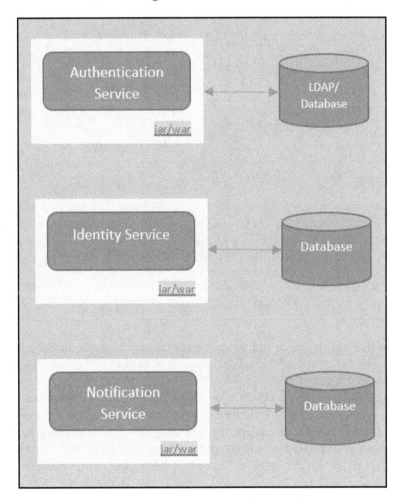

As shown in the preceding diagram, the application is composed of small services, each responsible for one functionality and each having its own store. Building, deploying, or upgrading services will have its own life cycle and these services exist independently of each other in the application, interacting with each other over the REST.

Here is a typical deployment model:

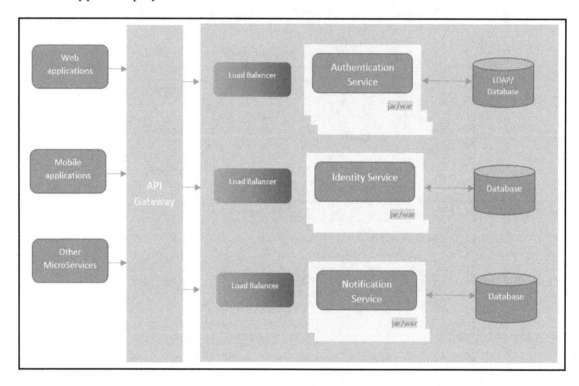

As shown in the preceding diagram, microservices each have their own database deployed and exposed as REST services. The number of service instances may vary from one service to another based on usage patterns. For example, we can deploy three instances of authentication service as it may be used more frequently, and two instances of each identity and notification service. The **Load Balancer** will be brought in to route the requests properly to these service instances as appropriate. An **API Gateway, service level agreement** (**SLA**), is also provided, which uniformly receives external requests, performs load balancing to invoke the backend service, and returns the results to the clients. It also performs some basic validation to prevent attacks and to decouple the exposed microservices from the consuming client. Any client (such as a mobile or web app) can use the APIs exposed over the **API Gateway**. This is a typical deployment model that may vary based on business needs and available infrastructure.

This is how the microservice architecture makes the application development more efficient and more manageable.

Developing real-world microservices

In previous chapters, we illustrated the **JSON Web Token** (**JWT**) and used that for a resource API authentication. If you remember, we wrote all of the code for this in a single module (though we used a different package) and violated the **single responsibility principle** (**SRP**). Needless to say, it was a monolith service. We were then able to familiarize ourselves with the problems encountered with the monolith. Let's split this monolith into small microservices, as follows:

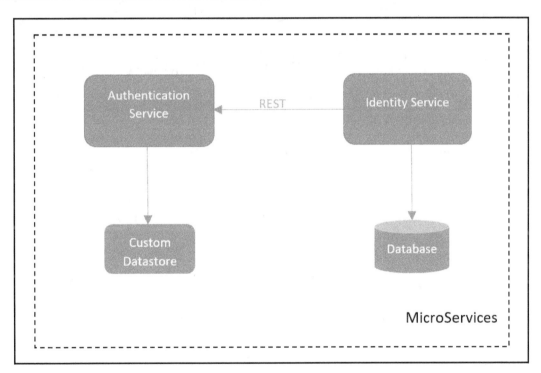

We will create two modules in a Maven project and these modules represent the microservices—one authentication service and one identity service. The authentication service will have the APIs for JWT, and identity service APIs are used to create identities, such as a person or an organization. All the APIs of the identity service require a valid JWT token obtained using the authentication service.

So let's start by creating a Maven project. The Maven project that we created looks like the following screenshot:

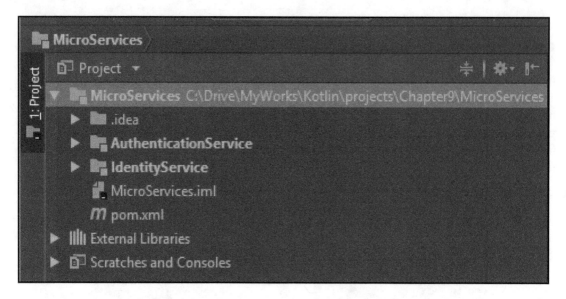

As we can see, this project has a parent module called **MicroServices** and two child modules—an **AuthenticationService** and an **IdentityService**.

All authentication- and authorization-related APIs go into the authentication service, while the identity APIs go into the identity service. Consequently, the API that issues a JWT is part of an authentication service and we will add an API to validate the JWT in the same module. Note that earlier we used the code directly to validate the JWT from the filter of the service. Now we provide an API so that the other services can consume it as a REST API.

For demonstration purposes, we create two APIs in the **Authentication Service**—the `/authorize/jwt/token` API to issue a jwt token, and the `/authorize/jwt/verify-token` API to verify the validity of the issued token:

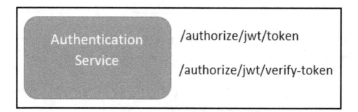

In the **Identity Service**, we will create the CRUD operations for organizations and person identities, and we will protect these APIs with jwt APIs. This means we will use the `/authorize/jwt/verify-token` API of the authentication service from the identity service. **Identity Service** is represented in the following diagram:

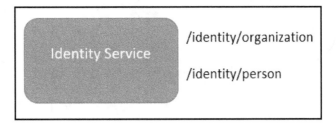

We will look into the details of these services in the next section and write the test cases for them.

Developing the microservices

Let's write some code to implement the APIs and see how the services can talk to each other over the REST. Then, we will learn how we can use Kotlin to develop these services and understand how easy it is to implement an API and to write a test case again using Kotlin. Importantly, we will look at the exception-handling code in Kotlin and how to handle exceptions for the APIs that we are going to implement.

Developing the authentication service

As previously mentioned, the authentication service will have two APIs—one for issuing a JWT token following authentication of the user, and another to check the validity of the issued JWT token.

First, let's add the following dependencies to the authentication service:

```
<dependency>
    <groupId>org.jetbrains.kotlin</groupId>
    <artifactId>kotlin-stdlib-jdk8</artifactId>
    <version>${kotlin.version}</version>
</dependency>
<dependency>
    <groupId>org.jetbrains.kotlin</groupId>
    <artifactId>kotlin-test</artifactId>
    <version>${kotlin.version}</version>
    <scope>test</scope>
```

```xml
        </dependency>

        <dependency>
            <groupId>com.sun.jersey</groupId>
            <artifactId>jersey-server</artifactId>
            <version>${jersey-server}</version>
        </dependency>
        <dependency>
            <groupId>com.sun.jersey</groupId>
            <artifactId>jersey-json</artifactId>
            <version>${jersey-json}</version>
        </dependency>
        <dependency>
            <groupId>com.sun.jersey</groupId>
            <artifactId>jersey-client</artifactId>
            <version>${jersey-client}</version>
        </dependency>

        <dependency>
            <groupId>javax.servlet</groupId>
            <artifactId>javax.servlet-api</artifactId>
            <version>${javax.servlet-api}</version>
        </dependency>
        <dependency>
            <groupId>javax.annotation</groupId>
            <artifactId>javax.annotation-api</artifactId>
            <version>${javax.annotation-api}</version>
        </dependency>
        <dependency>
            <groupId>javax.enterprise</groupId>
            <artifactId>cdi-api</artifactId>
            <version>${javax.enterprise.cdi.api}</version>
        </dependency>

        <dependency>
            <groupId>org.glassfish.soteria</groupId>
            <artifactId>javax.security.enterprise</artifactId>
            <version>${org.glassfish.soteria}</version>
        </dependency>
        <dependency>
            <groupId>org.glassfish</groupId>
            <artifactId>javax.security.auth.message</artifactId>
            <version>${javax.security.auth.message}</version>
        </dependency>

        <dependency>
            <groupId>io.jsonwebtoken</groupId>
            <artifactId>jjwt</artifactId>
```

```
        <version>${jjwt}</version>
    </dependency>
    <dependency>
        <groupId>com.auth0</groupId>
        <artifactId>java-jwt</artifactId>
        <version>${java-jwt}</version>
    </dependency>
```

Then, let's add the following packages to the **AuthenticationService**:

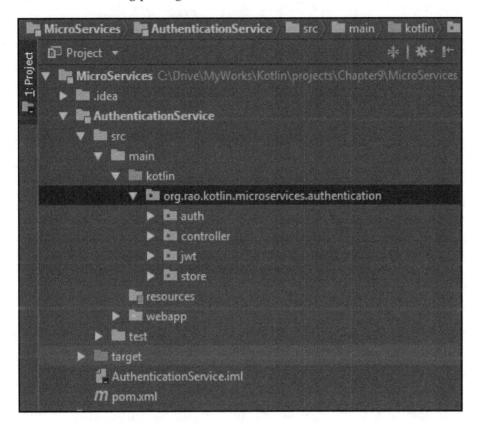

The `store` package is for the custom identity store that we explained earlier and this will be used for authentication. The `jwt` package will have the code construct for issuing and verifying the JWT. The authentication mechanism classes, which are used to interact with the data store, go into the `auth` package, while the controller will have the APIs that are exposed over the REST.

Implementing the /authorize/jwt/token API

Let's write a skeleton of the controller class:

1. Create an `AuthenticationController` class. The `@Path` annotation is used in the `AuthenticationController` class. `@Path` is from the jersey library, and this annotation maps the URI with `/authorize` to this class.

2. Inject `CustomAuthMechanism` and `HttpMessageContext`, which will be used with `AuthMechanism` to authenticate the user's credentials.

3. Create a function called `issueJwt()` with the `@Path` annotation. This maps the URI with `/authorize/jwt/token` to the `issueJwt()` function:

```
@Path("/authorize")
class AuthenticationController {

    @Inject
    private lateinit var customAuthMechanism: CustomAuthMechanism

    private val httpMessageContextImpl: HttpMessageContextImpl =
            HttpMessageContextImpl(CallBackHandlerImpl(),
MessageInfoImpl(), Subject())

    @POST
    @Path("/jwt/token")
    @Produces(MediaType.APPLICATION_JSON)
    fun issueJwt(@Context httpServletRequest: HttpServletRequest,
                 @Context httpServletResponse:
HttpServletResponse): Response {
        }
```

4. The `issueJwt()` function takes `httpServletRequest` and `httpServletResponse` as parameters. Let's add code to validate the user's credentials coming in via the request and to create a `jwt` token. The `issueJwt()` implementation looks as follows:

```
fun issueJwt(@Context httpServletRequest: HttpServletRequest,
             @Context httpServletResponse: HttpServletResponse):
Response {
        val isValid =
customAuthMechanism.validateRequest(httpServletRequest,
httpServletResponse,
             httpMessageContextImpl)
        if (isValid == AuthenticationStatus.SUCCESS) {
            var jwt: String = createJwt("1234", "localhost", "subject",
900000L)
```

```
            var resBody: JSONObject = JSONObject("{\"JWT\":$jwt}")
            return
Response.status(Response.Status.OK).entity(resBody).build()
        } else {
            return
Response.status(Response.Status.UNAUTHORIZED).entity("invalid
credentials").build()
        }
    }
```

Following a successful authentication, the createJwt() function will be invoked, creating the jwt token. Note that the expiry time is set to 900000L, which is equivalent to 15 minutes. The code for the createJwt() and validateRequest() functions is the same as we discussed in Chapter 9, *Securing JAVA EE Applications with Kotlin*. The jwt token will be wrapped around the JSONObject and a response with status code 200 will be returned. If the passed credentials are invalid, a response with status code 401 will be returned.

Let's verify this behavior with the following curl command:

```
curl -X POST \
    http://localhost:8080/authentication-service/authorize/jwt/token \
    -H 'Accept: application/json' \
    -H 'Content-Type: application/json' \
    -H 'UserId: testUser' \
    -H 'Password: ************'
```

This gives the following output:

```
Connected to localhost (::1) port 8080 (#0)
POST /authentication-service/authorize/jwt/token HTTP/1.1
User-Agent: curl/7.38.0
Host: localhost:8080
Accept: application/json
Content-Type: application/json
UserId: testUser
Password:

HTTP/1.1 200
Content-Type: application/json
Transfer-Encoding: chunked
Date: Sun, 02 Sep 2018 14:06:34 GMT

[data not shown]
00   207    0    207     0     0   2202     0 --:--:-- --:--:-- --:--:--  2653{"JWT":"eyJhbGciOiJIUzI1NiJ9.eyJqdGkiOiIxMjM0IiwiaWF0IjoxNTM1ODk3MTk0LCJzdWIiOiJ
dWIxMjMiLCJpc3MiOiJsb2NhbGhvc3QiLCJhdWQiOiIvand0Odg9rZW4iLCJleHAiOjE1MzU4OTgwOTR9.S15gRTUnA9_DI3rT1sfXio-uHGCPxP7K#MXbxQ4QvOE"}
```

The /authorize/jwt/token API responds with the JWT token.

Let's invoke the API with invalid credentials. This will give us the `401` status code:

```
Connected to localhost (::1) port 8080 (#0)
POST /authentication-service/authorize/jwt/token HTTP/1.1
User-Agent: curl/7.38.0
Host: localhost:8080
Accept: application/json
Content-Type: application/json
UserId: testUser
Password: testUserPass1

HTTP/1.1 401
Content-Type: application/json
Transfer-Encoding: chunked
Date: Sun, 02 Sep 2018 14:22:27 GMT

[data not shown]
00    19    0    19    0    0    202    0 --:--:-- --:--:-- --:--:--    243invalid credentials
```

Implementing the /authorize/jwt/verify-token API

Similar to the `issueToken()` function, we create a function called `verifyToken()` with the `@Path` annotation in the `AuthenticationController` class. This maps the URI with `/authorize/jwt/verify-token` to the `verifyToken()` function:

```
@POST
@Path("/jwt/verify-token")
@Produces(MediaType.APPLICATION_JSON)
fun verifyToken(@Context httpServletRequest: HttpServletRequest,
            @Context httpServletResponse: HttpServletResponse): Response
{

    var header: String = httpServletRequest.getHeader("Authorization")
    var token: String = extractJwtToken(header);

    val expiresIn:Long = verifyJwt(token)
    return Response.status(200).entity(JSONObject("{\"token\":\"active\","
+
            "\"expiresInSeconds\":$expiresIn }")).build()
}
```

The `verifyToken()` function takes servlet request and response objects. We extract the `Authorization` header from the request and verify the validity of the token using the `verifyJwt()` function. `verifyJwt()` will have the logic to check the token's validity.

Let's invoke the `/authorize/jwt/verify-token` API using cURL:

```
curl -X POST \
  http://localhost:8080/authentication-service/authorize/jwt/verify-token \
  -H 'Accept: application/json' \
  -H 'Content-Type: application/json' \
  -H 'Authorization: Bearer {{jwt}}'
```

This gives the following output:

```
{"token":"active","expiresInSeconds":1778}
```

We implemented two APIs, one for issuing a JWT token, and another to verify.

Developing the identity service

As we mentioned earlier, we will implement CRUD operations for the organization and person entities, and we will explain one flow of these operations here.

We will add the following mentioned dependencies to the identity service:

```
<dependency>
    <groupId>org.jetbrains.kotlin</groupId>
    <artifactId>kotlin-stdlib-jdk8</artifactId>
    <version>${kotlin.version}</version>
</dependency>
<dependency>
    <groupId>com.sun.jersey</groupId>
    <artifactId>jersey-server</artifactId>
    <version>${jersey-server}</version>
</dependency>
<dependency>
    <groupId>com.sun.jersey</groupId>
    <artifactId>jersey-json</artifactId>
    <version>${jersey-json}</version>
</dependency>
<dependency>
    <groupId>com.sun.jersey</groupId>
    <artifactId>jersey-client</artifactId>
    <version>${jersey-client}</version>
</dependency>
<dependency>
    <groupId>javax.servlet</groupId>
```

```xml
            <artifactId>javax.servlet-api</artifactId>
            <version>${javax.servlet-api}</version>
    </dependency>
    <dependency>
            <groupId>javax.enterprise</groupId>
            <artifactId>cdi-api</artifactId>
            <version>${cdi-api}</version>
    </dependency>

    <dependency>
            <groupId>org.hibernate.javax.persistence</groupId>
            <artifactId>hibernate-jpa-2.1-api</artifactId>
            <version>${hibernate-jpa}</version>
    </dependency>
    <dependency>
            <groupId>org.hibernate</groupId>
            <artifactId>hibernate-core</artifactId>
            <version>${hibernate-core}</version>
    </dependency>
    <dependency>
            <groupId>javax.persistence</groupId>
            <artifactId>javax.persistence-api</artifactId>
            <version>${javax.persistence-api}</version>
    </dependency>

    <dependency>
            <groupId>org.hibernate</groupId>
            <artifactId>hibernate-entitymanager</artifactId>
            <version>${hibernate-entitymanager}</version>
    </dependency>
    <dependency>
            <groupId>postgresql</groupId>
            <artifactId>postgresql</artifactId>
            <version>${postgresql}</version>
    </dependency>

    <dependency>
            <groupId>io.jsonwebtoken</groupId>
            <artifactId>jjwt</artifactId>
            <version>${jjwt}</version>
    </dependency>
    <dependency>
            <groupId>com.auth0</groupId>
            <artifactId>java-jwt</artifactId>
            <version>${java-jwt}</version>
    </dependency>
```

We will add the following packages to the identity service:

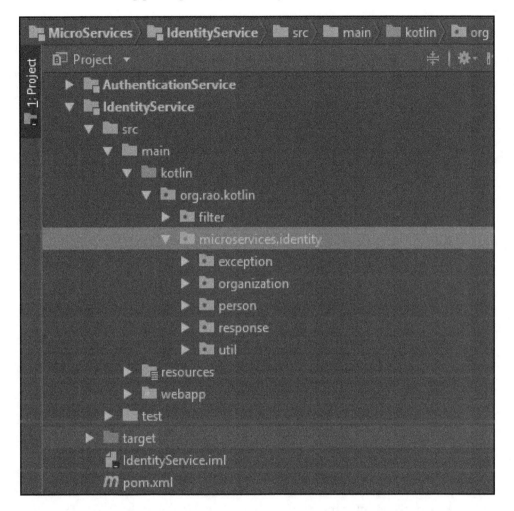

The exception package will have the classes for handling the exceptions in the module, while the response package will have general response classes, util for some constants and utility functions, and the organization and person packages will hold all the classes related to the operations of these entities.

These `organization` and `person` packages include other sub-packages, shown as follows:

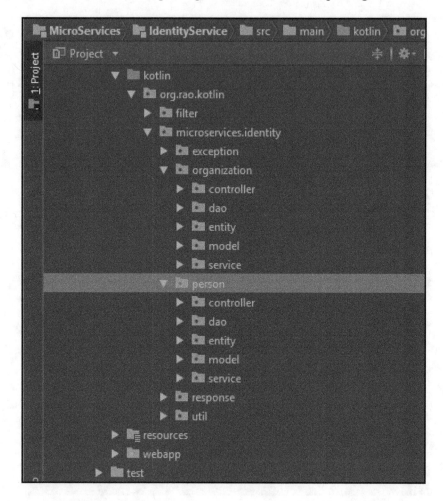

The `controller` package is for the classes that expose APIs over the REST. The `service` package holds service classes that connect the `controller` and `dao` classes and executes mapping of types that the `controller` and `dao` implementations can understand. The `model` package holds the request and response classes that are used at the API boundary, while the `entity` package includes the classes for mapping the entities to the table in the database. These are used by the dao layer. The `dao` package will have the classes that interact with the database and we use JPA entity manager for this. Note that this layered structure is mvc-based and repeated for the `organization` and `person` entities for the separation of concerns.

The `filter` package is common to these entities and will have logic to intercept the request to validate the JWT that is passed in the request header. It performs the validation by invoking the `/authorize/jwt/validate-token` API of the authentication service as a REST call.

Let's look at the create organization flow. This will give an understanding of the flow of control around these classes in different packages.

The controller code appears as follows:

```
@Path("/identity/organization")
class OrganizationController {
    @Inject
    private lateinit var serviceImpl: OrganizationServiceImpl

    @POST
    @Produces(MediaType.APPLICATION_JSON)
    fun createOrganization(organization: Organization): Response {
        try {
            var orgId: String =
serviceImpl.createOrganization(organization)
            var response: GenericResponse = GenericResponse()
            response.responseMessage = Constants.IDENTITY_CREATED
            return Response.status(Response.Status.CREATED)
                            .header("location", orgId)
                            .entity(response).build()
        } catch (e: IdentityAlreadyExistsException) {
            return sendErrorResponse(e.message!!,
Response.Status.CONFLICT.statusCode)
        } catch (e: IdentityException) {
            return sendErrorResponse(Constants.INTERNAL_SERVER_ERROR_MSG,
Response.Status
                    .INTERNAL_SERVER_ERROR.statusCode)
        }
    }
}
```

We inject the service class instance, `serviceImpl`, via the `@Inject` annotation, and we have the `@Path` annotation for mapping the request to this function and the class. Creating an organization is a post call, and the `createOrganization()` function takes the organization request that needs to be created. The `jersey` maps the request body to the organization parameter declared in the function. With this request, we pass the control to the service layer. The service layer returns `orgId` if it is created successfully, and this `orgId` will be included in the location header of the response object. A status code of `201` is then returned from the controller, indicating that the requested entity was created successfully in the system.

If the requested organization is already present, we will get `IdentityAlreadyExistsException` from the dao layer, this exception will be caught in our controller and sends a `409` conflict status code as response. In case of any other exception, we will send the error response. The `OrganizationServiceImpl` class implements the contract defined by the `OrganizationService` interface. The interface has declared the `createOrganization()` function and the implementing class provides the function definition. This is demonstrated by means of the following code:

```
class OrganizationServiceImpl : OrganizationService {
    @Inject
    private lateinit var organizationDao: OrganizationDaoImpl

    override fun createOrganization(organizationRequest: Organization):
String {
        var organizationEntity: OrganizationEntity =
OrganizationEntity(UUID.randomUUID().toString())
mapOrganizationToOrganizationEntity(organizationRequest,organizationEntity)

        var entity: OrganizationEntity =
organizationDao.createOrganization(organizationEntity)
        return entity.orgId
    }
}
```

The service class maps the request to the `entity` object and passes the control to the dao layer that is requesting to create the entity. From the service layer, an `orgId` is returned as a response if the organization is created.

The dao layer code looks as follows:

```
class OrganizationDaoImpl : OrganizationDao {

    private var entityManagerFactory =
Persistence.createEntityManagerFactory("local")
    private var entityManager = entityManagerFactory.createEntityManager()
```

```
      override fun createOrganization(organizationEntity: OrganizationEntity):
OrganizationEntity {
        try {
            entityManager.transaction.begin()

            entityManager.persist(organizationEntity)
            entityManager.transaction.commit()
            return organizationEntity
        } catch (exception: Exception) {
            if (exception is PersistenceException) {
                throw
IdentityAlreadyExistsException(Constants.IDENTITY_ALREADY_EXIST)
            } else {
                throw IdentityException(exception.message!!)
            }
        }
    }
```

We will load `EntityManagerFactory` from the persistence unit defined
in `persistence.xml`. We have defined the `postgresql` configuration in the XML file,
which we explained in `Chapter 5`, *Kotlin with JPA and EJB*.

Then we will create `entityManager` out of the `EntityManagerFactory` instance. We use
`entityManager` to interact with the database tables. The `createOrganization()`
function takes the organization entity. Using `entityManager`, a transaction will be started
and the entity will be persisted. When the transaction is committed, an entry will be made
in the organization table.

If the entity is already present, we will get `PersistenceException`, which we wrap into
`IdentityAlreadyExistsException`. In case of any other exceptions, that will be
wrapped inside `IdentityException`, which is handled by the controller layer.

 The other CRUD operations follow the same MVC model and the
complete implementation is available in the code repository.

The flow diagram

As depicted in the following flow diagram, the first user gets a token and then invokes the `/identity` APIs. The filter intercepts the request, takes the token passed in the request header, and validates it against the `/authorize/jwt/verify-token` API. If the token is valid and has not expired, it passes the control to the controller. Based on the request URI and the request method, the request is mapped to create, update, get, or delete functions defined in the **Controller**, and the **Client** request will be fulfilled by the **Server**:

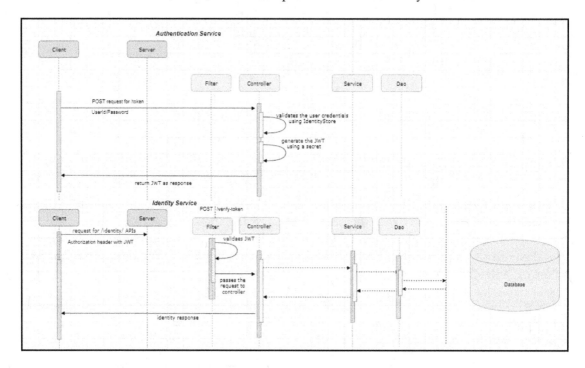

Exception handling

We have already seen how the dao layer throws the exception, and how the controller layer handles that exception and returns a proper error message to the requesting client. Let's quickly see the details of the exception-handling code.

We can create our own exception class, which we can use in our business cases as appropriate.

To create an exception class, we need to extend either the `Exception` or `Throwable` class, shown as follows:

```
class IdentityNotFoundException(message: String) : Exception(message) {

}
```

Alternatively, we can use the following code:

```
class IdentityNotFoundException(message: String) : Throwable(message) {

}
```

As shown in the preceding code, the custom exception class has to be inherited from either the `Throwable` or `Exception` class, and invoke its parent class constructor. To invoke the parent class constructor in Java, we can use the `super` or `this` keyword. In Kotlin, these keywords do not exist.

An exception type can be created without a constructor or an error message, as follows:

```
class IdentityException() :Throwable() {

}
```

An exception can be thrown using the `throw` keyword and an error message:

```
throw IdentityNotFoundException("Requested Identity not found")
```

The code can handle the exception using the `try...catch` block:

```
try {
    //...
} catch (e: IdentityNotFoundException) {
    //...
}
```

We can also provide the `finally` block for closing the resource of any that we have opened in the `try` block, as follows:

```
try {
    //...
} catch (e: IdentityNotFoundException) {
    //...
}finally {
    //...
}
```

Writing test code for microservices

One of the key points of developing the software is to ease the verification process, thus improving the quality of the system. For any change in the code, we should also be in a position to identify the impacted test cases and re-verify those sets of test cases, thus improving the predictability in the system. Writing the test case for the services is important for maintaining the quality and hygiene of the system.

There are multiple ways of testing the services. We will discuss two commonly used approaches—unit testing and integration testing.

Unit testing

We use unit tests to verify the individual code components as an independent unit without any external dependencies, mocking all the dependencies required. When we say testing the unit, this refers to testing a class and its functions. The response of all the functions of different classes and third-party libraries, if any, has to be mocked. We will write the test case for that particular class only. Here, the focus is on covering the test cases for a single class.

Let's write a unit test for our `createPerson()` function in the `PersonController` class.

We add the following dependencies to our `identity-service` module with a test scope for the purpose of unit testing the code:

```
<dependency>
    <groupId>junit</groupId>
    <artifactId>junit</artifactId>
    <version>${junit}</version>
    <scope>test</scope>
</dependency>
<dependency>
    <groupId>org.mockito</groupId>
    <artifactId>mockito-core</artifactId>
    <version>${mockito-core}</version>
    <scope>test</scope>
</dependency>
```

Writing the skeleton for the test class

We use `MockitoJUnitRunner` to run the unit test. We inject the required dependencies, such as the `PersonController` and `PersonServiceImpl` instances, by mocking the classes. We mock the `ResponseBuilder` class. We also use the `@InjectMocks` annotation to inject the `serviceImpl` instance into the controller object. This is shown in the following code:

```
@RunWith(MockitoJUnitRunner::class)
  class CreatePersonTest {
    @InjectMocks
    private lateinit var controller: PersonController

    @Mock
    private lateinit var serviceImpl: PersonServiceImpl

    private var builder = mock(Response.ResponseBuilder::class.java)
}
```

Setting up the test data

In the `createPersonTest()` function, we create the request object of the `Person` type and initialize this with some test data values, shown as follows:

```
@Test
fun createPersonTest() {
      val createPersonRequest = mock(Person::class.java)
      createPersonRequest.name = "test user"
      createPersonRequest.loginId = "user@some.com"
      createPersonRequest.orgId = "123"
      val uuid = UUID.randomUUID().toString()
  }
```

Mocking the response

We then mock the response for the identity-creation operation:

```
val mockResponse = TestUtil.getResponseForIdentityCreation(uuid)
```

When the `createPerson()` function is invoked on the `serviceImpl` instance, a `uuid` will be returned:

```
`when`(serviceImpl.createPerson(createPersonRequest))
                    .thenReturn(uuid)
```

When the `build()` method of the `Response` class is invoked, the mocked response will be returned:

```
`when`(builder.build())
            .thenReturn(mockResponse)
```

We invoke `createPerson()` on the mocked controller instance:

```
controller.createPerson(createPersonRequest)
```

Writing the assertions

We assert for the response status, the response message, and the location header:

```
assertTrue(mockResponse.status == 201)
assertTrue(mockResponse.entity.toString() == Constants.IDENTITY_CREATED)
assertNotNull(mockResponse.metadata["location"])
```

The unit test appears as follows:

```
@RunWith(MockitoJUnitRunner::class)
class CreatePersonTest {
    @InjectMocks
    private lateiit var controller: PersonController

    @Mock
    private lateinit var serviceImpl: PersonServiceImpl

    private var builder = mock(Response.ResponseBuilder::class.java)

    @Test
    fun createPersonTest() {
        val createPersonRequest = mock(Person::class.java)
        createPersonRequest.name = "test user"
        createPersonRequest.loginId = "user@some.com"
        createPersonRequest.orgId = "123"
        val uuid = UUID.randomUUID().toString()

        val response = TestUtil.getResponseForIdentityCreation(uuid)

        `when`(serviceImpl.createPerson(createPersonRequest))
```

```
                    .thenReturn(uuid)
        `when`(builder.build())
                .thenReturn(response)

        controller.createPerson(createPersonRequest)

        assertTrue(response.status == 201)
        assertTrue(response.entity.toString() ==
Constants.IDENTITY_CREATED)
        assertNotNull(response.metadata["location"])
    }
}
```

Let's run this unit test:

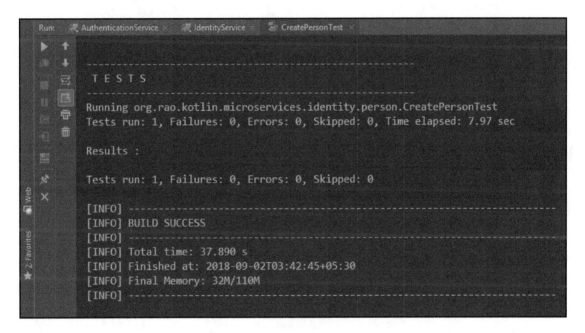

As we can see, this unit test case has executed successfully.

Integration testing

The purpose of integration testing—also known as **functional testing**—is to verify the system as a whole. This is also known as **black-box testing**. Throughout this process, we provide an input, expect the output, verify it, and don't worry about the internals of the code. We just give an input and compare the actual output against the expected one. This kind of testing is more suitable for verifying the RESTful APIs. Once the services are deployed, we make a call to the REST endpoints with an input and verify it for the HTTP status code, response body, response header (if any), and so on.

We will write a simple integration test for the GET organization API. Since this is an integration test case, the GET organization API is behind the `AuthFilter` that checks for a valid `JWT`. So, in our test case, first we have to get a `JWT` token using the `/authorize/jwt/token` API, and then invoke the `/identity/organization/{orgId}` API by passing the token in the request header.

Writing a REST client for the POST /authorize/jwt/token API

Let's write a simple REST client for getting a `JWT` token. We use the `Jersey` client to write our integration test case. This actually makes an API call and gets the response. We write the `getToken()` function, where we instantiate the `Jersey` client and invoke the API by passing the required headers, as follows:

```
fun getToken(): String {
    val client = Client.create()
    val webResource = client
.resource("http://localhost:8080/authentication-service/authorize/jwt/token
")

    val response = webResource
            .header("Accept", "application/json")
            .header("Content-Type", "application/json")
            .header("UserId", "testUser")
            .header("Password", "testUserPass")
            .post<ClientResponse>(ClientResponse::class.java)

    val responseBody = response.getEntity(String::class.java)
    return JSONObject(responseBody).get("JWT").toString()
}
```

Writing a REST client for the /identity/organization/{orgId} API

Let's write a REST client to invoke the GET organization API. This is similar to what we wrote in the getToken() function.

The getOrg() function takes the jwt token as an input parameter, which will be passed as a request header in the /identity/organization/{orgId} API. AuthFilter checks for the validity of the token. We then create a Jersey client instance, invoke the API and return the response, as shown in the following code:

```kotlin
fun getOrg(jwt: String):JSONObject {

    val client = Client.create()
    val orgId: UUID = "9dc30f1e-fb0f-48c1-bccb-f6d89f5e1108"
    val webResource = client
.resource("http://localhost:8090/identity-service/identity/organization/org
Id")

    val response = webResource
            .accept("application/json")
            .header("Authorization", "Bearer $jwt")
            .get<ClientResponse>(ClientResponse::class.java)

    val responseBody= response.getEntity(String::class.java)
    return JSONObject(responseBody)
}
```

Writing the assertions

Now, let's assert the response by invoking the getOrg() function by passing the token returned from the getToken() function:

```kotlin
@Test
fun testGetOrg() {
    var response = getOrg(getToken())
    assertNotNull(response)
    assertNotNull(response.get("orgName"))
    assertNotNull(response.get("orgId"))
}
```

Let's run this test case and see what happens:

As we can see, this integration test is able to invoke the APIs, and then the assertions are passed.

Refactoring the integration test cases

Let's refactor the integration test code that we wrote by removing some duplicates and hardcoded string values.

Note that the code for creating the `Jersey` client and invoking the API is the same for the `getToken()` and `getOrg()` functions. Consequently, we will create a new function that takes the URI and headers and an HTTP method type:

```kotlin
private fun execute(resourceUri: String, map: Map<String, String>,
httpMethod: String):
        JSONObject {
    val client = Client.create()
    val webResource = client.resource(resourceUri)
            .accept(MediaType.APPLICATION_JSON)
    for (entry in map) {
        webResource.header(entry.key, entry.value)
    }
```

```
    val response: ClientResponse = webResource
            .method(httpMethod, ClientResponse::class.java)

    val responseBody = response.getEntity(String::class.java)

    return JSONObject(responseBody)
}
```

Now, the `getToken()` and `getOrg()` function definitions become concise. At this point, we prepare the headers, use the proper resource URIs, and then invoke the `execute()` function, which, in turn, invoke the APIs, as follows:

```
private fun getToken(): JSONObject {

    var headers = HashMap<String, String>()
    headers.put(HttpHeaders.ACCEPT, MediaType.APPLICATION_JSON)
    headers.put(HttpHeaders.CONTENT_TYPE, MediaType.APPLICATION_JSON)
    headers.put(USERID_HEADER, USERID)
    headers.put(PASS_HEADER, PASS)

    return execute("$AUTHENTICATION_SERVICE_URL$TOKEN_API", headers,
HttpMethod.POST)
}

private fun getOrg(jwt: String, orgId: String): JSONObject {
    var headers = HashMap<String, String>()
    headers.put(HttpHeaders.AUTHORIZATION, "Bearer $jwt")
    return execute("$IDENTITY_SERVICE_URL$ORGANIZATION_API" + orgId,
            headers, HttpMethod.GET)
}
```

Then we assert the response in our test case:

```
@Test
fun testGetOrg() {
    val jwt = getToken().get("JWT").toString()

    val response = getOrg(jwt, "123")

    assertNotNull(response)
    assertNotNull(response.get(ORG_NAME))
    assertNotNull(response.get(ORG_ID))
}
```

This is how we write the test cases. If we now change anything in our code (for example, the status code of an API), the test case will fail. However, we can fix this at an early stage before the code goes to the production environment, ensuring that the quality of the product to be delivered is acceptable.

Summary

In this chapter, we discussed the following:

- A brief introduction to microservices. We described what microservices are and the benefits of using the microservice architecture style.
- What monolith services are and the various problems with this style of architecting the system.
- Microservice architecture.
- Developing the authentication service and identity service.
- Implementing APIs for issuing and verifying a JWT.
- Implementing CRUD operations for managing identities, such as organizations and people, as APIs in the identity service.
- Handling exceptions.
- The importance of writing test cases, and the test cases for the services that we developed.

10
Performance Monitoring and Logging

When we develop an application, we design it to function better by applying various design principles. In this context, it is also important to understand how the system behaves that we develop under different conditions. We also need to monitor the system to ensure that it is constantly available. Proper memory management and system monitoring are a vital part of the software life cycle and probably the longest stage in enterprise applications:

In this chapter, we will discuss the following:

- Different monitoring tools
- Detecting memory leaks
- Garbage collection
- Profiling

Technical requirements

We will discuss the different tools available for profiling and monitoring applications. Knowledge of the Java memory model is beneficial when it comes to understanding the concepts discussed in the chapter.

- We use jvisualvm, Java Mission Control
- Installing JProfiler is required

Finding Memory Leaks

Kotlin is a JVM-based language that has a garbage collector, which is a daemon thread that runs on the JVM and is responsible for automatic memory management. This reclaims the memory allocated to objects that are no longer referenced by the program running inside the VM. We will discuss more about garbage collector later in the chapter.

In execution, a program creates the objects required for the computation. Here, the memory is allocated for objects in the heap region. Once the program has finished using these objects, they are no longer needed by the program and it holds no reference to the objects that it has created. An object is garbage collected when it is no longer referenced by the program. A memory leak occurs when the program holds the reference to objects when they are not being used by it. Consequently, these objects are not eligible for garbage collection. This increases the program's memory usage, causing memory leaks in the system. If the program creates many such objects, the memory allocated for the system will become full, which may cause the system to crash. So, the program that we write is responsible for releasing object references when they are no longer needed.

There are monitoring tools available that help us to understand how memory is utilized in the system. If we see any abnormal behavior in memory usage, we can fix it and redeploy the services.

We will write a program to illustrate a memory leak and use `jvisualvm`, which comes with the JDK and is used for analyzing memory utilization. `jvisualvm` is available under the `{{path-to-jdk}}/bin` directory.

Let's write a simple program that creates a hashmap and goes on adding key-value pairs to it, and a statement to print in the console when an element is added to the map:

```
@JvmStatic
fun main(args: Array<String>) {
    try {
        val map = HashMap<MemoryLeakDemo, String>()
        while (true) {
            map[MemoryLeakDemo("myKey")] = "value"
            println("Element added to map")
        }
    } catch (e: Exception) {
        e.printStackTrace()
    }
}
```

The allocated memory for an entry in the map is no longer needed after it was added and printed in the console. While the program is running, we launch `jvisualvm` to monitor the memory. When `jvisualvm` starts up, we can see that the process that is running our code is already attached to `jvisualvm` and it shows the monitoring of that running program:

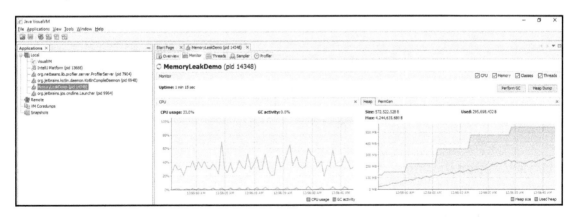

We can see from the preceding screenshot that the heap memory usage has already exceeded 200 MB and is growing. Once it reaches the upper limit and there is no memory left for objects to allocate, the program crashes with an `OutOfMemoryError` message. After crossing a certain limit before the program crashes, increasing the heap may appear to solve the problem, but eventually even that gets allocated and the program again runs out of memory. This is a clear indication that the program suffers from a memory leak problem.

There is also a sampler option in `jvisualvm` to indicate for what specific type of object the memory is being allocated. There is also an option to view the CPU usage, which is shown as follows:

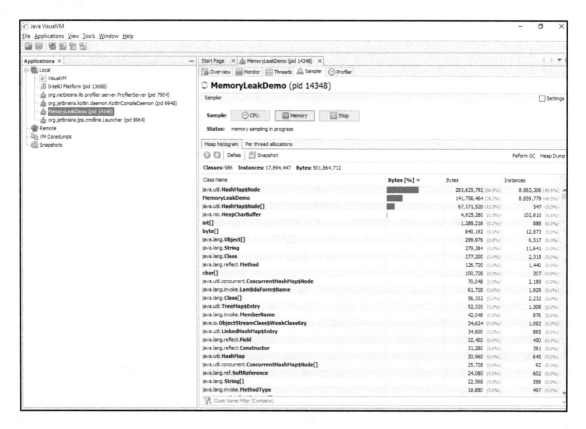

This shows that the majority of the memory is allocated to type `HashMap`, which is what our program is adding to. The program still holds the reference to the allocated objects, so it can never be reclaimed by the garbage collector. We see that the running `MemoryLeakDemo` thread, which is the class that we wrote, constantly adds to the memory. This an example of a memory leak. The `jvisualvm` tool helps to analyze the memory leak.

When we are developing a large system and check to see how memory is being utilized in order to identify any memory leaks, we can use `jvisualvm`. If we see a memory leak in the code, we now have a chance to fix it.

Application monitoring

Monitoring services is a key aspect in keeping track of system resource usage and the application's health. When the service or application is unresponsive or not working as expected, if the system's CPU usage is high or it is taking too long to respond to a request, monitoring helps troubleshoot issues. Application monitoring helps us understand CPU usage and other system resources. The result of the monitoring can be used to make decisions such as scaling services or notifying system administrators so that they can take appropriate actions.

We will discuss some of the popular monitoring tools to analyze a system's CPU and memory.

Java Mission Control

Java Mission Control (JMC) is a tool that is used for monitoring and profiling Java-based applications. We can use JMC for Kotlin applications as well. JMC consists of **Java Flight Recorder (JFR)** and the JMX console. JFR is a profiling tool that collects JVM runtime information, whereas the JMX console is a monitoring tool that presents the JVM data about CPU usage, memory, and garbage collection activities.

Let's explore how to use JMC to perform a recording of the CPU and other resource usage. Then, we will analyze the recorded information for resource utilization.

Consider the program that was used to illustrate the memory leak. This creates an empty `HashMap` with the default initial capacity(16) and then goes on adding key-value pairs to it, and prints a statement to the console to the effect that an element has been added to the map. This is shown with the following code:

```
@JvmStatic
fun main(args: Array<String>) {
    try {
        val map = HashMap<MemoryLeakDemo, String>()

        while (true) {
            map[MemoryLeakDemo("myKey")] = "value"
            println("Element added to map")
```

```
        }
    } catch (e: Exception) {
        e.printStackTrace()
    }
}
```

We need to set the `FlightRecorder` flag while starting the application. To do this, we need to set the following VM option:

```
-XX:+UnlockCommercialFeatures -XX:+FlightRecorder
```

The following screenshot is the output of the preceding code:

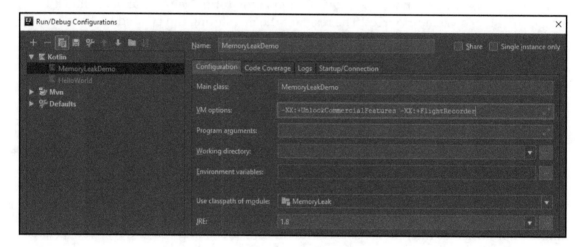

Start the application and then open the JMC, which is in the `bin` directory of the JDK. When it starts up, it looks like this:

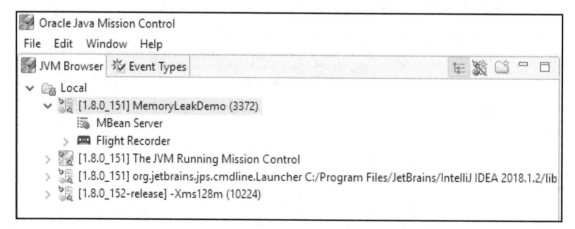

Note that this has already been attached to our Kotlin application. Now, we need to start recording the resource utilization using the **Flight Recorder**. We will record the data for five minutes while the application is running.

Once it has recorded the events, we can analyze the results as follows:

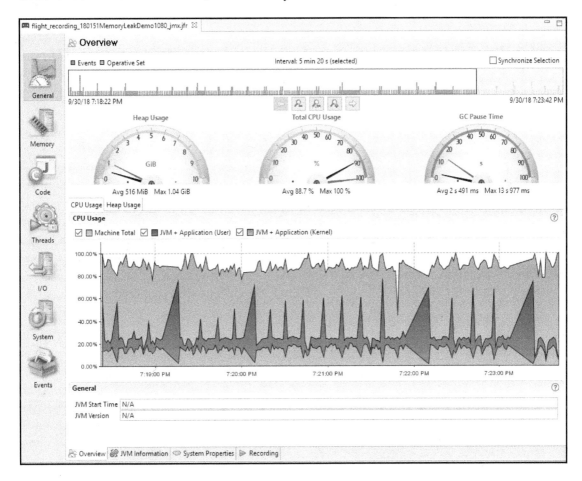

As we can see, the flight recorder has captured a lot of details and provided a summary of events. We can see that CPU usage is high; it has reached almost 80%. There is also a **Heap Usage** tab, which shows how much heap memory is consumed. The following screenshot shows this:

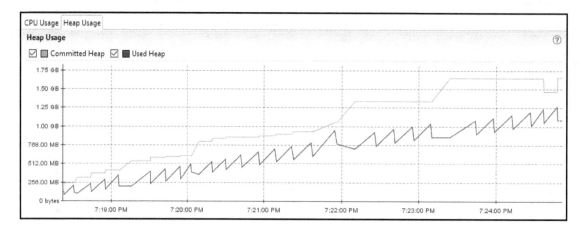

There is also a code section, which shows which class in the application has consumed the most memory. This section shows the memory consumption for the different classes in the application. The following screenshot shows this:

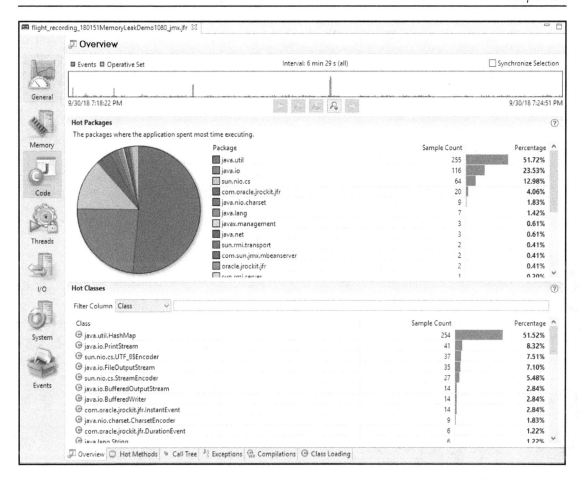

In this case, we can see from the recorded events that we are adding a `HashMap`.

The memory column shows how memory is used, capturing garbage collection information. The following screenshot shows this:

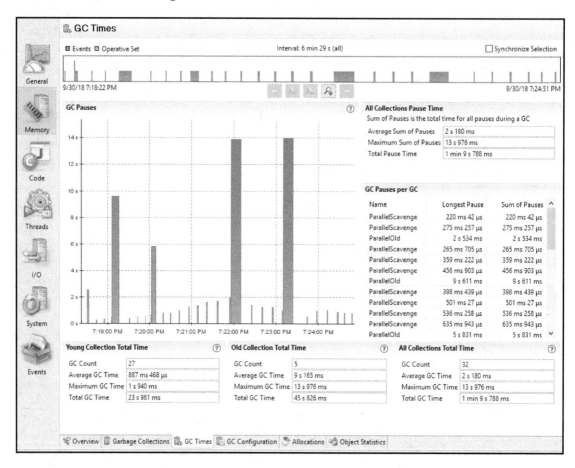

This shows **GC Times**, the application pause time during the GC event, details about the younger generation GC, the older generation GC, the GC count, and so on.

There is also a **Threads** section, which shows a list of threads running in the application. This shows the thread state and latency in thread executions, stating whether they are running, blocked, waiting, and so on. This is useful when monitoring concurrent applications.

 Until OpenJDK 10, JMC was not part of the OpenJDK. Instead, it was included in the Oracle JDK from version 7u40 and was a commercial tool used for monitoring and profiling Java-based applications. In Oracle JDK 11, JMC is removed and made available as a separate package, which is compatible with both OpenJDK and Oracle JDK. The open-source version was an early access build when this book was being written.

JMX is a powerful tool for monitoring applications. The data captured through this tool gives a lot of detailed information about the system's resource usage.

Java VisualVM

Java VisualVM (`jvisualvm`) is another tool that can be used for application monitoring. `jvisualvm` is useful for debugging memory and performance-related issues. It also provides a graphical representation of the runtime information captured. We already used `jvisualvm` to find a memory leak in the application.

Garbage collection

For programming languages that run on JVM such as Kotlin, Java, and so on, JVM automatically manages the memory. In our programs, we don't have to explicitly allocate and deallocate memory. In languages such as C and C++, it is the responsibility of programs to manage memory. This can become difficult when an application becomes big and could be erroneous when it has to manage memory explicitly.

Automatic garbage collection makes life easier, as the program doesn't need to handle memory in this case. JVM's garbage collector manages memory, allocating it to the objects that the program creates. It then reclaims it when these objects are no longer referenced by the program so that the memory becomes available to other objects in the application.

Automatic garbage collection reduces a lot of overhead that the program would have otherwise created in order to manage the memory that it uses during execution. The program doesn't have to worry about cleaning up objects that it uses, as the garbage collection handles this automatically.

There are two kinds of memory serving a program—stack and heap memory. Stack memory is used for storing temporary and local variables which are created by the functions. Heap memory is used for allocating the memory to objects at runtime.

Whenever we create an object, the memory for it is allocated in the heap memory and the reference variable that points to the object is stored in the stack memory or the heap memory, or it can be a local variable in the program context.

Consider the following small program to understand how an object is created and how it is referenced in the program:

```
object GCExample{
    internal fun foo() {
        val userList = ArrayList<Any>()
    }

    @JvmStatic
    fun main(args: Array<String>) {
        val obj = Any()
        val name: String = "test"
        foo()
    }
}
```

The simple class that we created has a main() function and a foo() function. These functions create some objects while in execution. The main() function creates an object of type Any and a variable of type String, which is initialized to the value *test*. The foo() function creates a userList, which is an ArrayList type.

Let's see the memory allocations for these objects:

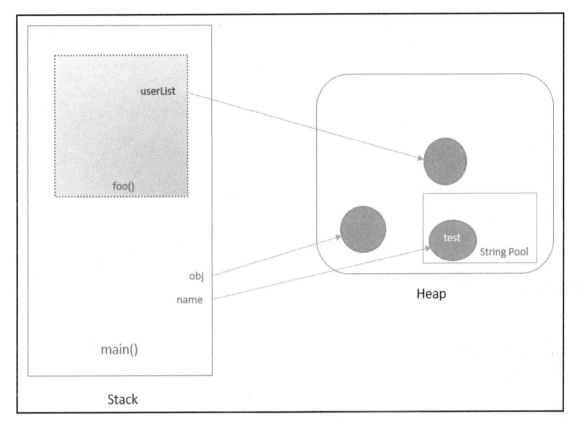

As shown in the preceding screenshot, the memory for objects is allocated in the heap memory and the references to these objects are maintained in the stack. Note that the `foo()` function has a separate stack for it. String literals are created in the pool and are reused. If we say `String ("test")`, then separate memory is allocated for it; it is outside **String Pool** and not reused by other references. Each time `String ("test")` is used, new memory is allocated in the heap area.

These objects stay in memory as long as the program holds the reference. When the program completes its execution, the references that were made to these objects are no longer reachable and objects on the heap are eligible for garbage collection. When the garbage collector runs, it reclaims the heap memory that is no longer needed by the program.

Memory model

In the Java memory model, the heap memory is divided into a young generation and old generation. The old generation is also known as **tenured**:

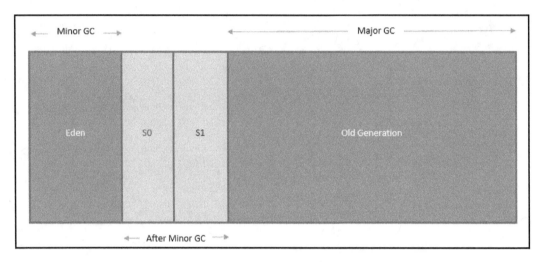

The young generation consists of **Eden** and Survivor spaces (**S0** and **S1**) and takes up about 40% of the heap memory, while the **Old Generation** takes up about 60% of the memory.

When the program creates an object, it is created in the **Eden** space first. When the **Eden** space is filled up, the partial GC runs, marks the objects that are still referenced, and cleans up the objects in the young generation that are no longer reachable by the program. The following diagram depicts this:

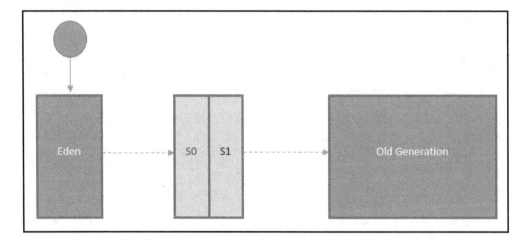

The objects that survive during the partial GC in the **Eden** space are now promoted to the Survivor space of the young generation. When the **Eden** space is filled up again, the partial GC runs and reclaims the memory for the objects that are no longer referenced. Any objects that survive during this GC are promoted to the **Old Generation**.

When the old generation fills up, the full garbage collection runs on the heap memory and deletes the objects that are no longer needed, keeping objects that are referenced by the program. The objects that are likely to live for a long time are moved to the old generation so that the partial GC doesn't have to clean up objects that are still referenced by the program.

Types of garbage collector

There are two types of garbage collectors:

- Serial/Parallel garbage collectors
- Concurrent collectors

The following diagram depicts garbage collectors:

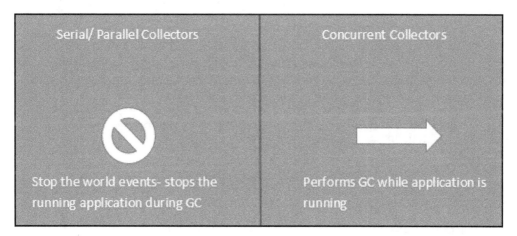

Serial and parallel collectors

Serial/parallel garbage collectors are *stop-the-world events*, meaning that they will stop all running application threads and perform the GC. Once this is done, collectors resume the application threads. While the GC runs, the application pauses for that time.

The difference between serial and parallel garbage collectors is that serial garbage collectors are single-threaded and parallel ones are multithreaded. When these collectors are running, the application will stop for that time.

Serial and parallel garbage collectors pause the application while they run GC, and the parallel collector is the default collector. These collectors work better for smaller heaps as it is quicker to clean them and stop the application while reclaiming the memory. With a smaller heap, the application pauses as the GC runs, is likely to be shorter, and mostly goes unnoticed.

Concurrent collectors

Concurrent collectors don't pause an application when they run. Instead, they reclaim the memory while the application is running.

There are two variants of concurrent collectors—concurrent mark-sweep (CMS) and G1 GC (Garbage First). G1 GC now replaces the CMS, and G1 GC cleans the old generation concurrently when the application is running. There are still some pauses while G1 GC runs to ensure consistency, but these are much shorter than the full GC that runs with a parallel collector.

The pauses in the concurrent collectors include the mark and remark phases. When GC starts, there is a pause for the initial marking of the objects and then again for the unused objects that are claimed from memory while the application is running. After this, there will be a small pause again at the end for remarking and cleanup.

Younger generation collectors are parallel by default and there is no way to make them concurrent.

Tuning the GC

Tuning the GC is not always required to achieve better performance or to reduce system downtime caused by any out-of-memory issues. The default settings are reasonable for reclaiming unused memory. The GC in the JVM is built to react to memory management adaptively. The GC is configured to run when the allocated memory reaches a certain threshold.

We can hint for the JVM to run GC programmatically using `System.gc()` or `Runtime.getRuntime().gc()`. However, it is up to the JVM to run the GC event. The `gc()` function is not guaranteed to run the GC.

The heap size can be specified using the following -Xms and -Xmx JVM options:

- -Xms is the heap area size when the JVM is starting
- -Xmx is the maximum heap size

JVM options can be used to set the GC types, as follows:

- -XX:+UseSerialGC is used to set the GC type to use serial GC collectors
- -XX:+UseParallelGC is used to set the GC type to use parallel collectors
- -XX:-UseConcMarkSweepGC is used to set the GC type to use concurrent mark-sweep collectors

When the application is running, there might be an out-of-memory-error. The reason for this might be that the application was allocated less memory or that it encountered a memory leak. Simply adding the memory seems to work, but this is not always the right solution. There will be a pause when GC is running, and this is not expected behavior for an application.

To address these issues, it's good to start with benchmarking, since tuning GC is not straightforward for the different memory problems that we face. While benchmarking, make small changes, measure the impact of each change, and repeat until you get the desired outcome. We can look for latency, throughput, and footprint while tuning for GC. Latency is the maximum individual pause time, throughput is the amount of time spent serving requests, and footprint is the size of the heap that we can tune for. The aim is to have high throughput and low latency in an application in order for it to perform better.

High throughput and low latency

In order to have maximum throughput and low latency, we need to use G1 GC and a large heap. When we have a large heap, a shorter pause time will lead to more time spent on serving the request, which is high throughput.

We use the -XX:+UseG1GC JVM option to indicate the JVM should use the G1 GC type.

High throughput and low footprint

If we need to have a small footprint and high throughput, then the best way to achieve that is to use a parallel collector and a small heap. In this case, what we have is a full garbage collection, which pauses the application for slightly longer in comparison to using G1 GC. This will allow the application to perform GC to claim the memory allocated to objects, but the application will pause while it performs GC. The pauses will be longer, but not as frequent. Consequently, we can still achieve more throughput while keeping the footprint low.

We use the -XX:+UseParallelGC JVM option to indicate that the JVM should use the parallel GC type.

Low pause time and small footprint

If we want low pause times and a smaller footprint then throughput will be lower. In this case, we have a lot of individual pauses that are very short. The pause time is split into smaller chunks, so it will go unnoticed.

The JVM manages these considerations for us. First, it tries to achieve low latency (that is, low pause times). If it achieves that, it next aims for throughput and more time spent serving requests. The JVM will increase the heap to the maximum specified in order to achieve high throughput.

Profiling

Profiling is another technique that is used to understand how the application behaves. In software engineering, profiling is a form of dynamic program analysis that measures various run-time performance parameters such as memory utilization, timing, control flow, and more.

Profiling is used to determine the time spent on each function when the application is running. Profiling tools gather runtime information and record resource utilization including memory, CPU usage, the time spent on functions, and so on. Profiling helps identify problems and looks at the code again to reevaluate the choice of data structures used to optimize for better application performance.

Different tools are available for profiling. Tools such as `jvisualvm`, `jstat`, JMC, JProfiler, and so on can be used for profiling applications.

Profiling with JProfiler

JProfiler is one of the most commonly used tools for profiling in enterprise applications. It is simple to use and integrated with IDEs such as Eclipse, IntelliJ Idea, and many more. It can be used to profile locally deployed applications or remote applications, and it also has support for profiling applications offline.

Let's launch JProfiler and attach the identity service application that we developed in `Chapter 9`, *Implementing Microservices with Kotlin*:

1. When **JProfiler** starts up, the start page is shown, as follows:

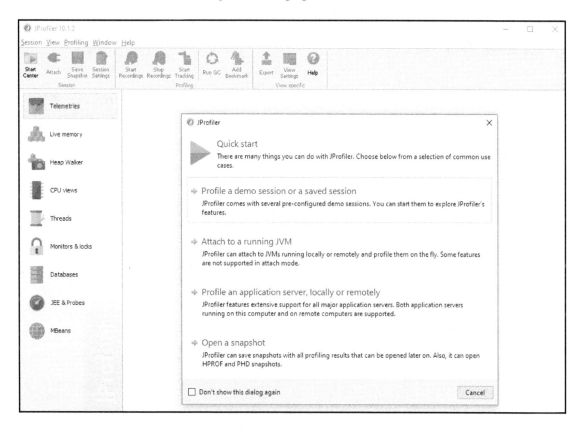

2. We will profile the get organization API of the identity service app.
3. Select the **Attach to a running JVM** option. This will list running Java processes. We select our identity service, which is running as follows:

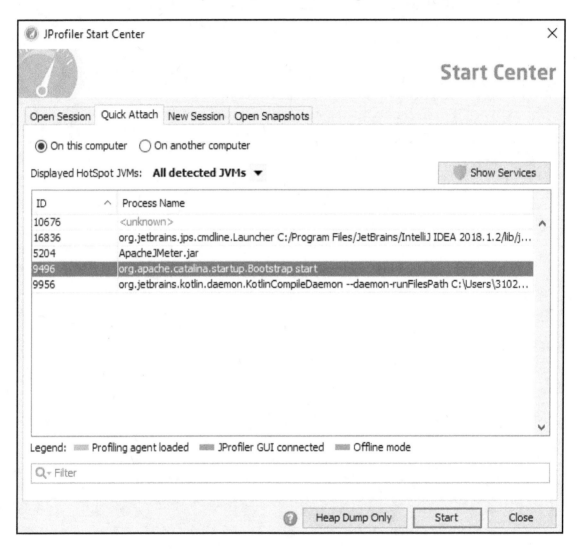

4. Then it prompts for initial profile settings. Here, we can select **Instrumentation** or **Sampling (Recommended)**. We choose **Sampling (Recommended)**:

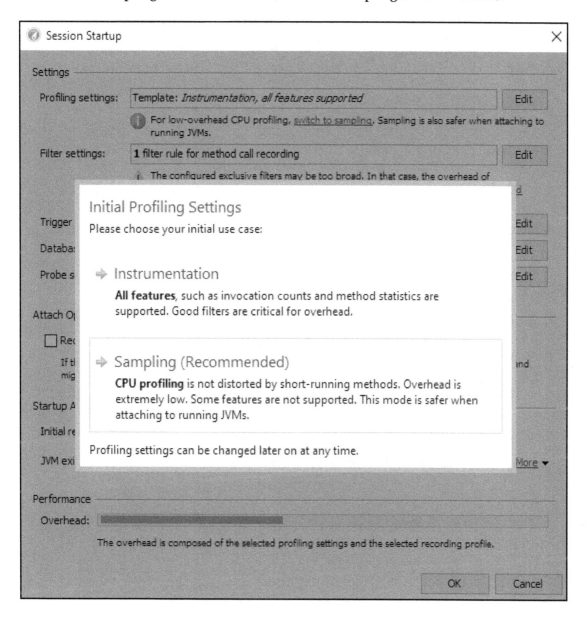

5. Then we select **CPU views** and elect to record CPU data, as follow. This starts to capture CPU recordings:

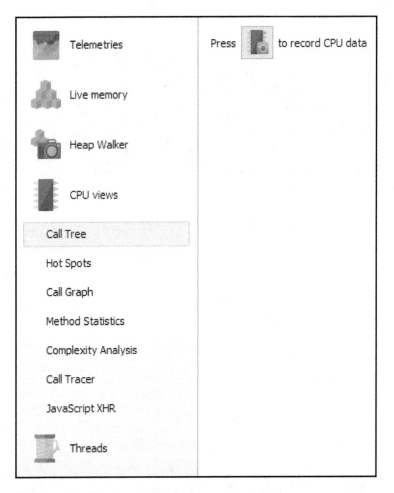

Now, let's execute a load test using Jmeter. We have created simple Jmeter scripts (JMX scripts) to invoke the REST APIs. At this point, we get the JWT token and access the get organization API. We then span five threads, which make concurrent requests to the identity service.

We run the tests for about 10 minutes and capture the CPU recordings. The function call breakdown is captured and shown as follows:

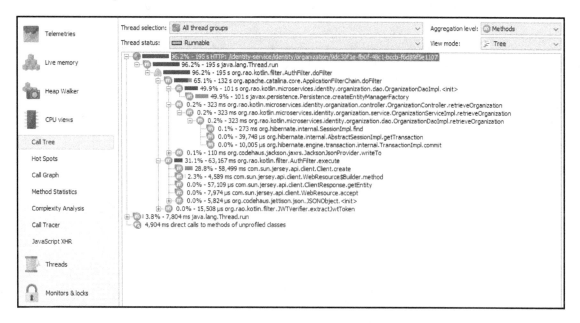

This breakdown shows how much time is spent on each function call.

As we can see, we have profiled a service written in Kotlin. Profiling helps identify performance bottlenecks in code.

Offline profiling

With JProfiler we can do offline profiling. We can do this for an application, save the result, and analyze it later. The key enabler for this offline profiling is triggered.

Firstly, we need to create a session and then add triggers to it; this will enable us to save recorded data, which can be used for analysis.

To create a session, perform the following steps:

1. Go to **Start Center** and select the **New Remote Integration** wizard, shown as follows:

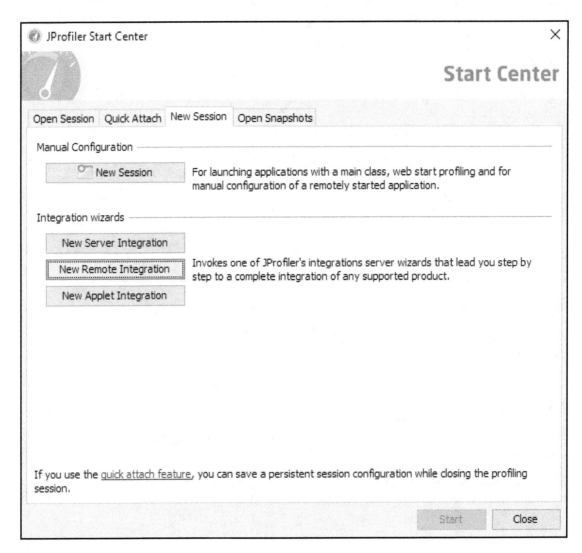

2. Select the JVM vendor and version, and then choose the profile offline option followed by **Finish**:

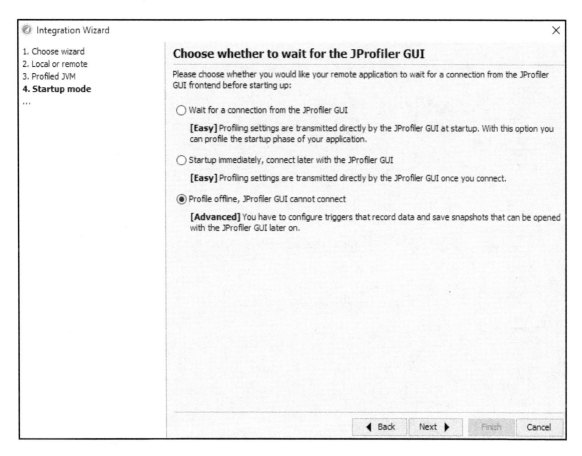

This has started the profiling session. We will now add a trigger to the session.

3. We have to create a session by selecting the running JVM, shown as follows:

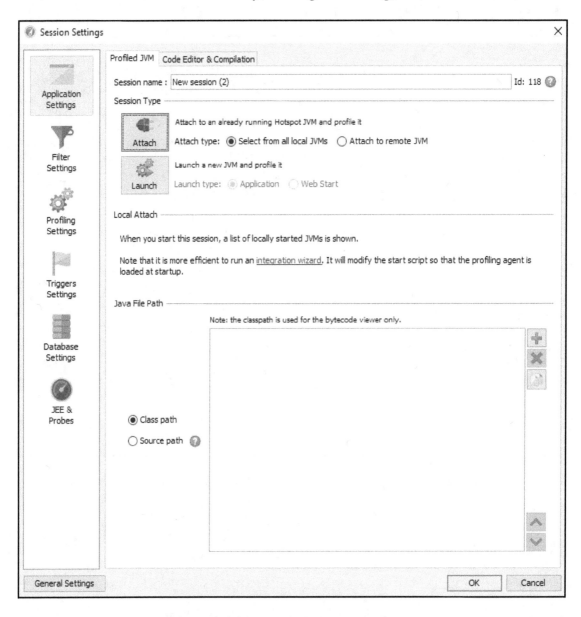

4. Now, click on **Trigger Settings** and add one or more triggers. A trigger is a list of actions that are executed when the defined condition becomes true. There are different trigger types to choose from in JProfiler:

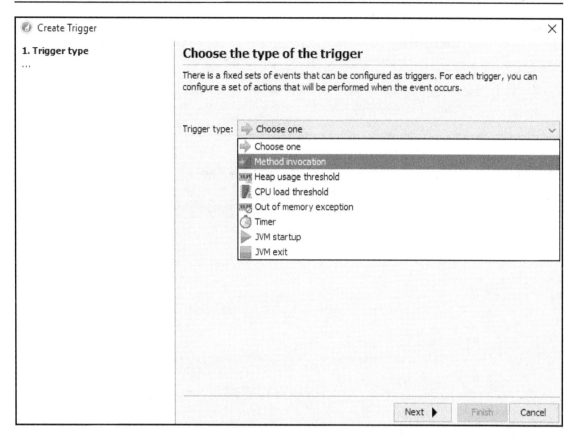

We have to select the appropriate **Trigger type** and define the action to be performed. We have the **Method invocation** trigger. Here, we can select a method of a class and define an action to be performed when the method is actually invoked. We have **Heap usage threshold** and **CPU load threshold**, where we can define an action to be taken when it crosses a certain threshold. There is one trigger for **Out of Memory exception**, which gets triggered when an application runs out of memory.

There is also a **Timer** trigger to perform some actions at regular intervals, as well as a JVM start and exit trigger, which is triggered during **JVM startup** and shutdown.

Let's see this in action. Say we want to record CPU usage whenever a call is made to the `issueJwt()` function defined in the `AuthenticationController` class, which we described in `Chapter 9`, *Implementing Microservices with Kotlin*:

1. In this case, we choose **Method invocation** as the trigger type and select the appropriate methods, as shown in the following screenshot:

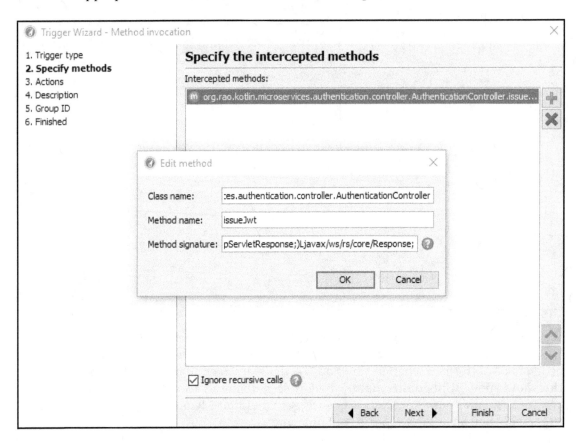

2. We can configure different methods or functions for the same set of actions:

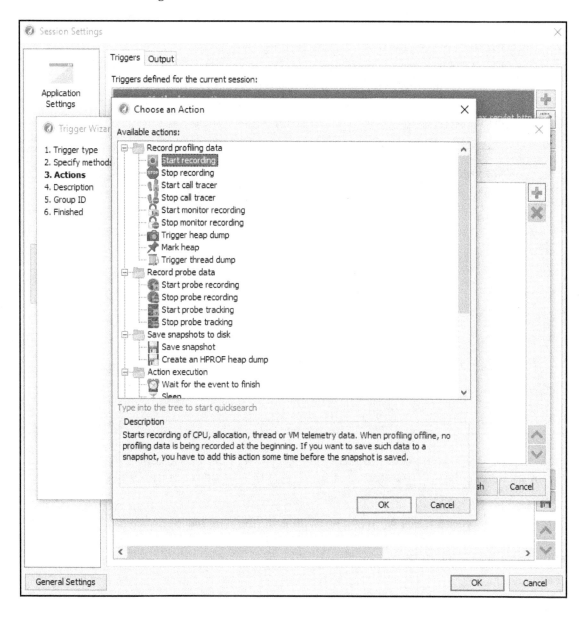

3. We will now select the **Start recording** option, where we will record CPU data, and click on **OK**.

4. Now, we have defined a trigger on a particular method invocation in the session that we created, by attaching the running application.

5. Using JMeter, we can now make continuous calls to the /authentication-service/authorize/jwt/token API, which will invoke the issueJwt() function in AuthenticationController. This automatically triggers the actions that we defined. The following screenshot shows this:

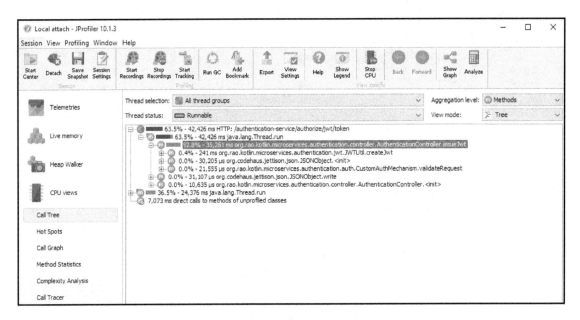

Note that we don't have to elect to record the CPU data manually after defining the trigger. When we invoke the API, it automatically triggers the recording of the CPU data for the function call.

Triggers are powerful tools. All we have to do is define which actions we have to perform on specific conditions. When the conditions become true, the actions will be triggered automatically.

Getting our real-world application production-ready

When developing services, we follow the concept of a microservice architecture and use design patterns to make the system flexible and reliable. However, there are a few points that we need to consider in order to make the system production ready. These are aimed at high availability and system performance. Let's discuss these points:

1. **Stability and reliability**: Stability and reliability are important to a system in order to make it production ready. Services tend to change and evolve over time. Any new code, any change in the existing code, and configuration changes should not break the existing functionality. Any changes in the system shouldn't result in reliability issues. Furthermore, no changes should result in instability in the system. Stability and reliability go hand in hand. To ensure the stability and reliability of the system, it is important to follow some standard practices when working through code and taking it to the end user.

   A standard development process is required so that the development of the system goes through a set of defined activities.

   Test cases play a vital role in ensuring the system's stability and reliability. It's important that the code is well tested. Writing unit test cases, integration test cases, system testing, and so on make the system reliable before it is used by an end user. The load testing and performance testing ensure the stability of the system under load and also ensure that the system is performant.

   A proper deployment pipeline ensures that any code that gets checked in goes through defined stages such as build, test, code quality checks, and so on:

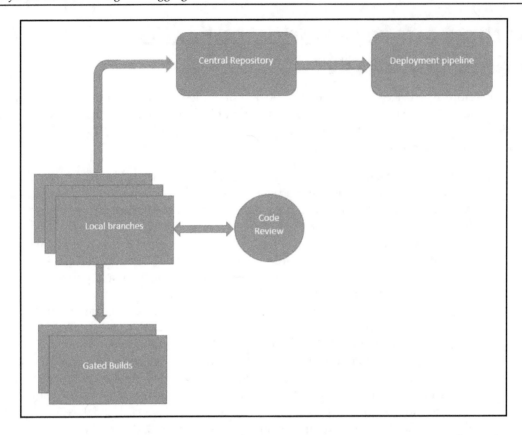

As shown in the preceding diagram, a central code repository is maintained. Developers working on the code create a local branch and work in that branch. Any code change in this branch will go to a code review. Gated builds will be configured so that any check-ins to the local branch trigger the code change to go through the build process, unit test execution, and quality checks. This ensures that basic hygiene is maintained while making the code change.

If the gated builds are fine, the code changes will be merged from the local branch to the central repository. Once the new code is in the central repository, it will trigger the deployment pipeline. This process is commonly known as **Continuous Integration and Continuous Deployment(CI/CD)**.

The **Deployment pipeline** goes through the build process and deploys the services, at which point regression test cases will be executed. Some pipelines will have a small set of regression test cases as smoke test cases to get early feedback and ensure that basic functionalities are working. Once all of the test cases are regressed, the change is pushed to the next stage in the pipeline. The following diagram depicts this:

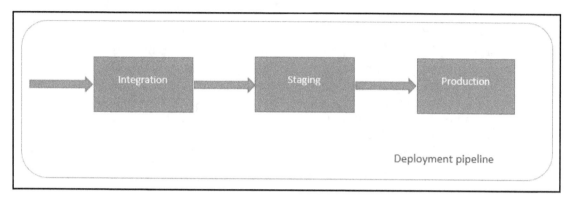

The deployment consists of multiple phases. Once the regression tests are passed in development, the services are deployed for integration. Again, a set of test cases is executed in integration and when they pass all the test cases, the changes are pushed to staging, which is a pre-production environment. Here, services are again deployed and tested, and will be rolled out to a production environment.

The development branch is where all code changes occur and regression tests are executed frequently. Integration environments are the candidates that follow development, where the different system integration tests are validated.

Services that are deployed to staging are release candidates for production. The staging and production environments are identical and will have a stable release version of the services. A production environment is consumed by end users and this is the last phase in the deployment pipeline. The build or services pass through the different stages before making it to production.

The majority of issues will be found and addressed in the development phase before any version is released. However, if releases have any issues, they will most likely be caught either in the integration or staging phases. Fixes will then be applied through patches or hotfixes, before being rolled out to production. Issues can be caught in the production stage also and patches will therefore be applied throughout the stages. It's not a good idea to put fixes directly into production. The pipeline ensures that any code change or new code is well tested and stable before it actually gets used by end users.

2. **Scalability:** Services that we develop and deploy have to be able to handle a large number of requests simultaneously. Systems have to be designed to be scalable so that they are able to respond to a bigger chunk of requests. Utilizing system resources efficiently is necessary for a system to handle many requests at the same time. Our code must also be written in a way that makes resource utilization optimal.

3. **Performance:** Performance is a measure of how well the system is handling and processing requests. This includes proper memory utilization and efficient use of computational resources.

4. **High availability:** Availability indicates the uptime of a service or an application. A system that is serving the request has to be up and running. Mission-critical systems are expected to have zero downtime. Furthermore, scaling services when load increases, adding multiple nodes to handle requests, and properly routing requests to nodes so that the load is shared between them increases the high availability of the system.

Summary

In this chapter, we discussed the following:

- Identifying memory leaks using `jvisualvm`
- Monitoring tools for monitoring applications
- The Garbage Collection process, Heap memory model, and different GC tuning options
- What profiling is and profiling the application using JProfiler
- Offline profiling with JProfiler
- How to make a service and application production-ready

11
Design Patterns with Kotlin

Enterprise applications encounter many common problems that have been known about for a long time, with some solutions being available for these. In some scenarios, design patterns are helpful for choosing the best possible solution—these are approaches that have already been created and optimized to solve recurring problems that are present in the programming world. Design patterns aim to solve some of these common design problems in an optimized fashion. Applying design patterns with Kotlin makes the code more elegant, concise, structured, flexible, reusable, and able to address these problems in an optimized way, which saves a lot of time and effort when developing applications or a piece of software.

The following topics will be covered in this chapter:

- What design patterns are and their benefits
- Different categories of design patterns
- Implementing different design patterns

Technical requirements

Being familiar with Kotlin or Java programming is necessary to understand the design patterns that we are going to discuss in this chapter.

Design patterns

Let's understand what design patterns are and how they will help us to design and develop applications or services.

Design patterns are a way of structuring code to solve commonly-occurring problems in designing software solutions. These are solutions to design problems that are common in the course of software design, unleashing the profundity of experiences to solve common problems of software development. The aim here is to use patterns to solve these problems in a more structured and elegant manner.

Software design or application design tends to change over the time. Any system has to be flexible for any change in the code. A change in the requirements, a new feature request, a defect fix, or a refactoring may require us to restructure the code. When a new piece of code is developed, it has to be gently integrated into the system. Existing code can be refactored without breaking the other working parts of the system. Any code change should not result in changing the code all over the system, so the software system has to be designed to handle the change and the impact on the code has to be minimized.

Design patterns help overcome some of the challenges that we face when designing a solution.

Advantages of design patterns

Patterns are well-tested solutions for common design problems and these address some of the concerns of how systems tend to evolve. Instead of starting from scratch, a proven pattern can be used to solve problems. These patterns are well-tested approaches and are already optimized and proven to work for these common design problems. If we need to improve the existing solution further in our application, we can do that as well. This will improve the software development life cycle.

Furthermore, these patterns support the reusability of solutions in different places within the system, providing transparent design solutions when designing an application.

Design patterns are not solutions for any domain-specific problems. Instead, they are the solution to common problems that are present in the design of software systems. Design patterns are a set of best practices that provide templates to address commonly occurring software-design problems. This provides a pattern that, when applied to these known problems, will save time, organize programming elements, and improve the architecture of the software. When these patterns are applied to any software application, it makes it more flexible, more maintainable, and more resilient.

Identifying the problem is important, but so is choosing the correct pattern to solve it. So, gaining an understanding of these patterns will give you an idea of what problems they can solve.

In the upcoming sections, we will discuss some patterns that are most commonly used to design enterprise applications.

Categorizing design patterns

Design patterns are categorized into three categories, based on some common considerations and the type of design problem they solve:

- Creational patterns
- Structural patterns
- Behavioral patterns

Creational patterns

Creational patterns focus on how objects are instantiated in a system. These patterns aim to reduce complexity in creating objects and allowing the instantiation of objects in a controlled way, thus providing flexibility in the way that objects are created and represented in the system.

These patterns enforce constraints for object creation, such as the number of instances that can be created in an application. This encourages the idea of coding to interfaces in which objects can be instantiated without knowledge of the specific implementation classes. It also reduces the tight coupling of objects within the system. The instantiation of objects will not be coupled directly into the code, but will be done in a way that can reduce complexity when we have to change from one implementation to another.

Patterns such as Factory, Builder, Singleton, and Prototype come under the category of creational patterns.

Structural patterns

Structural patterns focus on representing the relationship between objects. This includes looking at how classes can be composed to form a complex structure, thus providing a simple and efficient way to define class hierarchies and the relationships between objects.

Patterns such as Adapter, Decorator, Façade, Bridge, and Proxy come under the structural patterns category.

Behavioral patterns

These patterns provide a means by which common communication patterns can be identified between objects. These patterns encourage loose coupling and provide a flexible way for better interaction.

The Command, Observer, Interpreter, and Strategy patterns all come under the category of behavioral patterns.

We will implement some of these patterns in Kotlin and show how efficient it is to apply them using Kotlin for our use cases.

Implementing the singleton pattern

The singleton pattern is one of the best-known design patterns. This pattern ensures that only one instance of a class exists throughout the application running inside the virtual machine.

A singleton is a class whose instance can be created only once. This exists until the application is up and running. A singleton class provides a single access point that has to be used to get the instance of the class. It restricts the number of instances of a class to one and controls the creation of instances of the class.

A singleton class in an application is used when managing things such as memory, connection pools, threads, logging, and the registry. This ensures the consistency, reliability, and correctness of the data that classes handle in the application.

Writing a singleton class in Java

Let's understand how to write a singleton class in Java. We then compare it with the singleton class in Kotlin.

Let's consider the following class:

```
public class Singleton {
  public String getDetails() {
    System.out.println ("running the method");
    return "this is a singleton class";
  }
}
```

If we want to instantiate this class, we do it as follows:

```
new Singleton ();
```

Calling a constructor like this gives an instance of this class. If we repeatedly call this constructor, we get multiple instances of the same class and it is therefore not a singleton pattern.

Now we want only one instance of this class to be created and reused. To create a singleton class, we need to do the following:

- Make the constructor private and initialize it within the class.
- Provide a way to access the instance that is initialized.

Marking the constructor of the class private will ensure that the constructor is invoked only from that class, thus controlling the instantiation the class. This constructor can't be invoked outside of the class; only the code within the singleton class can invoke the constructor, as follows:

```
private Singleton() {}
```

If there is no zero-argument constructor and if the constructor takes some argument for initializing the member instance, we can mark that constructor as private:

```
private Singleton(String name) {
   this.name = name;
}
```

Now we need to use this private constructor to initialize the instance and provide a way to access it. This way, the instance is initialized within the class only and made available for usage in the application globally. Let's write a function that calls the private constructor of the singleton class:

```
private static Singleton singletonInstance;
   public static Singleton getInstance() {
     if(singletonInstance == null){
       singletonInstance = new Singleton ();
     }
     return singletonInstance;
   }
```

In the preceding code, we declared a static variable called `singletonInstance`, which holds the reference to the instance of the singleton class. Note that this is also private, meaning that this variable is again not accessible outside of the class; it is accessible only via the `getInstance()` function.

In the preceding code, we also defined a function named `getInstance()`, which is a static function and can be accessed directly using the class name.

In the `getInstance()` function, we check whether the `singletonInstance` member variable is initialized. If it is not, we initialize it with the private constructor of the class and return the instance.

When we make a call to the `getInstance()` function for the first time, `singletonInstance` will be null and it will be initialized using the constructor. When the call is made for the second time, the instance is not null and already holds a reference to the singleton class. This simply returns the same instance and we then have the same instance being returned from the `getInstance()` function.

Consequently, the code with the private constructor and the `getInstance()` function looks like the following:

```
public class Singleton {
  private static Singleton singletonInstance;
  private Singleton() {}

  public static Singleton getInstance() {
    if(singletonInstance == null){
      singletonInstance = new Singleton ();
    }
    return singletonInstance;
  }

  public String getDetails() {
    System.out.println ("running the method");
    return "this is a singleton class";
  }
}
```

In this Singleton class, we are instantiating the singleton instance only when required. `singletonInstance` is initialized only when the `getInstance()` function is invoked. Until then, the instance will not be initialized. This type of initialization is known as lazy initialization, as the object instantiation will be done only when required.

Lazy instantiation is good when the class is resource-intensive and has complex logic. This lazy instantiation will save the class loading time when JVM tries to load all the required classes in the application.

Writing the test case for a singleton

Now let's write a test class to verify the singleton class.

Consider the following test case:

```
@Test
public void testSingletonObject() {
  Singleton singleton = Singleton.getInstance ();
  Singleton anotherSingleton = Singleton.getInstance ();

  System.out.println (singleton);
  System.out.println (anotherSingleton);
  System.out.println (singleton == anotherSingleton);
```

```
        Assert.assertEquals (singleton, anotherSingleton);
    }
```

In this case, we are trying to instantiate the singleton class twice. We print the two instance objects that are initialized. Since the same object is returned every time the `getInstance()` function is invoked, it prints the same memory address at which these instances are loaded. The comparison of the instances is evaluated to true as it is the same instance:

```
singleton.Singleton@a38d7a3
singleton.Singleton@a38d7a3
true
```

Let's add another test case where we invoke a function on the singleton instance:

```
@Test
public void testSingleton() {
    Singleton singleton = Singleton.getInstance ();
    Assert.assertNotNull (singleton);

    String details = singleton.getDetails ();
    Assert.assertNotNull (details);
    Assert.assertEquals ("this is a singleton class", details);
}
```

In this test case, we initialize the instance by invoking the `getInstance()` function. On this instance, we call the `getDetails()` function that is defined in the singleton class. Furthermore, we assert for the non-null value for the instance, followed by the response that is returned from the `getDetails()` function, and then assert the actual message that is being returned by the function.

Note that the singleton code that we wrote is not thread-safe. If multiple threads access the `getInstance()` method at the same time, we end up with two instance of the class. To solve this, we use synchronized keywords or static initialization. The synchronized way is lazy initialization and the static initialization is known as eager initialization of the instance.

Lazy initialization

The code for lazy initialization is as follows:

```
public class Singleton {
    private static Singleton singletonInstance;

    private Singleton () {}
```

```
    public static synchronized Singleton getInstance() {
        if(singletonInstance == null){
            singletonInstance = new Singleton ();
        }
        return singletonInstance;
    }
}
```

The code for eager initialization is as follows:

```
public class Singleton {
    private static Singleton singletonInstance = new Singleton ();

    private Singleton () {}

    public static Singleton getInstance() {
        return singletonInstance;
    }
}
```

Singleton implementation in comparison to Kotlin

So far, we have explored how to implement a singleton pattern by making a constructor of the class private and providing a global way of accessing the instance that is initialized within the class in Java.

In Kotlin, it is much simpler to write a singleton class:

```
object Singleton {
}
```

The `object` keyword is used for a singleton class. Note that we used `object` to define constants and static functions in our examples in the previous chapters. We indeed created a singleton class in these examples. Unlike the class, the object does not have any constructors.

In addition, we don't need to create the instance to access any of its functions. Let's add the following function to the singleton class:

```
object Singleton {
    fun getDetails(): String {
        return "this is a singleton class"
    }
}
```

Our test case for the preceding code can be written as follows:

```
class SingletonTest {
    @Test
    fun testSingletonObject() {
        var details: String = Singleton.getDetails()
        Assert.assertEquals ("this is a singleton class", details);
    }
}
```

We can provide the `init` block for any initialization required:

```
object Singleton {
    init {
        //..
    }
}
```

There is no race condition when accessing the singleton class in Kotlin.

We looked at creating singleton instances in Java; to do so, we have to mark the constructor as private and provide a static method to access it. Furthermore, we need to have handled the race condition either by using the static initializer or the synchronized keyword on the `getInstance()` function. Then we looked at how easy it is to create a singleton in Kotlin, accessing the function in the singleton class. We also wrote test cases to verify the code.

Implementing the factory pattern

The factory pattern is another commonly-used creational design pattern. This pattern provides a way to create objects for clients without knowing the concrete object types. It simplifies the way we create objects when we are dealing with multiple implementations of a type and the implementation type has to be chosen based on the context provided.

Let's consider the following code snippet:

```
val sensor:Sensor = TemperatureSensor()
```

Here, we are directly instantiating the concrete type in our code. Our client code is directly dependent on the Sensor implementation types. If we have another type, such as HumiditySensor, to be used, then we have to modify our code to accommodate this change:

```
@JvmStatic
fun main(args: Array<String>) {
    var sensor: Sensor
    if (sensorType == "heat")
        sensor = TemparatureSensor()
    if (sensorType == "humid")
        sensor = HumiditySensor()
    if (sensorType == "optiical") {
        sensor = OpticalSensor()
}
```

In this code, we declare a variable of the Sensor type (which is an interface) and write conditional logic to instantiate the different sensor objects at runtime based on the sensor types. If this sensor type grows, we end up including all of these concrete types in our code. Furthermore, if we want to add or remove new sensors, we have to change the code in two places.

In principle, client code doesn't have to be aware of these concrete implementation types. Instead, it just has to say what type it needs and it will receive an object of the Sensor interface type:

```
val: Sensor = getSensor("humid")
```

To solve this design problem, we use the factory pattern. We will create a new class, called SensorFactory, that creates different sensors based on the type given:

```
object SensorFactory {
    fun getSensor(sensorType:String) :Sensor?{
        if (sensorType == "heat")
            return TemparatureSensor()
        else if (sensorType == "humid")
            return HumiditySensor()
        else if (sensorType == "optical")
            return OpticalSensor()
        else
            return null
    }
}
```

The `getSensor()` function is a factory function that creates sensors based on the type given.

The client code looks like the following:

```
object SensorClient {
    var sensor: Sensor ?= null

    @JvmStatic
    fun main(args: Array<String>) {
        sensor = SensorFactory.getSensor("optical")
    }
}
```

With this pattern, the client code doesn't need to worry about the concrete details of the Sensor. All it receives is an instance of the `Sensor` type. If any new sensor has to be added, that gets added to the factory class and we don't have to change the client code. When the client code wants to use a new type, it just passes the string input, and the factory function returns the appropriate type. With this pattern, the code becomes loosely coupled and more maintainable.

We can print the class name of the instance that's created by the factory class using Kotlin reflection, as follows:

```
fun main(args: Array<String>) {
        sensor = SensorFactory.getSensor("optical")
        if(sensor == null){
            println("requested sensor type not available yet")
        }else {
            println(sensor::class.simpleName)
        }
    }
```

Since we have hardcoded string literals for sensor types, we can use enum instead:

```
enum class SensorType private constructor(private val type: String) {
    HUMIDITY("humid"), TEMPARATURE("heat"), OPTICAL("optic")
}
```

In the Client class, we use enum as follows:

```
sensor = SensorFactory.getSensor(SensorType.OPTICAL.name)
```

Let's consider another use case in which we want to create a list of sensors given a type and quantity. Without the factory pattern, the client class will have to create `SensorType`, repeating this for the required number of quantities.

First this creates the required sensors, then it can have logic to process further. As stated earlier, the problem with this approach is that Sensor interface concrete classes are tightly coupled with the Client class, and the Client class violates the **single responsibility principle** (**SRP**).

Let's write code for this requirement with the factory pattern. We will add a new function to the SensorFactory class, which takes the sensorType and number of quantities as input parameters:

```
fun getSensorList(sensorType:String, quantity:Int): MutableList<Sensor> { }
```

The SensorFactory class looks like the following:

```
object SensorFactory {
    private fun getSensor(sensorType:String) : Sensor?{
        if (sensorType == "heat")
            return TemparatureSensor()
        else if (sensorType == "humid")
            return HumiditySensor()
        else if (sensorType == "optical")
            return OpticalSensor()
        else
            return null
    }

    fun getSensorList(type:String, quantity:Int): MutableList<Sensor> {

        var sensorList: MutableList<Sensor> = mutableListOf()
        for (i in 0 until quantity) {
            sensorList.add(SensorFactory.getSensor(type))
        }
        return sensorList
    }
}
```

SensorClient will invoke the getSensorList() function by passing the sensor type and the quantity:

```
var list = SensorFactory.getSensorList(SensorType.HUMIDITY.name,100)
```

In the factory pattern, we define an interface to create an object. However, the actual creation logic is not exposed to the clients. The concrete implementation of the interface type will be created and returned based on the context. This makes the class or interface flexible and easier to maintain.

Adding a new `SensorType` to the factory class still requires modification. We can avoid this by maintaining a map that consists of the class type of the sensors, and then adding a function that takes a new Sensor and puts that into the map. The `getSensor()` function reads the type from this map and returns the instance.

Implementing the builder pattern

The Builder pattern is a creational pattern whose goal is to simplify object construction. Instead of having complex constructors that take a large number of parameters, this pattern provides ways to create objects with different states of representation. It gives flexibility while instantiating a class. It provides builder functions to construct the object step by step, and the object will be returned in the final step.

Consider a class that represents a person. We will have to create person objects with different combinations of characteristics. Say, for example, person with `firstName`, `lastName`, `age`, `contactNumber`, `loginId`, and `address`. The class looks as follows:

```kotlin
class Person {
    var firstName: String? = null
    var lastName: String? = null
    var middleName: String? = null
    var loginId: String? = null
    var age: Int? = null
    var contactNumber: String? = null
    var address: String? = null

    constructor(firstName: String?, lastName: String?, middleName: String?,
loginId: String?, age: Int?,
            contactNumber: String?, address: String?) {
        this.firstName = firstName
        this.lastName = lastName
        this.middleName = middleName
        this.loginId = loginId
        this.age = age
        this.contactNumber = contactNumber
        this.address = address
    }
}
```

To create an instance of the `Person` type, let's say, we provide a complex constructor that takes all of these parameters. If we want to create a person object, we have to invoke the constructor by passing all the fields, as shown here:

```
object Test {
    @JvmStatic
    fun main(args: Array<String>) {
        val person = Person("Jane", "", "", "jane@test.org", 21,
"4561298421", "10, Charles ", "Street,NY")
    }
}
```

The problem with this approach is that the list of parameters supplied to create an object is long, and chances are we may pass the parameters in the wrong order if the parameters are of same type. This is slightly confusing. Also, sometimes all of the information may not be required or not available to create a `Person` object.

One way to solve this problem is to have multiple constructors, such as one that takes `firstName`, `lastName`, and then if needed another one that takes `firstName`, `lastName`, `loginId`. There could be yet another one that takes the first three arguments and age, and finally one constructor that takes all of the parameters. The problem with this approach is that the class ends up in having multiple constructors. As the parameter list grows, for every possible combination the number of constructors will also increase:

```
constructor(firstName: String?) {
    this.firstName = firstName
}

constructor(firstName: String?, lastName: String?) {
    this.firstName = firstName
    this.lastName = lastName
}

constructor(firstName: String?, lastName: String?, middleName: String?) {
    this.firstName = firstName
    this.lastName = lastName
    this.middleName = middleName
}

constructor(firstName: String?, lastName: String?, loginId: String?,
contactNumber: String?) {
    this.firstName = firstName
    this.lastName = lastName
    this.loginId = loginId
    this.contactNumber = contactNumber
}
```

```
constructor(firstName: String?, lastName: String?, middleName: String?,
loginId: String?, age: Int?,
          contactNumber: String?, address: String?) {
    this.firstName = firstName
    this.lastName = lastName
    this.middleName = middleName
    this.loginId = loginId
    this.age = age
    this.contactNumber = contactNumber
    this.address = address
}
```

The Builder pattern is a better alternative to solve this problem. The Builder pattern moves the construction of complex objects out of the constructor and provides flexibility in creating objects. Classes that use the builder pattern scale better, and it improves readability.

The Builder pattern consists of three components: **Product, Director,** and a **Builder**, as shown in the following diagram:

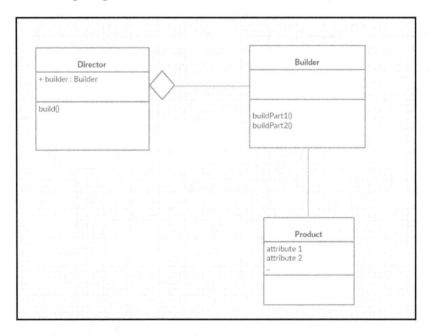

Product is a complex structure that needs to be constructed. In our case, the `Person` class is the product. A **Director** is a class that creates objects using the builder class. The `Test` class is the director in our case. Now we need to create a builder class that is used to build the components of the complex `Person` object.

The builder class looks as follows:

```
class PersonBuilder:Builder {
    var firstName: String? = null
    var lastName: String? = null
    var middleName: String? = null
    var loginId: String? = null
    var age: Int? = null
    var contactNumber: String? = null
    var address: String? = null

    fun withFirstName(firstName: String): PersonBuilder {
        this.firstName = firstName
        return this
    }

    fun withLastName(lastName: String): PersonBuilder {
        this.lastName = lastName
        return this
    }

    fun withMiddleName(middleName: String): PersonBuilder {
        this.middleName = middleName
        return this
    }

    fun withLoginId(loginId: String): PersonBuilder {
        this.loginId = loginId
        return this
    }

    fun withAge(age: Int): PersonBuilder {
        this.age = age
        return this
    }

    fun withContactNumber(contactNumber: String): PersonBuilder {
        this.contactNumber = contactNumber
        return this
    }

    fun withAddress(address: String): PersonBuilder {
        this.address = address
        return this
    }

    fun build(): Person {
        return Person(firstName, lastName, middleName, loginId, age,
```

```
contactNumber, address)
    }
}
```

In the `Test` class that creates the `Person` object, we now have the flexibility to use these builder functions than the constructor that take all the parameters.

Let's rewrite the code in the `Test` class:

```
var person = PersonBuilder()
        .withFirstName("Jane")
        .withLoginId("jane@test.org")
        .withContactNumber("4561298421")
        .build();
```

We implemented the builder pattern for our `Person` class, which gives flexibility to the classes creating the `Person` object to create it with the different argument list. Thus, we simplified the creation of a complex object with the Builder pattern.

Implementing the decorator pattern

The decorator design pattern is a structural, hierarchical pattern that is used to dynamically extend or alter the functionality of objects at runtime. This pattern builds the functionality at each level without altering the existing structure using the composition from similar data types. It does this by wrapping them in an object of a decorator class, providing the additional functionality and leaving the original object intact without any modification.

Using this pattern, we can add functionality by wrapping an object inside another without affecting the other parts of the hierarchy in the system. This is also known as a wrapper as it wraps the objects. This differs from adding functionalities to objects at design-time, which generally involves inheritance. To add any functionality, we have to create a new class and create a subclass that extends a base class. With inheritance, we can add functionalities to classes by extending a base class. A problem with this approach is that a new class is created for every possible combination of these types, resulting in a class explosion. This means that there will be many classes available just to have these functionalities. This can be achieved without actually creating a higher number of classes with the decorator pattern.

The decorator pattern attaches the additional responsibilities to an object dynamically without making any modifications to existing classes. This provides a flexible alternative to subclassing for adding the additional functionality.

The decorator pattern makes the design flexible. Applications have to be designed to be flexible enough to accommodate any functionalities for changing requirements. We also want to keep in mind that the base class should not be modified. This pattern is aligned with the open-closed design principle, which states that the classes should be open for extension, but closed to any modifications.

The decorator design pattern can be used when we don't want too many subclasses that would extend from a base class for every combination. This is more suitable when we want to add new functionality to a legacy system in cases in which we don't want to modify existing classes but still need a new responsibility to be handled. It makes more sense to use the decorator pattern to add the additional responsibilities than providing subclasses to add the functionality.

The key idea behind the decorator pattern is to wrap the object being decorated. Consequently, it is also known as a **wrapper pattern**.

Let's illustrate the decorator pattern via an example. Consider the example of purchasing windows. In this case, the windows can be different sizes, colors, and materials. If we follow inheritance, just imagine the number of classes that we have to create for all these sets of different combinations. Instead of using inheritance, we can use decorators for these combinations when choosing a window. For example, we may want to create a small, silver window made of glass. This is shown in the following diagram:

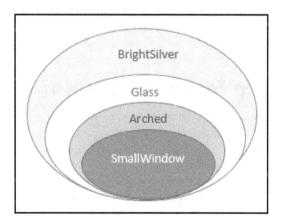

We wrap the **SmallWindow** object in a **GlassDecorator** object, which again gets wrapped in a **BrightSilver** color decorator object. Any combination of this sort can be created. We started with a window object and added the material type and color. We then wrapped one object in another. The price of the window will be calculated on the outermost decorator object, which is the sum of the window, material type, and the color. Note that these decorations can be wrapped dynamically at runtime:

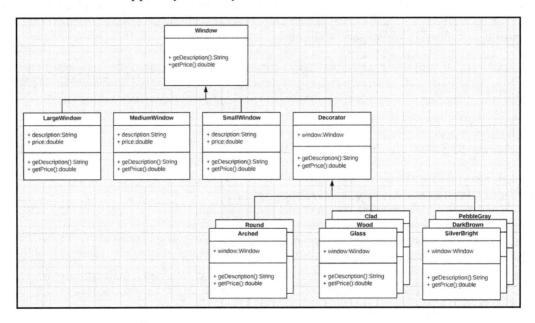

With these types, we can create any combination of windows, using the window shape, material type, and color. Let's see this in action.

Writing the code for the decorator pattern

To begin, we create four packages, each of which represents the components of the decorator pattern. These packages are named `component`, `concretecomponent`, `decorator`, and `concretedecorator`. This is shown in the following screenshot:

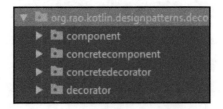

In our case, **Window** is our component. This is an interface that declares the getDescription() and getPrice() functions:

```
interface Window {
    fun getDescription(): String
    fun getPrice(): Double
}
```

We have three implementations of the component—LargeWindow, MediumWindow, and SmallWindow. These implementations are similar and look like the following:

```
class LargeWindow : Window {
    internal var description: String
    internal var price: Double

    init {
        description = "Large Window"
        price = 50.00
    }

    override fun getDescription(): String {
        return description
    }
    override fun getPrice(): Double {
        return price
    }
}
```

In these concrete implementations, we set the description and the price using the init block, which will be invoked during object initialization. The other two implementations vary in setting the description value to medium, small, and other appropriate prices.

Let's write a simple program that creates LargeWindow and print its description as well as the price:

```
fun main(args: Array<String>) {
    var window: Window = LargeWindow()
    println("Window description: ${window.getDescription()}")
    println("Window price: $${window.getPrice()}")

}
```

Now let's run this code. We should expect this to print the `Large Window` description as well as its cost of $50, which is what we have set for the `LargeWindow` class:

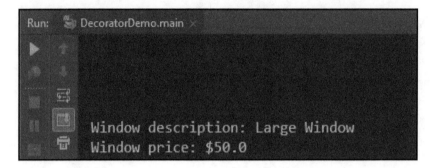

Adding decorators

Now we need to add the decorators to the window. To do this, we will create a `WindowDecorator` class, which is our decorator. This class implements the following `Window` component:

```kotlin
class WindowDecorator(private val window: Window) : Window {

    override fun getDescription(): String {
        return window.getDescription()
    }

    override fun getPrice(): Double {
        return window.getPrice()
    }
}
```

This class takes an instance of a `Window` type in its constructor, and this is the instance that is decorated. We also override the `getDescription()` and `getPrice()` functions.

Now let's write a concrete decorator. This is called **Arched**, which refers to the shape of the window:

```kotlin
class Arched(private val window: Window) : WindowDecorator(window) {
    internal var description: String
    internal var price: Double
    init {

        description = "Arched shape"
        price = 15.00
```

```
        }

    override fun getDescription(): String {
        var desc = super.getDescription()
        return "$desc, $description"
    }

    override fun getPrice(): Double {
        return super.getPrice() + price
    }
    }
}
```

This class extends from `WindowDecorator`, taking an object of the `Window` type that will be decorated. It then calls the parent class constructor. Note the syntax in Kotlin for this step. This is just one line that is used to declare a constructor, invoking the constructor of the parent class:

```
class Arched(private val window: Window) : WindowDecorator(window)
```

We also override the `getDescription()` and `getPrice()` functions in the Arched concrete decorator. As this is the wrapping of the window in an Arched type, we need to concatenate the description and find the total price for both the `Window` and the decorator classes. We do this by overriding the `getDescription()` and `getPrice()` functions in the decorator class.

Now we need to modify the `main()` function that we wrote for verifying the decorator pattern:

```
fun main(args: Array<String>) {

        var window: Window = LargeWindow()
        window = Arched(window)
        window = Glass(window)
        window = BrightSilver(window)

        println("Window description: ${window.getDescription()}")
        println("Window price: $${window.getPrice()}")

    }
```

In the main function, we create a `Window` instance, which happens to be `LargeWindow`, and then wrap it around the `Arched`, `Glass`, and `BrightSilver` decorator types.

When we run this code, we should expect the `Window` created to be `Arched` in shape, `BrightSilver` in color, and made of `Glass`. The price should also be the sum of the `Window` ($50), `Arched` ($15), `Glass` ($10), and `BrightSilver` ($20), which comes to $95. Consider the following screenshot:

We started with the `LargeWindow` type, wrapping this around the `Arched`, `Glass`, and `BrightSilver` decorator types. In the end, the instance window will be a `BrightSilver` type and when we invoke the `getDescription()` and `getPrice()` functions, this invokes the overridden version of these functions from the `BrightSilver` class.

Whenever we want to create a window of different combinations or add a new decor type, we just have to create a new decorator and wrap the component that needs to be decorated. Consequently, following the decorator pattern, we won't run into a class-explosion problem for all the possible combinations of the decor that we need to apply to an object type. This makes adding the new functionality/decor easier and the application therefore becomes more maintainable.

Implementing the observer pattern

The observer pattern is yet another design pattern that is widely used when developing applications or software. The observer pattern is useful when one object is dependent on the state of another object. This pattern defines one-to-many dependent models between the objects. Whenever an object changes its state, all the dependent objects are notified of the change and they are all updated with the new state information. Instead of periodically checking to see whether the object has changed, it's better to notify the objects that will take the new state information upon the notification. The object that changes state is called **State** and the other observing objects are **Dependent** objects:

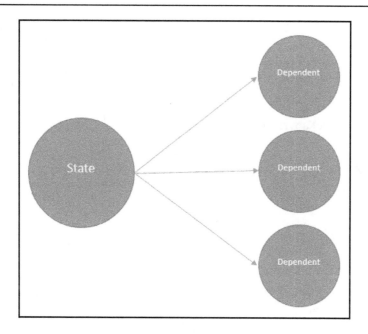

The preceding diagram represents a one-to-many model. With this, the state information is changed in a state object and a notification is then sent to many dependents. The object that changes state might not be aware of the other dependent objects that are monitoring the state change. This pattern allows the notification to be sent to the observing objects when the object changes its state without knowing that the other objects are observing the change.

The observer pattern can be used when the concerns of one class or the instances are unrelated and/or need to be hidden from the other classes or instances that are monitoring the object for any state changes. In fact, the *publisher* and *subscriber* model that is described in the messaging service chapter is based on the observer pattern. The *publisher* is the **subject** and the *subscriber* that listens to the messages is the **dependent** object.

Illustrating the observer pattern

Let's illustrate the observer pattern through the example of stock market data. Our use case here is that the observers will be registered for specific trades of a company and they will be observing for any changes in the data.

To design this model, let's write a simple contract. We will begin with the `Subject` and `Observer` interfaces.

The `Subject` interface has the following three functions:

- `fun register(observer: Observer)`
- `fun remove(observer: Observer)`
- `fun notify()`

The `register()` function registers an `Observer` for observing the subject. The `remove()` function will then remove dependent objects from observing `Subject`. The `notify()` function then sends a notification to all registered observers about the state change.

The `Observer` interface has one function:

```
fun update()
```

This function will be invoked by the subject while sending the notification. When this function is invoked, dependent objects will see the updated value for the stock price.

Let's provide an implementation class for the `Subject` interface, as follows:

```kotlin
class StockData : Subject {
    internal var observerList: MutableList<Observer> = ArrayList()
    var symbol: String ?= null
    var price: Float? = null

    override fun register(observer: Observer) {
        observerList.add(observer)
    }

    override fun remove(observer: Observer) {
        val i = observerList.indexOf(observer)
        if (i >= 0) {
            observerList.removeAt(i)
        }
        observerList.remove(observer)
    }
}
```

```
override fun notify() {
    for (i in observerList.indices) {
        observerList[i].update()
    }
}

fun setStockData(symbol: String, price: Float?) {
    this.symbol = symbol
    this.price = price
    notifyObservers()
}
}
```

This `StockData` class maintains a list of observers for the stock-data change event. Here, the `register()` function adds the observer to the list and the `remove()` function takes the observer out of the list. The `notify()` function simply invokes `update()` on the observers that are registered.

An implementation of the `Observer` interface will have the definition for the `update()` function, which updates the required data in the observer.

We have now described the *observer pattern* and illustrated it using an example. This pattern is useful when we have multiple observers that are monitoring state-information changes.

Implementing the chain of responsibility pattern

The chain-of-responsibility pattern is a behavioral pattern that decouples a request from a handling object in a chain of handlers until the handler is recognized as processing the request. This pattern avoids tight coupling between the sender and the receiver, and gives more than one chance to handle the request.

With this pattern, requests are sent to a sequential chain of potential handlers. One of the handlers is expected to take the request and return the response. If the request is not accepted by any of the handlers, it will not be handled by the application. This is depicted by the following diagram:

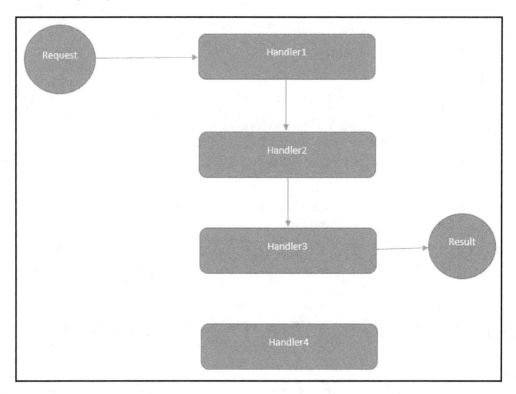

Each of the handlers handles a single responsibility, which makes the design cleaner, loosely coupled, and easy to extend.

This pattern is useful when we want to perform different operations based on a request as well as keeping these operations separate. Instead of putting all operations in a single class, we can have different classes, each of these performing specific operations to process an incoming request and to return a result.

Illustrating the chain-of-responsibility pattern

Consider audit messages for different identity types, including `Person`, `Group`, `Organization`, and `Device`. These identities will have different audit messages and must be handled separately. Keeping all audit-related code in a single class increases the overhead when we want to add audits for new identities.

The chain-of-responsibility pattern would be a good fit in this case. We will illustrate the chain of responsibility through this pattern, handling audits for different identities.

We will start with the `Handler` interface, which defines the contract for concrete handlers. Then we write an `AbstractHandler`. Some of the reusable code that can be used in the concrete implementation goes here. Then we have concrete handlers for handling the request. The following is the *UML* diagram for this implementation:

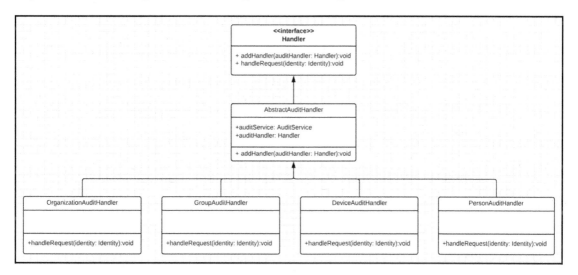

Defining the contracts

Let's write the `Handler` interface:

```
interface Handler {
    fun addHandler(auditHandler: Handler)
    fun handleRequest(identityRequest: Identity)
}
```

As shown in the preceding code, we declare the following two functions:

- The `addHandler()` function is for adding the next handler in a chain.
- The `handleRequest()` function is for handling the request. In our case, we will implement this function to generate audit message.

Writing the implementation

The `AbstractAuditHandler` class will have some reusable components that are used by concrete implementation classes. We declare a field, `auditHandler`, of the `Handler` type, and set this using the `addHandler()` function. This handler instance is used in concrete implementation classes to add the next handler in the chain. Note that we override the `addHandler()` function in the abstract class itself, as in our case this function does not differ in concrete classes; the implementation is the same. We also have an instance of `AuditServiceImpl` for which we write the following audit message:

```
abstract class AbstractAuditHandler : Handler {
    protected lateinit var auditHandler: Handler
    protected lateinit var auditService: AuditService
    override fun addHandler(auditHandler: Handler) {
        this.auditHandler = auditHandler
    }
}
```

In the handler implementations class, we override the `handleRequest()` function. This function takes an identity object as a request . This can be an `Organization`, `Group`, a `Device`, or a `Person` type, as shown in the following code:

```
abstract class Identity {
    var id: String? = null
    var name: String? = null
    var description: String? = null
    var identityType: IdentityType? = null
    var requestMethod: String? = null
}
```

`Identity` is an abstract class that contains basic information about an identity, including `identifier`, name, and `identityType`. `IdentityType` is an enum that represents the identity types that we use. Consider the following code example:

```
enum class IdentityType {
    ORGANIZATION, GROUP, PERSON, DEVICE
}
```

The information that is specific to the identities can go in the class extending the abstract `Identity` class. We have the `Person`, `Device`, `Group`, and `Organization` classes, which extend the `Identity` type, and these will have details specific to that identity.

Defining the concrete handlers

Now let's add a concrete audit handler. We write four handlers at this point: `PersonAuditHandler`, `DeviceAuditHandler`, `GroupAuditHandler`, and `OrganizationAuditHandler`. Here, we will explain `PersonAuditHandler`.

In the `handleRequest()` function, we take the `Identity` instance as the request. If `identityType` is a person, we process the request in the handler class. If not, we pass the control to the next handler in the chain:

```
override fun handleRequest(identityRequest: Identity) {
        if (identityRequest.identityType == IdentityType.PERSON) {
            //..
        } else {
            auditHandler.handleRequest(identityRequest)
        }
}
```

If the identity is a *person,* then we prepare an audit message and a participant object, as follows:

```
  if (identityRequest.identityType == IdentityType.PERSON) {
      var auditMessage: AuditMessage =
AuditUtil.prepareAuditMessage(Constants.PERSON_AUDIT_MESSAGE)
      auditMessage.participantObject =
AuditUtil.createParticipantObject(identityRequest)
  }
```

The `AuditMessage` class looks as follows:

```
class AuditMessage {
    var auditMessageId: String? = null
    var auditEventDate: Date? = null
    var auditMessage: String? = null
    var participantObject: ParticipantObject? = null
    var event: Event? = null
}
```

AuditMessage has the following information: `message`,
`date`, `auditMessageId`, `participantObject`, and `event`.

`ParticipantObject` will have identity-specific information such as `id`, `name`, and `type`.
We map `requestIdentity` to `ParticipantObject` for auditing purposes:

```
class ParticipantObject {
    var participantObjectId: String? = null
    var participantObjectName: String? = null
    var participantObjectType: String? = null
}
```

The Event class has code that is a defined constant for each of the operations on the
entities. This includes GET, CREATE, UPDATE, and DELETE.

```
class Event {
    var code: String? = null
    var displayName: String? = null
}
```

We can input whichever type of operation is requested on the identity that we get from the
`requestIdentity` object, as follows:

```
when (identityRequest.requestMethod) {
    "GET" -> {
        event.code = Constants.PERSON_READ_EVENT_CODE
        event.displayName = Constants.PERSON_READ_EVENT_DISPLAYNAME
    }
    "POST" -> {
        event.code = Constants.PERSON_CREATE_EVENT_CODE
        event.displayName = Constants.PERSON_CREATE_EVENT_DISPLAYNAME
    }
    //..
}
```

We embed the event details in the audit message. Consequently, we have now constructed
the audit message with a participant object and the event details of the request identity. We
then use the AuditService instance that we have created in our AbstractAuditHandler
class to invoke the audit() function, as follows:

```
auditServiceImpl.audit(auditMessage)
```

For our demo, we print the details of the audit message. In a real-world implementation, an audit service can be a rest API or it can push the audit messages to a queue or to a database. These stored audit messages can be used later by querying the audit record. So, our `PersonAuditHandler` class looks as follows:

```
class PersonAuditHandler : AbstractAuditHandler() {

    private var participantObject: ParticipantObject

    override fun handleRequest(identityRequest: Identity) {

        if (identityRequest.identityType == IdentityType.PERSON) {
            var auditMessage: AuditMessage =
AuditUtil.prepareAuditMessage(Constants.PERSON_AUDIT_MESSAGE)
            auditMessage.participantObject =
AuditUtil.createParticipantObject(identityRequest)
            var event: Event = Event()

            when (identityRequest.requestMethod) {
                "GET" -> {
                    event.code = Constants.PERSON_READ_EVENT_CODE
                    event.displayName =
Constants.PERSON_READ_EVENT_DISPLAYNAME
                }
                "POST" -> {
                    event.code = Constants.PERSON_CREATE_EVENT_CODE
                    event.displayName =
Constants.PERSON_CREATE_EVENT_DISPLAYNAME
                }
                "PUT" -> {
                    event.code = Constants.PERSON_UPDATE_EVENT_CODE
                    event.displayName =
Constants.PERSON_UPDATE_EVENT_DISPLAYNAME
                }
                "DELETE" -> {
                    event.code = Constants.PERSON_DELETE_EVENT_CODE
                    event.displayName =
Constants.PERSON_DELETE_EVENT_DISPLAYNAME
                }
            }
            auditMessage.event = event
            auditService.audit(auditMessage)
        } else {
            auditHandler.handleRequest(identityRequest)
        }
    }
}
```

The other handler-implementation classes, such as `GroupAuditHandler` and `DeviceAuditHandler`, are similar, but these classes create the audit message with details that are specific to a group or device identities.

Verifying the handler implementation

Now let's write a test class to verify the chaining of handlers:

```
fun main(args: Array<String>) {

        val personAuditHandler = PersonAuditHandler()
        val organizationAuditHandler = OrganizationAuditHandler()
        val groupAuditHandler = GroupAuditHandler()
        val deviceAuditHandler = DeviceAuditHandler()

        organizationAuditHandler.addHandler(groupAuditHandler)
        groupAuditHandler.addHandler(deviceAuditHandler)
        deviceAuditHandler.addHandler(personAuditHandler)

        organizationAuditHandler.handleRequest(creaeSamplePersonRequest())
    }
```

In this class, we created instances of handler implementations and chained them using the `addHandler()` function. We also created a sample `Person` identity that we pass to the `handleRequest()` function.

The function to generate the sample identity of a person is as follows:

```
fun creaeSamplePersonRequest(): Person{
        val identity = Person()
        identity.id = "person123"
        identity.description = "Person identity"
        identity.identityType = IdentityType.PERSON
        identity.name = "Name"
        identity.organizationId = "orgId123"
        identity.requestMethod = HttpMethod.POST
        return identity
    }
```

Note that the handlers will be executed in the order that we mention here when chaining them. So, the request is first sent to `OrganizationAuditHandler`. From there, since the identity type is `Person`, it goes to the next handler in the chain, which is `GroupAuditHandler` – this handler is for the `Group` identity type. It then goes to `DeviceAuditHandler`, which is not a match either. The request now goes to `PersonAuditHandler`, which prepares the audit message specific to the `Person` identity and will be sent to `AuditService`. With `AuditService`, we print the audit message contents.

For the purpose of this demo, we have added `println()` messages in each handler's `handleRequest()` function to show the execution order. After that, we print the audit message to the console. Let's run this test class and see the output:

```
Run:  org.rao.kotlin.designpatterns.chain.ChainOfResponsibilityDemo

------------------------------ OrganizationAuditHandler.handleRequest() invoked ------------------------------
------------------------------ GroupAuditHandler.handleRequest() invoked ------------------------------
------------------------------ DeviceAuditHandler.handleRequest() invoked ------------------------------
------------------------------ PersonAuditHandler.handleRequest() invoked ------------------------------

------------------------------ audit message ------------------------------
MessageId: 6866d75a-dc4b-4637-826a-fd66e0f5762c
Message: Person identity audit data
ParticipantObjectId: person123
ParticipantObjectName: Name
AuditEventDate: Thu Sep 13 02:02:08 IST 2018
AuditEventCode: P1000031
AuditEventDisplayName: CREATE PERSON
------------------------------ audit message ------------------------------
```

As expected, the control went through the chain of handlers for request processing until it found a handler, processed the request, generated the audit message, and printed it to the console.

There may be a situation in which a request may come with an unknown identity type or a type that is not yet supported in the system. In that case, we need a default handler to handle such requests and we may also choose to audit it. Let's take a look at our test class where we add the default handler to the chain:

```
organizationAuditHandler.addHandler(groupAuditHandler)
groupAuditHandler.addHandler(deviceAuditHandler)
deviceAuditHandler.addHandler(personAuditHandler)
personAuditHandler.addHandler(defaultAuditHandler)
```

Now let's invoke the `handleRequest()` function by changing the `IdentityType` to `TEST`. This is shown as follows:

```
Run:    org.rao.kotlin.designpatterns.chain.ChainOfResponsibilityDemo

    --------------------- OrganizationAuditHandler.handleRequest() invoked ---------------------
    --------------------- GroupAuditHandler.handleRequest() invoked ---------------------
    --------------------- DeviceAuditHandler.handleRequest() invoked ---------------------
    --------------------- PersonAuditHandler.handleRequest() invoked ---------------------
    --------------------- DefaultAuditHandler.handleRequest() invoked ---------------------

    --------------------- audit message ---------------------
    MessageId: 45d7af07-aba3-4bcb-9cc9-337f4e3250c6
    Message: A request made with a unknown identity type
    ParticipantObjectId: 123
    ParticipantObjectName: Name
    AuditEventDate: Thu Sep 13 07:00:43 IST 2018
    AuditEventCode: NA
    AuditEventDisplayName: NA
    --------------------- audit message ---------------------
```

As we can see, since the identity type in unknown, the request has finally reached `DefaultAuditHandler` and created an audit message with some values that the handler can recognize.

With these patterns, it is easy to add a new `Identity` to the system, and adding a request handler for the type is also easy. We just have to create a new handler and chain it to the other handlers.

Selecting design patterns

Design patterns are intended to solve common design problems. These patterns provide guidelines for solving a design issue, and their techniques are proven to work. There are 23 original patterns, categorized into *creational*, *structural*, and *behavioral* patterns. Different design patterns exist for different types of known design issue. In this chapter, we discussed some commonly-used patterns in enterprise applications.

Design patterns introduce transparency and clarity to the system's design, and provide reusable constructs that help to build a better enterprise system. Selecting a design pattern from the set of patterns is important for solving a design issue that we are trying to solve.

The first thing that we need to do before selecting a pattern is to understand the problem and see whether it is related to object creation, or its behaviors, or how it has to be structured. We should then map this to the categories of the design patterns. Some problems may fall into more than one category and may require mix-and-matching more than one pattern.

Once we are clear on the type of problem we are trying to solve, the next thing that we need to do is understand what problems different design patterns solve. We need to understand the purpose of these patterns to see which patterns fit with the design problems that we are going to solve.

If the solution requires choosing between more than one pattern, we need to understand how these have to be interlinked for the problem that we are solving.

Once you're clear on the intent, prepare a model and try to establish a relationship between the classes and objects. We should then gain an understanding of how these classes and objects have to be composed and collaborated, and how they relate to each other. If required, we may have to reconsider the chosen patterns, providing implementations for them and maintaining consistency during this.

Patterns are there to aid design issues and provide templates for designing a system in a better way. Identifying the appropriate patterns in the context of the problem that we are trying to solve makes the solution easier and creates a common solution to addressing the problem, making it easier for other people to understand the design. We might already be following some of these patterns unknowingly in our system's design. However, having an understanding of the patterns—and their intent for solving design problems, recognizing a pattern in an existing system, and implementing these patterns—will make the system design cleaner and easier to maintain over time.

Summary

In this chapter we discussed the following:

- What design patterns are and the benefits of using design patterns to design a system.
- How patterns are categorized into creational, structural, and behavioral patterns.
- The Singleton pattern and how it compares with Java and Kotlin implementations.
- Implementing the factory pattern.
- Implementing the observer pattern.
- Implementing the decorator and handler patterns.
- Selecting appropriate patterns for the problem that we are trying to solve.

Other Books You May Enjoy

If you enjoyed this book, you may be interested in these other books by Packt:

Hands-on Design Patterns with Kotlin

Alexey Soshin

ISBN: 9781788998017

- Get to grips with Kotlin principles, including its strengths and weaknesses
- Understand classical design patterns in Kotlin
- Explore functional programming using built-in features of Kotlin
- Solve real-world problems using reactive and concurrent design patterns
- Use threads and coroutines to simplify concurrent code flow
- Understand antipatterns to write clean Kotlin code, avoiding common pitfalls
- Learn about the design considerations necessary while choosing between architectures

Hands-On Object-Oriented Programming with Kotlin
Abid Khan

ISBN: 9781789617726

- Get an overview of the Kotlin programming language
- Discover Object-oriented programming techniques in Kotlin
- Understand Object-oriented design patterns
- Uncover multithreading by Kotlin way
- Understand about arrays and collections
- Understand the importance of object-oriented design patterns
- Understand about exception handling and testing in OOP with Kotlin

Leave a review - let other readers know what you think

Please share your thoughts on this book with others by leaving a review on the site that you bought it from. If you purchased the book from Amazon, please leave us an honest review on this book's Amazon page. This is vital so that other potential readers can see and use your unbiased opinion to make purchasing decisions, we can understand what our customers think about our products, and our authors can see your feedback on the title that they have worked with Packt to create. It will only take a few minutes of your time, but is valuable to other potential customers, our authors, and Packt. Thank you!

Index

advantages 315
categorizing 315
selecting 348, 349
domain entities
mapping, with JPA 139, 141
domain events
building, with CDI 123
defining 123
firing 124
listening to 124

E

Eclipse Enterprise for Java (EE4J) 76
Eclipse
Kotlin, configuring 59, 60, 62, 63
EJB component model
about 100, 102
entity bean 100
message-driven bean 101
session bean 100
enterprise applications (EA). 75
Enterprise Java Beans (EJBs)
about 114
advantages 99
Bean validation 103, 104
EJB component model 100
Kotlin, working with 99
overview 99
versus CDI-managed beans 114
entity bean, EJB
about 100
bean-managed persistence 100
container-managed persistence 101
exception handling 158, 159
Expression Language (EL) 228
expressions
comparing, with statements 20
Extensible Markup Language (XML) 206
extension functions 35, 36

F

factory pattern
implementing 322, 324, 325
features, Kotlin
concise code 54

functional paradigms 47, 48, 53
immutability 48, 49
Java, interoperability 46
null safety 50, 51
for loop 25, 26, 27, 28
functional testing 274
functions
defining, in Kotlin 20, 21, 22

G

garbage collection
about 289, 290, 291
memory model 292, 293
garbage collectors
about 293
concurrent collectors 294
high throughput and low footprint 296
high throughput and low latency 295
low pause time and small footprint 296
serial/parallel garbage collectors 293
tuning 294
GlassFish Message Queue (glassfishmq) 179
GlassFish
configuring 176, 178
Glassfish
installing 174, 176

H

HTTP status codes
100 series 211
200 series 211
300 series 212
400 series 212
500 series 213
about 210
HttpAuthenticationMechanism
about 232
BasicAuthenticationMechanismDefinition 233
Custom form-based HTTP authentication 234
FormAuthenticationMechanismDefinition 233
SecurityContext API 235, 236
Hyper Text Transfer Protocol (HTTP) 207

Q

qualifiers 117, 119
query language (QL) 138

R

real-world application production
  preparing 309, 312
real-world microservices
  developing 253, 254, 255
Representational State Transfer (REST) 204
resources, REST verbs
  HTTP status codes 210
REST verbs
  about 208
  resources 208, 209
RESTful service
  implementing, with Jersey 217, 218
RESTful web services
  about 207
  create organization API, invoking with cURL 222
  GET function, writing for read operation 223, 225
  get organization API, invoking with cURL 225
  implementing 219
  layers, defining 219
  POST function, writing for create operation 221, 222

S

SAM-with-receiver compiler plugin
  about 86
  using, in CLI 88
  using, in Gradle 88
  using, in Maven 87
secondary constructor 39
security API
  about 228
  HttpAuthenticationMechanism 232
  IdentityStore mechanism 229
  implementing 228, 229
  implementing, Kotlin used 236, 237, 238, 239
security
  technical requisites 228
service level agreement (SLA) 252

servlet life cycle
  destruction phase 93
  initialization phase 92
  service phase 93
servlets
  about 91
  life cycle 92
session bean, EJB
  about 100
  singleton bean 100
  stateful bean 100
  stateless bean 100
simple servlet application
  creating, with Maven and Kotlin 93, 94, 95, 97, 98
single abstract method (SAM) 34
Single Responsibility Principle (SRP) 253, 325
Singleton class
  writing, in Java 317, 318
Singleton pattern
  implementing 317
  implementing, in comparison to Kotlin 321, 322
  lazy initialization 320
singleton pattern
  test case, writing 319, 320
spread keyword 24, 25
statement 20
string templates
  about 17
  multiline String Literals, creating 19
structural patterns 316
Structured Query Language (SQL) 138
syntactic rules and coding guidelines
  class name 42
  comments 43
  imports 42
  operators 43
  packages 42
  variables 43
system exceptions 159
system monitoring
  technical requisites 280
system performance
  high availability 312
  performance 312